Studying Bilinguals

To Lysiane, Marc, and Eric... bilingual, trilingual, and quadrilingual

Studying Bilinguals

FRANÇOIS GROSJEAN

OXFORD
UNIVERSITY PRESS

OXFORD
UNIVERSITY PRESS

Great Clarendon Street, Oxford OX2 6DP

Oxford University Press is a department of the University of Oxford.
It furthers the University's objective of excellence in research, scholarship,
and education by publishing worldwide in

Oxford New York

Auckland Cape Town Dar es Salaam Hong Kong Karachi
Kuala Lumpur Madrid Melbourne Mexico City Nairobi
New Delhi Shanghai Taipei Toronto

With offices in

Argentina Austria Brazil Chile Czech Republic France Greece
Guatemala Hungary Italy Japan Poland Portugal Singapore
South Korea Switzerland Thailand Turkey Ukraine Vietnam

Oxford is a registered trade mark of Oxford University Press
in the UK and in certain other countries

Published in the United States
by Oxford University Press Inc., New York

© François Grosjean 2008

British Library Cataloguing in Publication Data

Data available

Library of Congress Cataloging in Publication Data

Data available

Typeset by SPI Publisher Services, Pondicherry, India
Printed in Great Britain
on acid-free paper by
Biddles Ltd., King's Lynn, Norfolk

ISBN 978–0–19–928128–2 (Hbk.)
       978–0–19–928129–9 (Pbk.)

1 3 5 7 9 10 8 6 4 2

Contents

Part VI Methodological Issues in Bilingualism Research

1

Introduction

When I was asked to give a special options seminar at Oxford University in the spring of 2004 on my research on bilingualism, I used the opportunity to approach Oxford University Press with the idea of writing a book based on my lectures. This is the outcome. The book covers the work done over a period of twenty-five years since the publication of *Life with Two Languages*. The latter was a fine starting point for my research program as it had allowed me to survey the field in depth and had given me many new directions along which to guide my own studies.

The present book is an effort to contribute to four areas of bilingualism. The first concerns our thinking about the bilingual person: how we define and describe the bilingual in a wholistic perspective, the role of the complementarity principle, of language restructuring, and of language mode. The second area concerns the experimental psycholinguistics of bilingualism, in particular the processing of spoken language (as opposed to written language, a modality which is covered by many other researchers). In this area, I examine such topics as the bilingual's movements along the language mode continuum in language production, the base-language effect, the factors that account for the recognition of code-switches and borrowings, and how best to model this latter process. The third area concerns a different form of bilingualism, that of the Deaf where one language is sign language and the other is an oral language, in its written or spoken modality. Finally, the fourth area pertains to methodological and conceptual issues in research on bilingualism. Here I venture into the fields of linguistics (e.g. characterizing bilinguals), psycholinguistics (processing issues, tasks and stimuli used, modeling), and neurolinguistics (aspects to take into account when using modern imaging techniques with bilinguals). These four areas of research are arranged sequentially in the book although there is some overlap at times: Chapters 2 to 4 cover the first area; Chapters 5 to 11 deal with the second area; Chapters 12 and 13 concern the third area, and Chapters 14 and 15, the fourth. A short overview of each chapter is presented below.

Chapter 2, "A Wholistic View of Bilingualism", is, in many ways, a belated epilogue to *Life with Two Languages*. A number of points that emerged whilst writing the book deserved further attention: the dominant role played by the monolingual view of bilingualism in our study of people who use two or more languages; the importance of a newer—wholistic—view of bilingualism which states that bilinguals are fully competent speakers-hearers; and the contribution this latter view makes when we compare monolinguals and bilinguals, study language learning and language forgetting, and attempt to understand the bilingual's speech modes as well as the so-called "semilingualism" of the bilingual child. Chapter 3, "The Complementarity Principle and Language Restructuring", stresses the fact that bilinguals usually acquire and use their languages for different purposes, in different domains of life, and with different people. It describes the consequences this has on both language performance and language competence. Two studies that have examined the impact of the complementarity principle on bilingual language production—language mixing in particular—are summarized. In addition, research that pertains to language restructuring, that is, the long-term influence of one language on the other (in our case, a second language on a first language) is reviewed. The first area of the book ends with Chapter 4, "The Bilingual's Language Modes", which covers the many facets of language mode, that is the state of activation of the bilingual's languages and language processing mechanisms at any given point in time. This phenomenon was alluded to over the years by respected bilingualism researchers such as Uriel Weinreich, Nils Hasselmo, Michael Clyne, and Hugo Baetens Beardsmore, and the chapter simply follows in their footsteps. The following topics are covered: a description of language mode, the factors that influence it, the impact it has on language behavior, evidence that has been found for it, and the dangers of not controlling for it when doing research on bilingualism. The chapter ends with a review of what will have to be undertaken to better understand the phenomenon.

With Chapter 5, "Manipulating Language Mode", we enter the second area of interest of the book, the experimental psycholinguistics of bilingualism. The chapter describes research in which language mode is manipulated experimentally in language production and language perception studies. In the first part of the chapter, the original language mode production study that was done in Boston with French-English bilinguals is summarized. Two other studies are then described: one undertaken with Swiss German-French bilinguals, and one that involved Brazilian Portuguese-French bilinguals. In the second part of the chapter, the reasons why it is so difficult to control for language mode in perception experiments, in particular the monolingual language mode, are discussed. The factors that move bilingual subjects towards a bilingual mode are reviewed. Chapters 6, 7, and 8 concern the base-language effect, that is the impact that the base language has on the processing of guest words in bilingual speech. In perception, the question is whether the base language influences the perception of guest sounds and the recognition of guest words. In production, the question concerns the influence of the base language on the actual pronunciation of guest words. Chapter 6, "The Base-language Effect in Speech Perception", reviews evidence from different studies that show that the base-language effect is indeed present in perception and that it does have an impact on processing. A number of different tasks were used and, each time, the effect was shown to be present, even if momentarily. Chapter 7, "Base-language Effect and Categorical Perception" examines, by means of categorical perception experiments, the base-language effect on the identification of words in bilingual speech. It shows that the nature of the effect may depend, in part, on the acoustic-phonetic characteristics of the code-switched words. Finally, Chapter 8, "Is There a Base-language Effect in Speech Production?", investigates whether the base language also has an impact during speech production. It contains two sections. The first asks whether, when code-switches are produced, the phonetic momentum of the base language carries over into the guest language and hence affects the beginning of code-switches. How complete is a code-switch therefore? The second section examines the base-language effect on prosody. It is shown that the suprasegmentals (prosody) of a code-switch do not always follow the same trend as that found at the segmental (sound) level.

Chapters 9, 10, and 11 deal with research on spoken word recognition in bilinguals. Chapter 9, "The Gender Marking Effect in Bilinguals", takes up a factor, gender marking, which is common to both monolinguals and bilinguals in the recognition of nouns in French. It examines how early English-French bilinguals who make no gender errors in production, and late English-French bilinguals who make such errors, react to gender marking when listening to French. The results obtained open up interesting questions about the "critical period" for particular processing phenomena such as the use of gender marking in word recognition. Chapter 10, "The Role of Guest Word Properties", revolves around the impact of three factors (phonotactics, interlanguage neighbor proximity, and language phonetics) during the recognition of code-switches and borrowings. In addition to showing their differential role, it examines two other variables, sound specificity and interlanguage neighbor frequency. The chapter ends with the description of an interactive activation model of word recognition for bilinguals. It is governed by two basic assumptions: first, bilinguals have two language networks which are both independent and interconnected, and second, in the monolingual mode, one network is strongly activated while the other is weakly activated, whereas, in the bilingual mode, both networks are activated but one—that of the base language—more so than the other. In Chapter 11, "The Léwy and Grosjean BIMOLA Model", a short unpublished account written by Nicolas Léwy and myself is presented of BIMOLA, a computational model of bilingual lexical access. After having discussed how such a model needs to take into account the bilingual's language modes, a general overview of the model is given along with a number of its characteristics (e.g. shared phonetic features for the two languages but a language independent organization at the phoneme and word levels, excitation links within and between levels, one type of inhibition link, etc.). The chapter ends with an assessment of the model as it stood when the document was written.

Chapters 12 and 13 deal with the third area covered by the book, the bilingualism and biculturalism of the Deaf. Chapter 12, "The Bicultural Person: A Short Introduction", is concerned with several aspects. First, the bicultural is characterized as someone who takes part, to varying degrees, in the life of two or more cultures, who adapts, at least in part, to these cultures, and who combines and blends aspects of the cultures. This is followed by a discussion of points such as becoming bicultural, cultural dominance, and the lack of coextensiveness between bilingualism and biculturalism. The chapter ends with a presentation of how biculturals choose to identify with the cultures they belong to. Chapter 13, "The Bilingualism and Biculturalism of the Deaf", contains three parts. In the first, what it means to be bilingual in sign language and the oral (majority) language is explained. Similarities with hearing bilinguals are discussed as are differences. The second part examines the biculturalism of Deaf people: like hearing biculturals, they take part in the life of two worlds (the Deaf world and the hearing world), they adapt their attitudes, behaviors, languages, etc., to both worlds, and they combine and blend aspects of the two. The decisional process they go through in choosing a cultural identity is discussed and the difficulties met by some Deaf subgroups are examined. The chapter ends with a discussion of the Deaf child and why it is so important for him/her to be able to grow up bilingual in sign language and the oral (majority) language. The role of both languages is explained and it is argued that pursuing solely an oral approach puts the child at risk cognitively, linguistically, and personally.

The final two chapters, 14 and 15, are dedicated to the fourth area of the book: methodological and conceptual issues in research on bilingualism. In Chapter 14, "Methodological and Conceptual Issues", it is argued that because the field of bilingualism is still relatively new, studies in the linguistics, psycholinguistics, language development, and neurolinguistics of bilingualism have often produced conflicting results. It is suggested that some of the difficulties encountered by researchers could have been lessened, if not avoided, had close attention been paid to methodological and conceptual issues. Among the issues covered are bilingual participants, language mode, stimuli, and tasks as well as models of bilingual representation and processing. Each issue is dealt with in the following way: first it is explained, then the problems it causes are discussed, and, finally, tentative solutions are proposed. Chapter 15, "Imaging Bilinguals", is a dialogue between two neuroscientists (Thomas Münte and Antoni Rodriguez-Fornells) and two language scientists (Ping Li and myself). The object of the discussion is a paper which appeared in *Nature* in 2002 authored by the two neuroscientists, among others. The intention of the authors is to start bridging the gap between the neurosciences and language sciences on a number of methodological and theoretical issues. The authors come to the conclusion that a two-way collaboration between these two sciences should be encouraged in order to make headway in our understanding of language processing and representation in bilinguals.

A few additional points should be made. The first is that the chapters in the book were either written specifically for the book or are reprints of existing articles and/or chapters. This mingling of two types of chapters was decided with Oxford University Press and has some merit. It allows the reader, for example, to read the original papers of some of the research done instead of being presented with a summary of them. Care was taken not to have too many repeats (it is amazing how, over the years, one has a tendency to restate certain things!). Where some duplication does appear, the slant is slightly different. For example, language mode is dealt with in an introductory way in Chapter 4 and taken up again in Chapter 5 (here I discuss how it has been manipulated) and Chapter 14 (methodological issues and language mode). The second point is that the research covered in the book was conducted by myself, singly or with colleagues, and sometimes by Master's students under my supervision. Since the work of the latter was written up in French, mentioning their studies is a way of making them known to others. Of course, the research of many others is referred to throughout the book when presenting and discussing various findings, issues, and models.

I would like to end by thanking a number of people who have made this book possible. I wish to express my appreciation to John Davey of Oxford University Press and anonymous reviewers he called upon when I sent in the book proposal. Without John's support, especially when he learned that the book would be delayed for health reasons, I would not be telling him now how much I appreciated his kindness. I would also like to thank the person who made my stay in Oxford possible and, as a consequence, was one of the sources of this book: Kim Plunkett of the Experimental Psychology Department and of St. Hugh's College was a wonderful host to whom I owe much. My heartfelt thanks also go to a number of my co-authors who have kindly accepted that I repro-duce some of our writings or extracts from them: Judith Bürki-Cohen, Delphine Guillelmon, Nicolas Léwy, Ping Li, Joanne Miller, Thomas Münte, Bernard Py, Antoni Rodriguez-Fornells, and Carlos Soares. My appreciation is also extended to Emmanuelle de Dardel and Murielle Roth who helped me with various secretarial tasks. Finally, my deep gratitude goes to my wife, Lysiane, who has been such a fine support during trying times (and whose bilingualism is still enlightening) and to my two sons, Marc and Eric, who have divested themselves of their monolingualism and who are respectively trilingual and quadrilingual. It is amazing what moving back to Europe can do to one's knowledge and use of languages!

PART I
The Bilingual Person

Introduction

This first part contains two chapters. Chapter 2, "A Wholistic View of Bilingualism", was first published in 1985 under the title, "The bilingual as a competent but specific speaker-hearer". Parts of it appeared again in other publications such as, "Neurolinguists, beware! The bilingual is not two monolinguals in one person" (see the Appendix at the end of the book for the references). The article was written only three years after the publication of *Life with Two Languages: An Introduction to Bilingualism* (Harvard University Press) and was, in many ways, a belated epilogue to the book. A number of points that emerged whilst writing the book deserved further attention: the dominant role played by the monolingual view of bilingualism in our study of people who use two or more languages; the importance of a newer—wholistic— view of bilingualism which states that bilinguals are fully competent speakers-hearers; and the contribution this latter view makes when we compare monolinguals and bilinguals, study language learning and language forgetting, and attempt to understand the bilingual's speech modes as well as the so-called "semilingualism" of the bilingual child. Topics such as the complementarity principle, language restructuring, and language mode are mentioned in this chapter and are dealt with in more detail in the next two chapters.

Chapter 3, "The Complementarity Principle and Language Restruc- turing", stresses the fact that bilinguals usually acquire and use their lan- guages for different purposes, in different domains of life, and with dif- ferent people. It describes the consequences this has on both language performance and language competence. Two studies that have exam- ined the impact of the complementarity principle on bilingual lan- guage production—language mixing in particular—are summarized. Research that examines language restructuring, that is, the long-term influence of one language on the other (in our case, a second language on a first language) is then reviewed. It was conducted by Bernard Py and myself, and by one of our Master's students in Neuchâtel, Switzerland.

2

A Wholistic View of Bilingualism*

Only rarely do researchers working on the many facets of bilingualism take the opportunity to sit back from their on-going work and reflect on some fundamental issues regarding bilingualism and the bilingual person. Among the many issues that should be kept at the forefront of research, we find the following:

1. What do we mean when we use the terms "bilingual" and "bilingualism"?
2. Is the bilingual person the "sum" of two monolinguals or a specific speaker-hearer in his or her own right?
3. Can one adequately compare monolinguals and bilinguals, and if so, can one continue to do so with traditional procedures?
4. Can the linguistic tools and methods developed to study monolinguals be used without reservation to study bilinguals?

These are some of the questions I wish to raise as I examine the bilingual as a specific speaker-hearer. I will first discuss and criticize a particular view of bilingualism that has been prevalent in the field for decades; this I will term the monolingual (or fractional) view of bilingualism. I will then propose a different, much less accepted, view of bilingualism which I will name the bilingual (or wholistic) view. Finally, I will examine a number of areas of bilingual research that are affected by

* This chapter first appeared as an article: Grosjean, F. (1985c). "The bilingual as a competent but specific speaker-hearer", *Journal of Multilingual and Multicultural Development* 6: 467–77. The author thanks Multilingual Matters for permission to reprint it here. A note in the original article stated the following: "Readers may be surprised that there are no references in the text. This comes from the fact that this position paper is in many ways a belated epilogue to my book *Life with Two Languages: An Introduction to Bilingualism* (Cambridge, MA: Harvard University Press, 1982). It is in this latter work that I acknowledge the many scholars and researchers who have influenced my thinking on bilingualism."

this different perspective. Before proceeding, however, it is important that I state what I mean by the terms "bilingualism" and "bilingual". Bilingualism is the regular use of two or more languages (or dialects), and bilinguals are those people who use two or more languages (or dialects) in their everyday lives. A more detailed description of these concepts is given in later pages of this chapter.

2.1 The monolingual (or fractional) view of bilingualism

I wish to argue that a monolingual (or fractional) view of bilingualism has played too great a role in our study of people who use two languages in their everyday lives. According to a strong version of this view, the bilingual has (or should have) two separate and isolable language competencies; these competencies are (or should be) similar to those of the two corresponding monolinguals; therefore, the bilingual is (or should be) two monolinguals in one person.

It is interesting to ask why this view of bilingualism has been so prevalent among researchers and educators, as well as among laypersons, be they monolingual or bilingual. Perhaps the main reason is that language sciences have developed primarily through the study of monolinguals who have been the models of the "normal" speaker-hearer. The methods of investigation developed to study monolingual speech and language have been used with little, if any, modification to study bilinguals; strong monolingual biases have influenced bilingual research, and the yardstick against which bilinguals have been measured has inevitably been the ideal—monolingual—speaker-hearer. (One should add to this the strong impact of writing systems which are always monolingual.) It is worth asking how the research on bilingualism would have evolved and what state it would be in today, had the scholars in the field all been bi- or multilingual (in fact *and* in spirit) and had the research been conducted in societies where bi- or multilingualism is the norm and not the exception.

The monolingual (or fractional) view of bilingualism has had a number of consequences, among which we find:

(a) Bilinguals have been described and evaluated in terms of the fluency and balance they have in their two languages
The "real" bilingual has long been seen as the one who is equally and fully fluent in two languages. He or she is the "ideal", the "true", the "balanced", the "perfect" bilingual. All the others (in fact, the vast

majority of people who use two languages in their everyday life) are "not really" bilingual or are "special types" of bilinguals; hence the numerous qualifiers found in the literature: "dominant", "unbalanced", "semilingual", "alingual", etc. This search for the "true" bilingual has used traditional language tests as well as psycholinguistic tests which are constructed around the notion of "balance"; among these we find tests in which visual stimuli have to be named as fast as possible in one language or the other, or tests in which associations have to be given to stimuli in each of the two languages. Invariably, the ideal bilingual subject is the one who does as well in one language as in the other. All other subjects are somehow "less bilingual" and are put into an indeterminate category—they are neither monolingual nor "really bilingual"!

(b) Language skills in bilinguals have almost always been appraised in terms of monolingual standards

The tests used with bilinguals are often quite simply those employed with the monolinguals of the two corresponding language groups. These tests rarely take into account the bilingual's *differential needs* for the two languages or the *different social functions* of these languages (what a language is used for, with whom and where). The results obtained from these tests invariably show that bilinguals are less proficient than the corresponding monolinguals. This, in turn, is seen as a problem by the monolingual environment. It would appear that much of the controversy surrounding so-called "semilingualism" or "alingualism" in children is affected by the prevalence of the monolingual viewpoint and by the monolingual tests which have been used. These may be appropriate for monolingual children but not for other kinds of children: those who are monolingual in the other language, those who are in the process of becoming bilingual, or those who have attained a stable level of bilingualism. Monolingual tests are, for the most part, quite inappropriate to evaluate the language skills of bilinguals.

(c) The effects of bilingualism have been closely scrutinized

Because the monolingual viewpoint considers bilingualism as the exception (when, in fact, half of the world's population is bilingual) and because bilinguals should be two monolinguals in one person, the cognitive and developmental consequences of bilingualism have received close scrutiny. (As a bilingual myself, I have often wondered why the cognitive consequences of *monolingualism* have not been investigated with the same care!) Numerous studies have "pushed" the apparent negative effects or the apparent positive effects of bilingualism, and have done so with such force that it is rare to find an educator or a layperson who does not have an opinion on the subject. What we fail to remember is that numerous problems still surround the "effects" literature: children have rarely been tested in the appropriate language or languages (how many tests use mixed language with children whose normal input and output is mixed language? how many tests use the language variety the child is used to?, etc.); matching and sampling procedures remain questionable despite all the criticisms that have been made; and few studies manage to show a direct, unambiguous, causal relationship between using two languages in one's everyday life and various cognitive effects.

(d) The contact of the bilingual's two languages is seen as accidental and anomalous

Because bilinguals are (or should be) two separate monolinguals in one person, covert or overt contact between their two languages should be rare. The two language systems should be autonomous and should remain so at all times. If there is contact, it is accidental and is simply the result of language interference; "borrowings" and "code-switches", which are often ... intentional in conversations with other bilinguals, are either included in the interference category or are explained away as the product of "sloppy" language.

(e) Research on bilingualism is in large part conducted in terms of the bilingual's individual and separate languages

The monolingual view of bilingualism has influenced the many domains of bilingualism research. For example, researchers studying language acquisition have too often concentrated solely on the development of the new language system and, with some exceptions, have paid no real attention to what happens concurrently to the first language as it restructures itself in contact with L2. In addition, researchers have invariably used the monolingual child as the yardstick against which to judge the bilingual. Sociolinguists have long been interested in what the bilingual's languages are used for, when they are used, with whom, etc. and yet many surveys are still done solely in terms of the two separate languages; they then have problems categorizing the "both languages at the same time" answers. Psycholinguists have been interested in how the bilingual's two languages are activated one at a time, how one language gets switched on while the other gets switched off, and hence have paid little attention to the simultaneous activation of the two languages as in the case of borrowing and code-switching. Linguists have shown little interest in the bilingual's language competence in the Chomskyan sense, maybe because the bilingual can never be an "ideal speaker-hearer" in the same way that the monolingual supposedly can; there is no real acceptance among linguists that the bilingual's two grammars can be quite different from the corresponding monolingual grammars or that language competence (and especially first language competence) can actually change when it comes into contact with another language. Finally, many speech therapists and neurolinguists are still using standard monolingual tests with their bilingual subjects; these tests very rarely take into account the situations and domains the languages are used in, nor do they take into account the type and amount of code-mixing the person is involved in on a daily basis. Thus, much of what we know about bilingualism today is tainted—in part at least—by a monolingual, fractional, view of bilingualism.

(f) **Bilinguals rarely evaluate their language competencies as adequate**
The monolingual view of bilingualism is assumed and amplified by most bilinguals, and they exteriorize this in different ways. Some criticize their own language competence: "Yes, I use English every day at work, but I speak it so badly that I'm not really bilingual"; "I mix my languages all the time, so I'm not a real bilingual", etc.; others strive their hardest to reach monolingual norms (how many bilinguals have been put down by other bilinguals who strive to be "pure" monolinguals?); and still others hide their knowledge of their "weaker" language.

To conclude this section, it is important to stress how negative—often destructive—the monolingual view of bilingualism has been, and in many areas, still is. It is time that we accept the fact that bilinguals are not two monolinguals in one person, but different, perfectly competent speaker-hearers in their own right. It is this view that I will now develop.

2.2 The bilingual (or wholistic) view of bilingualism

The bilingual or wholistic view of bilingualism proposes that the bilingual is an integrated whole which cannot easily be decomposed into two separate parts. The bilingual is *not* the sum of two complete or incomplete monolinguals; rather, he or she has a unique and specific linguistic configuration. The co-existence and constant interaction of the two languages in the bilingual has produced a different but complete language system. An analogy comes from the domain of track and field. The high hurdler blends two types of competencies, that of high jumping and that of sprinting. When compared individually with the sprinter or the high jumper, the hurdler meets neither level of competence, and yet when taken as a whole the hurdler is an athlete in his or her own right. No expert in track and field would ever compare a high hurdler to a sprinter or to a high jumper, even though the former blends certain characteristics of the latter two. A high hurdler is an integrated whole, a unique and specific athlete, who can attain the highest levels of world competition in the same way that the sprinter and the high jumper can. In many ways, the bilingual is like the high hurdler: an integrated whole, a unique and specific speaker-hearer, and not the sum of two complete or incomplete monolinguals. Another analogy comes from the neighboring domain of biculturalism. The bicultural person (the Mexican-American, for example) is not two monoculturals; instead, he or she combines and blends aspects of the two cultures to produce a unique cultural configuration.

According to the wholistic view, then, the bilingual is a fully competent speaker-hearer; he or she has developed competencies (in the two languages and possibly in a third system that is a combination of the first two) to the extent required by his or her needs and those of the environment. The bilingual uses the two languages—separately or together—for different purposes, in different domains of life, with different people. Because the needs and uses of the two languages are usually quite different, the bilingual is rarely equally or completely fluent in the two languages. Levels of fluency in a language will depend on the need for that language and will be extremely domain specific, hence the "fossilized" competencies of many bilinguals in each of their two languages (see Chapter 3).

Because the bilingual is a human communicator (as is the monolingual), he or she has developed a communicative competence that is sufficient for everyday life. This competence will make use of one language, of the other language or of the two together (in the form of mixed speech) depending on the situation, the topic, the interlocutor, etc. The bilingual's communicative competence cannot be evaluated correctly through only one language; it must be studied instead through the bilingual's total language repertoire as it is used in his or her everyday life.

A number of areas of research are affected by this wholistic view of bilingualism; a few will be discussed below.

2.2.1 Comparing monolinguals and bilinguals

A wholistic view of bilingualism should lead, hopefully, to a more complete and fairer comparison of bilinguals and monolinguals in terms of language competence, language performance, language learning, etc. The comparison will need to stress the many specificities of the bilingual:

- the structure and organization of the bilingual's language competencies; it may well be that these competencies are in some ways different from those of the two corresponding monolinguals;
- the structure and organization of the bilingual's mixed language competence; that is, the language system(s) that is (are) activated when the bilingual is in a bilingual (mixed) speech mode and is borrowing and code-switching with other bilinguals;
- the bilingual's language processing systems when the language input and output are monolingual (as when the bilingual is speaking to monolinguals; we know that in such cases the other language is never totally deactivated);
- the linguistic and psycholinguistic operations involved in producing and perceiving mixed speech.

But the comparison of bilinguals and monolinguals will also need to stress the many similarities that exist between the two at the level of communicative competence. A first question that needs to be answered is the following: Does the stable bilingual (and not the person in the process of learning or restructuring a language) meet his or her everyday communicative needs with two languages—used separately or together—and this to the same extent as the monolingual with just one language? Because the bilingual, like the monolingual, is a human communicator with similar needs to communicate with others, I hypothesize that the answer to this question can only be affirmative. The bilingual will develop a communicative competence that is equivalent to that of other speaker-hearers, be they monolingual, bilingual, or multilingual, even though the outward manifestations of this competence may at first appear quite abnormal to the monolingual researcher (as in the case of mixed speech, which so often is seen as a reflection of semilingualism or alingualism). To answer the communicative needs question, we will need to develop new testing procedures. Traditional language tests that put more stress on the *form* of the language than on the speaker's ability to communicate in context are not appropriate.

Having shown that bilinguals do indeed have the same communicative competence as monolinguals, one will then need to study in more detail how the two types of speaker-hearers implement this competence; that is, how the bilingual and the monolingual meet their everyday communicative needs so differently on the surface: the former with his or her two languages, used separately or together, and the monolingual with just the one language. The issue has started to be addressed and we will return to it below.

2.2.2 Language learning and language forgetting

If the bilingual is indeed an integrated whole, then it is interesting to study the wax and wane of languages in that person; in other words, how changes in the language environment, and therefore in language needs, affect his or her linguistic competence in the one language and in the other, but not in his or her communicative competence in general. The following hypothesis can be made: a person can go in and out of bilingualism, can shift totally from one language to the other (in the sense of acquiring one language and forgetting the other totally), but will never depart (except in transitional periods of language learning or restructuring) from a necessary level of communicative competence needed by the environment. Because bilinguals, like monolinguals, have an innate capacity for language and are, by essence, communicators, they will develop competence in each of their languages to the extent needed by the environment (the competence in one language may therefore be quite rudimentary, as the interlanguage literature has shown) but they will always maintain a necessary level of communicative competence. New situations, new environments, new interlocutors will involve new linguistic needs in one language, in the other, or in both simultaneously, and will therefore change the language configuration of the persons involved; but this will in no way modify his or her communicative competence. After a period of adjustment (of language restructuring) the person will meet his or her new communicative needs to the fullest.

It is critical to differentiate between the process of restructuring a language and the outcome of restructuring, in other words, between becoming bilingual or readjusting one's bilingualism and attaining stability in one's bilingualism. It is also important to study what is happening to the two languages (and to the interaction of the two) during this period of readjustment. In the long run, the really interesting question of language learning and language forgetting is how the human communicator adjusts to and uses one, two, or more languages—separately or together—to maintain a necessary level of communicative competence, and not what level of grammatical competence is reached in each language taken individually and out of context. Unfortunately, too much stress has been put on the latter in bilingual research, especially when children are being studied.

2.2.3 The bilingual's speech modes[1]

An aspect of bilingual behavior that takes on added dimensions when seen from the wholistic perspective concerns the bilingual's speech modes (see also Chapter 4). In everyday life, bilinguals find themselves at various points along a situational continuum which induces a particular speech mode. At one end of the continuum, bilinguals are in a totally monolingual speech mode in that they are speaking to monolinguals of *either* language A *or* language B. At the other end of the continuum, bilinguals find themselves in a bilingual speech mode in that they are speaking to bilinguals who share languages A and B and with whom they normally mix languages (code-switch and borrow). For convenience, we will refer to the two ends of the continuum when speaking of the monolingual or bilingual speech modes, but we should keep in mind that these are endpoints and that intermediary modes do exist between the two.

It is important to note two things before describing these endpoints. First, bilinguals differ among themselves as to the extent they travel along the continuum; some rarely find themselves at the bilingual end (purists, language teachers, etc.) whereas others rarely leave this end (bilinguals who live in tight knit bilingual communities where the language norm is mixed language). Second, it is critical to know which speech mode a bilingual is in before making any claims about the individual's language processing or language competence. For example, what might be seen as the accidental (or permanent) interference of one language on the other during language production may in fact be a perfectly conscious borrowing or code-switch in the bilingual speech mode. Rare are the bilingual corpora that clearly indicate the speech mode the bilinguals were in when their speech was recorded; as a consequence, many unfounded

---

[1] In later writings (see Chapters 4, 5, and 14), "speech mode" is referred to as "language mode" so as not to exclude written language and sign language.

claims are made about the bilingual's knowledge of his or her languages.

In the monolingual speech mode, bilinguals adopt the language of the monolingual interlocutor. They also deactivate, as best they can, the other language. This deactivation has led to much theorizing and much controversy around the notion of a language switch or a monitor system. What is certain, however, is that bilinguals rarely deactivate the other language totally, and this leads to the following question: In what way is the language processing of bilinguals in the monolingual speech mode different from that of monolinguals, given that there is always some residual activation of the other language in bilinguals? The specific processing operations that will be uncovered in the future will only strengthen the view that the bilingual is a unique speaker-hearer.

In the bilingual speech mode, where both languages are activated, bilinguals become quite different speaker-hearers. Once a particular language has been chosen as the base language, they bring in the other language in various ways. One of these ways is to code-switch, that is to shift completely to the other language for a word, a phrase, a sentence (for example, "Va chercher Marc *and bribe him* avec un chocolat chaud *with cream on top*"). Code-switching has received considerable attention from linguists who have asked questions such as: What rules or constraints govern the switching? Is there a code-switching grammar? Sociolinguists have also studied code-switching extensively and have concentrated on when and why it takes place in the social context. The actual production and perception of code-switches have received much less attention and psycholinguists will ultimately have to answer questions such as: How does the bilingual speaker program and execute an utterance that contains code-switches? At what point in the acoustic-phonetic stream does the speaker actually switch from one language to the other? How complete is the switch? How does the bilingual listener perceive and comprehend a mixed language input? What strategies and operations lead him or her to process the utterance appropriately? How does the listener keep up with the interlocutor who is producing code-switches? These and other questions will find the beginnings of answers in the chapters that follow.

The other way a bilingual can mix languages is to borrow a word from the other language and to adapt it phonologically and morphologically into the base language ("bruncher" or "switcher" in French, for example). Again, the linguistic aspects of borrowings have been investigated carefully, but much less is known about their processing. One question of interest here is: How do bilingual listeners access (look up) a borrowing in the appropriate lexicon when the acoustic-phonetic (and sometimes morphological) information signals a word from the base lexicon? Note that this question only pertains to speech borrowings as opposed to language borrowings; the latter are already part of the base language lexicon and are therefore accessed normally.

Future bilingual research on the production and perception of languages will have to take into account the speech mode the bilingual is in when speaking or listening. As things stand, many published studies have not controlled for this variable and much of the data obtained is thus quite ambiguous. It is time that the complexity of the bilingual's speech modes is taken into account by researchers.

2.2.4 The bilingual child and "semilingualism"

So much has been written about the "semilingualism" or "alingualism" of certain bilingual children and adolescents. And yet before coming to rapid conclusions about language deficit in these children, it is important that we consider the points made so far on comparing bilinguals to monolinguals, on language learning and language forgetting, and on the bilingual's speech modes. We will then be ready to answer the following questions:

- Is the child in the process of becoming bilingual (structuring or restructuring his or her language competencies), either because he or she is learning two languages simultaneously and is in the fusion stage (a stage (sometimes) found in infant bilinguals[2]), or because he or she is simply in the process of learning a second language (or a different variety of the first language)? Could so-called "language deficit" simply be a reflection of language learning or language restructuring in process?
- Is the child mostly in a "bilingual speech mode" at home? Is the language input usually mixed and the output therefore also mixed? Is the child only just discovering the monolingual versions of the two languages? Can one expect the child to know how to behave in the monolingual mode when he or she has had no experience with this mode? Learning to use only *one* language at a time, when the two have always been used in a mixed language mode, takes

---

[2] Since writing this article, evidence has been produced showing that children acquiring two or more languages simultaneously may not go through a fusion stage.

time to get used to and needs the appropriate environment and feedback.
- Finally, is the child meeting his or her communicative needs in the home environment? Could "language deficit" simply be a reflection of the absence of particular formal skills that the child has never needed until he or she arrived in school?

These questions, among others, must be asked before concluding that a child really is "semilingual". It is important that we do not talk of "language deficit" until we are sure the child has had the chance, and has been given every opportunity, to learn and use the new language or new language variety that is employed in school. Learning or restructuring a language (or variety) takes time, and yet the child is often tagged as "semilingual" or "alingual" *before* he or she has had the time to adjust to the new language environment. Time is a critical factor, as are need and motivation: the child must feel the necessity to learn the new language and must be motivated to do so. If neither need nor motivation is present, then the child will not become bilingual, but through no fault of his or hers. It is clearly up to the school system and the adult environment to motivate language acquisition and to create the opportunity for the child to learn the new language or language variety. Does the child meet his or her everyday communicative needs by remaining monolingual (in the minority language)? In a sense, the answer is "yes", but communicating in school, with the majority language, is just not one of those needs. The child has not been given the opportunity to become bilingual and therefore remains monolingual.

Conclusion

To conclude, I wish to express a hope, the hope that the bilingual or wholistic view of bilingualism will increasingly affect our thinking and our research on bilingualism, and that consequently we will consider the bilingual as an integrated whole, a unique and specific speaker-hearer, a communicator of a different sort.

This will have a number of positive consequences:

1. It will encourage us to study the bilingual as a whole. We will no longer examine one of the bilingual's languages without examining the other(s); rather we will study how the bilingual structures and uses the two or more languages, separately or together, to meet his or her everyday communicative needs.

2. It will force us to use tests that are appropriate to the domains of language use: domains that involve mixed language will be tested in mixed language; domains requiring a monolingual speech mode will be tested monolingually, etc. Great care will be taken not to give bilinguals (and especially bi- or monolingual children) batteries of tests that have little to do with their knowledge and use of the two languages.

3. It will stimulate us to identify (or control) the speech mode the bilingual is in before recording or testing him or her. Too many studies have failed to pay attention to the speech mode issue and the results or data they have obtained are therefore difficult to appraise (see Chapter 4).

4. It will force us to differentiate between the person or child who is in the process of becoming bilingual, and the one who has reached a (more or less) stable level of bilingualism (whatever the ultimate level of proficiency attained in the two languages).

5. Finally, it will encourage us to study the bilingual as such and not always in relation to the monolingual, unless it is at a level of analysis that makes the comparison possible (for example, the level of communicative competence as opposed to formal competence). We should keep in mind that half the world's population is bilingual and that using the monolingual as a yardstick is questionable.

Each type of human communicator, whether he or she uses a spoken or a sign language, one or two languages, has a particular language competence, a unique and specific linguistic configuration. Our role as researchers is to recognize this and to develop our methods of analysis to reflect this. It is only when we start studying bilingualism in itself and for itself that we will make additional headway in this field.

3

The Complementarity Principle and Language Restructuring*

In Chapter 2, "A Wholistic View of Bilingualism", the bilingual's differential needs for the two (or more) languages were mentioned as were the different social functions these languages have (what the language is used for, with whom, and where). It was also shown that new situations, new environments, new interlocutors will involve new linguistic needs in one language, in the other, or in both simultaneously, and will therefore change the language configuration of the person involved (what has also been called language restructuring). In what follows, the differing needs of the bilingual for the two (or more) languages—what is now known as the complementarity principle—will be examined. This will be followed by a discussion of language restructuring. In each case, research that we have conducted in the French speaking part of Switzerland over the last several years will be called upon.

3.1 The complementarity principle

We know that in language contact situations, that is where two or more languages are used in everyday life, it is rare that all facets of life require the same language. If that were so, people would not be bilingual as they could lead their lives with just one language. It is also rare that both languages are required all the time, for example, language

* This chapter was written specifically for the book and is based in part on two articles (Grosjean, F. (1997b). "The bilingual individual", *Interpreting: International Journal of Research and Practice in Interpreting* 2: 163–87, and Grosjean, F. and Py, B. (1991). "La restructuration d'une première langue: l'intégration de variantes de contact dans la compétence de migrants bilingues", *La Linguistique* 27: 35–60) and on three Master's theses by Christine Gasser, Eliane Girard, and Roxane Jaccard and Vanessa Cividin.

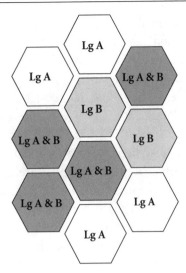

FIGURE 3.1 An illustration of the complementarity principle. The domains covered by languages A and/or B in a hypothetical bilingual are represented by the hexagons

A *and* B at work, language A *and* B at home, language A *and* B with friends, etc. The reasons that bring the two or more languages together (e.g. migration of various kinds, nationalism and federalism, education and culture, trade and commerce, intermarriage, etc.) create varied linguistic needs in people who are in contact with these languages. I have entitled this phenomenon, which most bilinguals know and live with, the complementarity principle (see Grosjean, 1997b). I describe it as follows:

Bilinguals usually acquire and use their languages for different purposes, in different domains of life, with different people. Different aspects of life often require different languages.

Figure 3.1 depicts the principle and shows the domains covered by languages A and/or B in a hypothetical bilingual. We see that in the case of this person, language A only is used in four domains of life, language B only in two domains of life, and both languages A and B in four other domains. Some domains, therefore, are specific to one language (six in all) and others are shared by the two languages (four in all). Any bilingual can be characterized in this way and will have a pattern that is specific to him or her.

The consequences of the complementarity principle are several. First, the level of fluency attained in a language (more precisely, in a language skill) will depend on the need for that language and will often be domain specific. It is precisely because the needs and uses of the languages are usually quite different that bilinguals rarely develop equal and total fluency in their languages. If reading and writing skills are not needed in a language, they will not be developed. If a language is spoken with a limited number of people in a reduced number of domains, it may be less fluent and more restricted than a language used extensively. If a language is never used for a particular purpose, it will not develop the linguistic properties needed for that purpose (specialized vocabulary, stylistic variety, some linguistic rules, etc.). Notions such as "dominance" and "balance" are, in fact, reflections of the complementarity principle. Thus, in the case of our hypothetical bilingual in Figure 3.1, we see a slight dominance for language A as more domains are covered by it (eight in all, counting shared domains) than by language B (six in all). In some bilinguals the dominance will be even greater for one or the other language; in a few, one will find a balanced situation with as many domains covered by one or the other language (or the two together).

Another consequence of the complementarity principle is that regular bilinguals are often not very good translators and interpreters. In domains covered by just one language, they do not always have translation equivalents in the other language (words, phrases, set expressions, etc.) which in turn will lead to perception and production problems. Unless they acquired their second language in a manner which involves learning translation equivalents (the approach often used in more traditional second language learning), many bilinguals will find themselves lacking vocabulary in certain domains covered by the other language (e.g. work, religion, politics, sports, etc.) even though they may appear to be rather fluent in their two languages. They may also be lacking the stylistic varieties needed in a domain and/or they may not have the cultural knowledge (pragmatic competence) required to understand and/or produce an utterance in a domain covered by the other language. A third consequence of the complementarity principle is that new situations, new interlocutors, and new language functions will involve new linguistic needs and will therefore change the language configuration of the person involved. The bilingual's languages will restructure in the sense that they will expand or retract based primarily on need, and the weaker language will often be influenced by the stronger language. Extreme cases of restructuring can be language forgetting and a return to functional monolingualism, be it in the person's first, second, or third language. We will turn to language restructuring a bit later on in this chapter; first, we will show empirical evidence for the complementarity principle in bilinguals.

Gasser (2000), from the University of Basle, Switzerland, wanted to show that the languages of bilinguals are distributed as a function of topic and activity, that is sub-aspects of the domains above, and to capture the impact the complementarity principle has on bilingual language production and, in particular, language mixing. She expected that bilinguals who had to talk about a topic or do an activity in the "wrong language" would be less fluent in that language and, if the situation allowed it (the language mode was appropriate), she expected that they would mix their languages more. She asked twenty first generation English-German bilinguals who had grown up in an English-speaking environment and had then moved to the German part of Switzerland as adults to assess how often they talked about various topics in English and in German, topics such as immediate family, home, shopping, leisure, clothes, health, education, politics, religion, etc. She also asked them to say how often they undertook various activities in the one and the other language, for example writing at work, writing mail, attending local circles and clubs, counting, expressing one's feelings, etc. Gasser worked out a "Complementarity Index" for each bilingual where 100 percent represents no overlap between the languages (all topics and activities are covered by one or the other language, never the two), 50 percent signals that half of the topics and activities are covered by the two languages (the other half by just one language) and 0 percent means that all topics and activities are covered equally by the two languages. She found that when you combine self reports on both topics and activities, the mean complementarity index is 80.35 percent for the twenty bilinguals who took part in her study. Thus, most topics and activities seem to be categorized as either English related or German related, exactly what the complementarity principle states.

Gasser went on to explore the impact of the principle on bilinguals' language behavior. For a subset of her bilinguals, she worked out, for each of their two languages, the strong and the weak topics. Thus, for example, she found that for bilingual X, work was a strong English topic (she spoke about work mainly in English), home was a weak English topic (she spoke about home matters mainly in German), education was a strong German topic (she spoke about this topic mainly in German), and sports was a weak German topic (she rarely spoke about this subject in German). She interviewed them in the one and in the other language on their strong and weak topics, and she examined how much language mixing took place. (Note that the interviewee was in a bilingual language mode as Gasser herself was an English-German bilingual and the situation was conducive to language mixing). She examined the percentage of mixed syllables per topic and found more than twice the amount of mixing took place in the weak language condition (significant at the 0.05 level), and this for both languages. In sum, when bilinguals were forced to talk about a topic in the "wrong" language, they would bring in the other language to compensate for the lack of terms and expressions they had in that language. Thus, Gasser not only showed that the complementarity principle is very much present in bilinguals' lives but that it also had an impact on their language behavior.

As Gasser was doing her study in Basle with English-German bilinguals, Jaccard and Cividin (2001) were investigating the same subject in French-Italian bilinguals in the French speaking part of Switzerland. They worked with second-generation bilinguals (the parents had immigrated to Switzerland) whereas in Basle Gasser had studied first generation bilinguals. Jaccard and Cividin proceeded in the same way as Gasser, first working out a Complementarity Index for their bilinguals and then studying their language mixing when talking about various strong and weak topics in their languages. The mean Complementarity Index they found was 67.02 which is less than Gasser's (80.35 percent) but which still shows the complementarity principle at work (recall that 50 percent signals that half of the topics and activities are covered by just one language, the other half being covered by the two). As for the amount of language mixing that occurred when the bilinguals were asked to talk about a strong or weak topic in one or the other language, Jaccard and Cividin found about five times more mixed speech in the weak language condition than in the strong language condition (significant at the 0.01 level). Once again, talking about a topic in the "wrong" language had a real impact on how much the speaker called upon the other language (in a language mode that was conducive to language mixing). Thus both studies found evidence for the complementarity principle and both showed the very real impact it has on language behavior.

3.2 Language restructuring

We saw above that one of the consequences of the complementarity principle is that new situations, new interlocutors, and new language functions will involve new linguistic needs and may therefore change, over time, the language configuration of the person involved. We have known for a long time that there can be a long-term influence of one language on the other, usually the first language on the second. It involves static interferences (permanent traces of one language on the other) and concerns language competence. What we have known for less time is that a first language can also be influenced at the level of competence by a second language, such as in the case of immigration where, over the years, the first language starts to be used much less often and its domains of use are restricted as compared to those of the second language, the language of the host country. In a series of studies, Bernard Py and I (see, for example, Grosjean and Py 1991), with the help of Eliane Girard, have examined the restructuring of Spanish, the first language of Spanish immigrants in Neuchâtel, Switzerland, under the influence of French, their second language, in a situation of prolonged bilingualism. Over a period of some thirteen years, we tested first generation Spanish immigrants and their adult bilingual children (second generation), as well as a monolingual Spanish control group in Spain.

The five features we examined concern primarily the level of syntax, with one exception, and are characterized by a standard Spanish variant (S) and a Neuchâtel immigrant Spanish variant (N). They are:

1. complement of movement verbs;
2. object complement;
3. infinitive complement;
4. focus;
5. loan shifts.

Feature 1 has to do with the complement of movement verbs. Spanish subcategorizes verbs with the feature [+/− moving]; [+ moving] takes the preposition "a" before the complement, as in *Fuimos de vacaciones a España* (We went on vacation to Spain), whereas [− moving] takes the preposition "en", as in *Hemos pasado unos días en Granada* (We have spent a few days in Grenada). Neuchâtel Spanish, after many years of contact with French, is starting to lose the distinction and to use the French equivalents "a", "en", "dans", etc. Hence we find in Neuchâtel, *Fuimos de vacaciones en España* (based on French "en") and *Hemos pasado unos días a Granada* (based on French "à"). Feature 2 has to do with the object complement. In Spanish, it is preceded by the preposition "a" if it concerns a person; this marks the difference between the subject and object. Hence one finds in standard Spanish,

El león quería morder <u>al</u> hombre (The lion wanted to bite the man). Neuchâtel Spanish has a tendency to stabilize the SVO order of Spanish and hence no longer needs the preposition. This gives, for example, *El león quería morder Ø el hombre* (where Ø corresponds to the missing preposition). Feature 3 concerns the infinitive complement. In Spanish, when a main verb is followed by an infinitive complement, either there is no preposition between the two or the preposition is determined by the main verb, for example *Decidió Ø llamar al médico* (He decided to call the doctor) where Ø marks the missing preposition. Neuchâtel Spanish, under the influence of French, tends to add a "de" before an infinitive that is not in an initial position, for example *Decidió <u>de</u> llamar al médico* (based on French "d'appeler"). Feature 4 involves focus. In standard Spanish, putting elements in focus can be done in one of two ways. In the first, the verb "ser" is used and is made to agree with the main verb, a relative pronoun (or phrase) is added based on the function of the focused phrase, and sometimes the preposition is repeated before the relative pronoun. This gives, for example, *<u>Fue</u> la lluvia <u>la que</u> lo mojó todo* (It was the rain that wet him completely). Another route is to use word order and prosody. In Neuchâtel Spanish, the approach is simplified: "es" is used, based on French "c'est", alongside the use of "que", for example *<u>Es</u> la lluvia <u>que</u> lo mojó todo*. Finally, Feature 5 concerns lexical semantics and more precisely, loan shifts. In Neuchâtel Spanish, a number of Spanish words have taken on an additional meaning based on French. Hence, *No <u>oigo</u> el ruido del tren* (I can't hear the noise made by the train) often becomes *No <u>entiendo</u> el ruido del tren*. Here the Spanish verb "entender", which means "understand", has taken on a second meaning ("hear") based on French "entendre".

In a first study (Grosjean and Py 1991), we asked fifteen first generation immigrants to give presence and acceptability judgments of sentences of the type given above. The mean age of the participants was 40. They had all been born in Spain and had arrived in Switzerland as adults with no knowledge of French. Since then, they had become bilingual and they used their two languages on a regular basis: Spanish with their family, their friends, on holiday, etc. and French at work, in the community, and sometimes with their children. We wanted to know if the Neuchâtel variants were recognized as being present in Neuchâtel Spanish (we had picked them up in free conversation but wanted to see if the bilinguals acknowledged their presence). We also wanted to know if they were accepted and what relationship existed between their perceived presence and their acceptability. Finally, we were interested in finding out if the bilinguals could still differentiate between the Spanish and the Neuchâtel variants. The participants were given two booklets with the sentences in them (we underlined the grammatical aspect we were interested in) and the instructions were in Spanish. The first booklet was for the presence test; they had to circle a number on a 1 to 7 scale, where 1 corresponded to the variant never being used in Neuchâtel and 7 to it always being used. The second booklet was for the acceptability test; again there was a 1 to 7 scale where 1 corresponded to the variant being unacceptable and 7 to it being totally acceptable.

When describing the results we obtained, we will concentrate on the Neuchâtel variants as the standard Spanish variants were always perceived as highly present and highly acceptable. We found that the Neuchâtel variants ranged from not being perceived as present (Feature 1 received a mean presence rating of 2.42 on the 1 to 7 scale) to being perceived as present (Feature 4 received a mean rating of 5.13). The rank ordering we obtained, from least present to most present, with a stepwise increase in values, was as follows:

1. N1: complement of movement verbs;
2. N5: loan shifts;
3. N2: object complement;
4. N3: infinitive complement;
5. N4: focus.

We also found a very strong relationship between perceived presence and acceptability—a variant that was present was also a variant that was accepted. The rank ordering for the acceptability judgments was exactly the same as that of the presence judgments (see above). Finally, we noted that first generation immigrants differentiate between the two types of variants. With the exception of one variant (N4: focus), the Neuchâtel variants were perceived as less present and less acceptable than the Spanish variants (as we saw above, the latter always received very high ratings, be it for their presence or their acceptability). We concluded that as concerns the participants' Spanish competence, there appeared to be a continuum of integration for the Neuchâtel variants: from the not so well integrated (e.g. N1 and N5) to the fairly well integrated (e.g. N3 and N4).

In a second study (again in Grosjean and Py 1991), we asked ourselves how a group of monolingual Spanish speakers would react to the two variants of each grammatical feature. We therefore asked fifteen native speakers of Spanish, in Spain, of the same mean age (40) but with

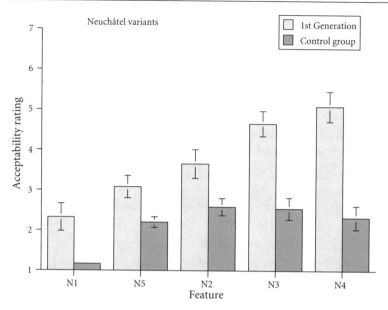

FIGURE 3.2 Mean acceptability ratings of five Neuchâtel Spanish variants for the Spanish control group (darker bars; $n = 15$) and the first generation immigrant group (lighter bars; $n = 15$). Error bars represent $+/-$ one standard error of the mean

no knowledge of French, to fill in the acceptability booklet. Figure 3.2 shows the results obtained for the Neuchâtel variants for both the Spanish control group (darker bars) and the first generation immigrant group (lighter bars). (Note that the two groups had very similar results for the Spanish variants.) As can be seen in the figure, at no time did the control group produce a mean acceptability judgment that was greater than 2.6 whereas the first generation immigrants produced mean values that ranged from 2.3 (Feature 1) all the way to 5.1 (Feature 4), with four of the means being greater than 3. There is a very real difference therefore between the Neuchâtel immigrants who seem to be adding variants to these features (based on French) and the native speakers back in Spain who do not accept the Neuchâtel variants.

We asked ourselves why it was that some Neuchâtel variants were more fully accepted than others in the Spanish of our first generation immigrants (compare N1 and N4 in Figure 3.2, for example). We proposed that the degree of integration of a variant depends on the feature's position (central or peripheral) in each of the two languages. This position will allow it either to resist when confronted with the feature of the other language or be influenced by it. Among the factors which contribute to the position of a feature (central or peripheral) and hence to its level of resistance are the number of rules involved in the structure of the feature (the fewer, the more central the position; the more numerous, the more peripheral) and the types of rules involved (the more general, the more central; the more specific, the more peripheral). For example, Feature 1 (complement of movement verbs) has fewer and more general rules in Spanish and hence it can resist the influence of French. On the other hand, Feature 4 (focus) has a greater number of rules in Spanish and these are rather specific, as compared to French, and hence it resists less well.

Some twelve years later (the first generation group was tested in 1983), Eliane Girard (1995) used the same acceptability test with second generation bilinguals (most of whom were the children of first generation bilinguals). She wanted to know to what extent they accepted the Neuchâtel variants and whether the distinction between the Spanish and the Neuchâtel variants was as strong as that of the first generation group. She used fifteen participants, with a mean age of 20, all of whom had been born in Switzerland, with the exception of two who had arrived at age two. They had all attended the local French speaking school and they had also attended the Spanish consular school for eight years. They used their two languages on a regular basis and they all gave high subjective ratings to their four basic language skills in Spanish (the means ranged from 5.06 to 6.33 on 7). The results expected could go either way. They could be similar to those of their first generation elders as French was their stronger language and they had heard the first generation use Neuchâtel Spanish variants with them. On the other hand, they could be different as they had attended the consular school where much emphasis is put on "good" Spanish devoid of French influence. They had also gone back to Spain several times a year and hence were in contact with standard Spanish. As can be seen in Figure 3.3 where we present mean acceptability ratings for the first and second generation groups, it is the first alternative that is correct. The rank ordering is the same for the two groups (N1, N5, N2, N3, N4) and, apart from very minor fluctuations here and there, one cannot differentiate the group results. In fact, the grand means, across the five features, is 3.76 for the first generation group and 3.78 for the second generation group. Before returning to the Neuchâtel variants, we should say a word on the standard Spanish variants. Although they were perceived as highly present and strongly accepted by all three groups, there seems to be the beginning of a difference between the control group (Spanish native speakers) and the second generation

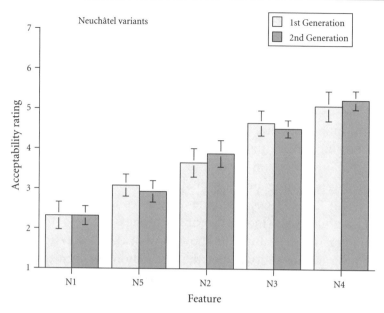

FIGURE 3.3 Mean acceptability ratings of five Neuchâtel Spanish variants for the first generation group (lighter bars; $n = 15$) and the second generation group (darker bars; $n = 15$). Error bars represent $+/-$ one standard error of the mean

bilinguals. When we examined the acceptability judgments, we found almost a one point difference between the two groups' grand means: 6.50 for the control group and 5.66 for the second generation, a statistically significant difference at the 0.05 level. This might be showing that the standard Spanish variants are losing a bit of ground in the Spanish of the second generation group. But to be sure, one would need to test that group at age 40 (and not 20), like the other groups, and a third generation group would also need to be tested on the condition that the latter still use Spanish.

When speaking to Noam Chomsky about the acceptability ratings of the Neuchâtel variants during a 1985 interview, he suggested that the results could be due to a change in cognitive style and not a change in native language competence. He said, "One possible explanation is that when you move into a foreign language environment ... your standards on acceptability are going to be lowered because you're going to have to accept all sorts of things that don't make any sense to you, and it could be that it's a change in cognitive style. It might influence the way you decide to react to your native language, but not your knowledge of your native language." To try to get to the bottom of this, Eliane Girard (1995) sought to confirm the integration level of the Neuchâtel variants in the second generation bilinguals without resorting to acceptability judgments. She asked the same fifteen bilinguals to interpret, from French to Spanish, sentences which contained the same five features. The task was done before the acceptability test so that they would not be aware of what it was we were examining. The bilinguals heard French sentences over headphones and had to interpret them into Spanish; their productions were recorded. Thus, for example, a Feature 1 sentence was, "Cet été nous allons en vacances en Espagne" (This summer we are going on vacation to Spain) and Girard checked to see if they responded with *Este verano vamos de vacaciones a España* (Standard Spanish variant) or *Este verano vamos de vacaciones en España* (Neuchâtel Spanish variant). A Feature 3 sentence was "Il feint d'ignorer la vérité" (He's pretending not to know the truth) and Girard looked out for either *Finge ignorar la verdad* (Standard Spanish variant) or *Finge de ignorar la verdad* (Neuchâtel Spanish variant). The results obtained confirmed the rank ordering found in the acceptability study and hence speak against a simple change in cognitive style as suggested by Chomsky. The productions with the Neuchâtel Spanish variants were least numerous for Feature 1 (some 10 percent) and most numerous for Feature 4 (80 percent) with Features 5, 2, and 3 in-between.

From these studies, we concluded that under the impact of a dominant language, and over time, the competence that native speakers have in their first language can in fact change, even if moderately. We should recall that in our case, members of the first generation group did not know any French before the age of 20. But twenty years later, at age 40, and under the influence of French, their Spanish was being modified with the introduction of French influenced variants. This change was present in the competence of the next generation several years later.

Conclusion

We have seen in this chapter that the complementarity principle can explain bilinguals' level of fluency in their languages. Notions such as "dominance" and "balance" are, in fact, reflections of the complementarity principle. We have also seen that the principle explains the difficulties bilinguals can have when using a language or translating from one language to another. For example, they will find themselves lacking in vocabulary in a language when certain domains are covered by the other language, even though they may appear rather fluent in their two languages. Finally, we have seen how the principle may actually cause a weaker language to restructure itself under the influence of the stronger (dominant) language. All of this has to be kept in mind when assessing the competence bilinguals have in their languages and when testing them experimentally in a laboratory situation.

PART II
Language Mode

Introduction

Chapter 4, "The Bilingual's Language Modes", is a reprint of my chapter in Janet Nicol's book, *One Mind, Two Languages: Bilingual Language Processing* (2001). Language mode, which is the state of activation of the bilingual's languages and language processing mechanisms at any given point in time, has a very real impact on the bilingual's everyday behavior. As is clear from the introduction to the chapter, this phenomenon was alluded to over the years by respected bilingualism researchers such as Uriel Weinreich, Nils Hasselmo, Michael Clyne, and Hugo Baetens Beardsmore. In the chapter, which simply follows in their footsteps, the following topics are covered: a description of language mode, the factors that influence it, the impact it has on language behavior, evidence that has been found for it, and the dangers of not controlling for it when doing research on bilingualism. The chapter ends with a review of what will have to be undertaken to better understand the phenomenon.

Chapter 5, "Manipulating Language Mode", describes research in which language mode is manipulated experimentally in language production and language perception studies. In the first part of the chapter, the original language mode production study that was done in Boston with French-English bilinguals is summarized. Two other studies are then described: a replication with an interesting twist undertaken in Basle, Switzerland, with Swiss German-French bilinguals, and an investigation in Neuchâtel, Switzerland, with Brazilian Portuguese-French bilinguals. In the latter study, the fluency of the participants was also manipulated. In the second part of the chapter, the reasons why it is so difficult to control for language mode in perception experiments, in particular the monolingual language mode, are discussed. The factors that move bilingual subjects towards a bilingual mode even though every effort is made to put them in a monolingual mode are reviewed. The difficulties encountered are illustrated with two perception studies, done by others, who sought to induce a monolingual mode but who failed to do so.

4

The Bilingual's Language Modes*

Bilinguals who have reflected on their bilingualism will often report that they change their way of speaking when they are with monolinguals and when they are with bilinguals. Whereas they avoid using their other language with the former, they may call on it for a word or a sentence with the latter or even change over to it completely. In addition, bilinguals will also report that, as listeners, they are sometimes taken by surprise when they are spoken to in a language that they did not expect. Although these reports are quite anecdotal, they do point to an important phenomenon, language mode, which researchers have been alluding to over the years. For example, Weinreich (1966) writes that, when speaking to a monolingual, the bilingual is subject to interlocutory constraint which requires that he or she limit interferences (Weinreich uses this as a cover term for any element of the other language), but when speaking to another bilingual there is hardly any limit to interferences; forms can be transferred freely from one language to the other and often used in an unadapted way. A few years later, Hasselmo (1970) refers to three sets of "norms" or "modes of speaking" among Swedish-English bilinguals in the United States: English only for contact with English monolinguals, American Swedish with some bilinguals (the main language used is Swedish), and Swedish American with other bilinguals (here the main language is English). In the latter two cases, code-switching can take place in the other language. The author also notes that there exist two extremes in the behavior of certain bilinguals, one extreme involves minimal and the other maximal code-switching. A couple of years later, Clyne (1972)

* This chapter first appeared as: Grosjean, F. (2001). "The bilingual's language modes", in J. Nicol (ed.) *One Mind, Two Languages: Bilingual Language Processing*. Oxford: Blackwell, 1–22. The author thanks Wiley-Blackwell Publishing for permission to reprint it here.

talks of three communication possibilities in bilingual discourse: in the first, both codes are used by both speakers; in the second, each one uses a different code but the two understand both codes; and, in the third, only one of the two speakers uses and understands both codes whereas the other speaker is monolingual in one of the codes. Finally, Baetens Beardsmore (1986) echoes these views when he writes that bilinguals in communication with other bilinguals may feel free to use both of their language repertoires. However, the same bilingual speakers in conversation with monoglots may not feel the same liberty and may well attempt to maximize alignment on monoglot norms by consciously reducing any formal "interference" features to a minimum.

What is clear from all of this is that, at any given point in time and based on numerous psychosocial and linguistic factors, the bilingual has to decide, usually quite unconsciously, which language to use and how much of the other language is needed—from not at all to a lot. If the other language is not needed, then it will not be called upon or, in neural modeling terms, activated. If on the other hand it is needed, then it will be activated but its activation level will be lower than that of the main language chosen. The state of activation of the bilingual's languages and language processing mechanisms, at a given point in time, has been called the language mode. Over the years, and in a number of publications, I have developed this concept. Already in Grosjean (1982, ch. 6), the bilingual's language behavior was presented in two different contexts: when the bilingual is speaking to a monolingual and when he or she is speaking to a bilingual. The notion of a situational continuum ranging from a monolingual to a bilingual speech mode was presented in Grosjean (1985c). In the monolingual speech mode, the bilingual deactivates one language (but never totally) and in the bilingual mode, the bilingual speaker chooses a base language, activates the other language, and calls on it from time to time in the form of code-switches and borrowings. The notion of intermediate modes and of dynamic interferences was presented in Grosjean (1989); the latter were defined as those deviations from the language being spoken due to the involuntary influence of the other deactivated language. The expression "language mode" replaced "speech mode" in Grosjean (1994) so as to be able to encompass spoken language and written language as well as sign language, and the current two-dimensional representation of the base language and the language mode was introduced in Grosjean (1997a) as was the notion that language mode corresponds to various levels of activation of the two languages. Finally, in Grosjean (1998a) perception was taken into account, and the many problems that arise from not controlling the language mode sufficiently in bilingualism research were discussed.

Researchers in bilingualism will need to take into account language mode for a number of reasons: it has received relatively little attention in bilingualism research; it gives a truer reflection of how bilinguals process their two languages, separately or together; it helps us understand data obtained from various bilingual populations; it can partly account for problematic or ambiguous findings relating to such topics as language representation and processing, interference, code-switching, language mixing in bilingual children, bilingual aphasics, etc.; and, finally, it is invariably present in bilingualism research as an independent, control, or confounding variable and hence needs to be heeded at all times.

In this chapter, language mode will be described, the factors that influence it will be spelled out, and the impact it has on language behavior will be examined. Next, existing evidence for the bilingual's language modes in language production, language perception, language acquisition, and language pathology will be described. Language mode as a confounding variable will then be evoked and suggestions for controlling it will be proposed. Finally, future research topics related to language mode such as assessment, processing mechanisms, highly language dominant bilinguals, and modeling will be considered.

4.1 Language mode

4.1.1 Description

Language mode is the state of activation of the bilingual's languages and language processing mechanisms at a given point in time. Given that activation is a continuous variable ranging from no activation to total activation and that two languages are concerned,[1] language mode is best visualized in a two dimensional representation such as that in Figure 4.1. The bilingual's languages (A and B) are depicted on the vertical axis by a square located in the top and bottom parts of the figure, their level of activation is represented by the degree of darkness of the square (black for a highly active language and white for a deactivated language), and the ensuing language mode is depicted by the position of the two squares (linked by a discontinuous line)

---

[1] At this stage, only the regular use of *two* languages in relatively stable bilinguals will be considered. People who use three or more languages in their everyday life will be evoked in the last section.

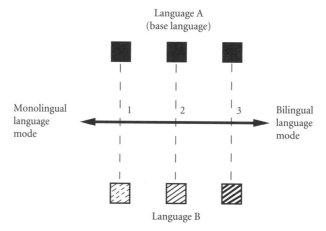

FIGURE 4.1 Visual representation of the language mode continuum. The bilingual's positions on the continuum are represented by the discontinuous vertical lines and the level of language activation by the degree of darkness of the squares (black is active and white is inactive)

Source: This figure first appeared in Grosjean (1998a). It is reprinted with the permission of Cambridge University Press.

on the horizontal axis which ranges from a monolingual mode to a bilingual mode. Three hypothetical positions are presented in the figure, numbered 1 to 3. In all positions it is language A that is the most active (it is the base language, i.e. the main language being produced or perceived at a particular point in time) and it is language B that is activated to lesser degrees. In position 1, language B is only very slightly active, and hence the bilingual is said to be at, or close to, a monolingual language mode. In position 2, language B is a bit more active and the bilingual is said to be in an intermediate mode. And in position 3, language B is highly active (but not as active as the base language) and the bilingual is said to be in a bilingual language mode. Note that in all three positions, the base language (language A) is fully active as it is the language that governs language processing. Examples taken from production and perception will illustrate these three positions on the continuum. As concerns production, bilingual speakers will usually be in a monolingual mode when they are interacting with monolinguals (speakers of language A in Figure 4.1) with whom they simply cannot use their other language (language B). When they are in this kind of situation, they deactivate their other language (most often unconsciously) so that it is not produced and does not lead to miscommunication. Speakers will be in an intermediate position (such as position 2) when, for example, the interlocutor knows the other language but either is not very proficient in it or does not like to mix languages. In this case, the speaker's other language (language B in the figure) will only be partly activated. And speakers will be in bilingual mode (position 3) when they are interacting with other bilinguals who share their two languages and with whom they feel comfortable mixing languages. In this case, both languages are active but one language (language B in the figure) is slightly less active than the other language (language A) as it is not currently the main language of processing. The same applies to bilingual listeners. In position 1, for example, a bilingual may be listening to a monolingual who is using language A and who simply does not know language B. In position 2, the same person may be listening to another bilingual who very rarely code-switches and borrows from the other language, and in position 3, the listener may be listening to mixed language being produced by his or her bilingual interlocutor.[2]

Language mode concerns the level of activation of two languages, one of which is the base language, and hence two factors underlie the concept. The first is the base language chosen (language A in the above figure) and the second is the comparative level of activation of the two languages (from very different in the monolingual mode to quite similar in the bilingual mode). As these two factors are usually independent of one another (for possible exceptions, see Section 4.3), there can be a change in one without a change in the other. Thus, the base language can be changed but not the comparative level of activation of the two languages (e.g. a bilingual can change the base language from A to B but remain in a bilingual mode). Similarly, there can be a change in the comparative level of activation of the two languages without a change in base language (e.g. when a bilingual goes from a bilingual to a monolingual mode but stays in the same base language). Since these two factors are always present, it is crucial to state both when reporting the bilingual's language mode. Thus, for example, a French-English bilingual speaking French to a French monolingual is in a "French monolingual mode" (French is the base language and the other language, English, is deactivated as the mode is monolingual). The same bilingual speaking

---

[2] As much of the psycholinguistics of bilingualism has concerned language perception (spoken or written) in the laboratory, it is important to stress that depending on the stimuli presented (monolingual or bilingual), the task used, the laboratory setting, and the instructions given, a bilingual listener in an experiment can be situated at any point along the language mode continuum but is usually at the bilingual end. We will come back to this in a later section as well as in Chapter 5.

English to an English monolingual is in an "English monolingual mode". If this person meets another French-English bilingual and they choose to speak French together and code-switch into English from time to time, then both are in a "French bilingual mode". Of course, if for some reason the base language were to change (because of a change of topic, for example), then they would be in an "English bilingual mode", etc. Saying that a bilingual is in an English language mode leaves totally open whether the mode is monolingual or bilingual. It should be noted that the expressions "language set", "language context", and even "language mode" have been used in the literature to refer to the base language the bilingual is using (or listening to) but they do not tell us anything about the comparative level of activation of the bilingual's two languages (for use of such terminology, see e.g. Caramazza *et al.* 1973; Elman *et al.* 1977; Beauvillain and Grainger 1987; etc.).

4.1.2 Factors that influence language mode

Any number of factors can help position a bilingual speaker or listener at a particular point on the language mode continuum, that is, set the activation level of the bilingual's languages and language processing mechanisms. Among these we find the participant(s), that is the person(s) being spoken or listened to (this includes such factors as language proficiency, language mixing habits and attitudes, usual mode of interaction, kinship relation, socioeconomic status, etc.), the situation (physical location, presence of monolinguals, degree of formality and of intimacy), the form and content of the message being uttered or listened to (language used, topic, type of vocabulary needed, amount of mixed language), the function of the language act (to communicate information, to request something, to create a social distance between the speakers, to exclude someone, to take part in an experiment, etc.), and specific research factors (the aims of the study taking place (are they known or not?), the type and organization of the stimuli, the task used, etc.). Thus, a monolingual mode will arise when the interlocutor or the situation is monolingual and/or other factors require that only one language be spoken to the exclusion of the other. This is the case, for example, when a bilingual adult or child is speaking with, or listening to, a monolingual family member or friend, or when a bilingual aphasic is speaking to a monolingual examiner, etc. Of course, no physical interactant need be present for a bilingual to be in a monolingual mode. If a bilingual is reading a book written in a particular language, watching a TV program in just one language or, more experimentally, taking part in a study in which only one language is used and where there is absolutely no indication that the other language is needed (but see below for the very real difficulty of creating this situation), then the bilingual is probably in a monolingual mode. The same factors apply for any other position on the continuum. Thus, if two bilinguals who share the same languages and who feel comfortable mixing languages are interacting with one another, there is a fair chance that they will be in a bilingual mode. This will be reinforced if, for example, the topic being dealt with is one that cannot be covered without having recourse to the other language in the form of code-switches and borrowings. A bilingual mode will also arise when a bilingual child is interacting with a bilingual parent (or adult), when a bilingual is simply listening to a conversation which contains elements of the other language or, more experimentally, when the study concerns bilingualism, the stimuli come from both languages and the task asked of the participants requires processing in the two languages.[3] As for intermediate positions on the continuum, they will be reached by different combinations of the above factors. If the bilingual's interlocutor is not very proficient in the other language (but still knows it a bit), if he or she does not like to mix languages, if the topic has to be covered in the base language but the other language is needed from time to time (e.g. in the case of a bilingual child speaking one language to a bilingual researcher about a topic usually talked about in the other language), if the situation is more formal, if only a few stimuli in an experiment are similar in the two languages (e.g. cross-language homographs, cognates), etc., then we can expect an intermediate language mode. Movement along the continuum, which can happen at any given point in time depending on the factors mentioned above, is usually an unconscious behavior that takes place smoothly and effortlessly. It is probably akin to changing speech style or register based on the context and the interlocutor.

4.1.3 Impact on language behavior

The effects a particular language mode has on language behavior are quite varied. Among these we find the amount of use of the other (guest) language during language production and language perception, the amount and type of mixed language used, the ease of processing of the two languages and the frequency of base-language change. In

---

[3] See Chapter 5 also.

the monolingual mode, the language not being processed is deactivated (some researchers such as Green (1986, 1998) would even say that it is inhibited). This in turn prevents changing base language as well as producing mixed speech, that is code-switches and borrowings or, at least, reducing them drastically. However, dynamic interferences may still take place, that is speaker-specific deviations from the language being spoken due to the influence of the other deactivated language. (Note that interferences can also occur in the bilingual mode but they are more difficult to separate from other forms of language mixing such as code-switches and borrowings.) As for the impact on listening in the monolingual mode, the bilingual will not make much use of the deactivated language (if any) and this may speed up the processing of the base language (but this still has to be proved experimentally).[4] As concerns the bilingual mode, both languages will be active but one language (language B in Figure 4.1) will be slightly less active than the other language (language A) as it is not currently the main language of communication. In production, bilinguals usually first adopt a base language through the process of language choice (language A in our case) and, when needed, they can bring in the other language, often referred to as the guest language, in the form of code-switches and borrowings. A code-switch is a complete shift to the other language for a word, a phrase, or a sentence whereas a borrowing is a morpheme, word, or short expression taken from the less activated language and adapted morphosyntactically (and sometimes phonologically) to the base language. Borrowings can involve both the form and the content of a word (these are called nonce borrowings) or simply the content (called loan shifts). It should be noted that given the high level of activation of both languages in the bilingual mode, not only can code-switches and borrowings be produced but the base language can also be changed frequently, that is the slightly less activated language becomes the base language and vice versa. A change of topic, of situation, of interlocutors, etc. may lead to a change in base language. In our example, language B would then become the more active language (it would be represented by a black square) and language A would be slightly less active (the black square would contain white diagonal lines). When this happens repeatedly within the same interaction, it gives the impression that the two languages are equally active but there is evidence in the

---

[4] To my knowledge, no experiment aimed at this question has given all the necessary guarantees that the participants were in a truly monolingual mode. See Chapter 5 for further discussion of this.

sociolinguistic and psycholinguistic literature that, at any one point in time, one language is always more active than the other and that it is this language that governs language processing. As concerns perception, both languages will be processed in the bilingual language mode but the base language will usually play a greater role (see Grosjean 1997a for a review of work on mixed language processing). Finally, the impact of an intermediate mode will be somewhere in between: more code-switching and borrowing than in the monolingual mode, some flagged switches, fewer dynamic interferences, some involvement of the other language during perception, etc.

4.1.4 Additional points

Several additional points need to be made concerning language mode. First, it should be noted that bilinguals differ among themselves as to the extent they travel along the language mode continuum; some rarely find themselves at the bilingual end (for example, bilinguals who rarely code-switch, sometimes on principle, or who do not hear mixed language very much) whereas others rarely leave this end (for exam-ple, bilinguals who live in communities where mixed language is the norm). Second, movement along the continuum can occur at any time as soon as the factors underlying mode change, be it during a verbal exchange between bilinguals or, in a more controlled situation, during an experiment. In addition, the movement usually takes place uncon-sciously and can be quite extensive. Thus, for example, if a bilingual starts off speaking to a "monolingual" and then realizes, as the conver-sation continues, that he/she is bilingual, there will invariably be a shift towards the bilingual end of the continuum with such consequences as change of base language, code-switching, etc. During perception, if bilingual listeners who start off in a monolingual mode determine (consciously or not) as they go along, that what they are listening to can contain elements from the other language, they will put themselves in a bilingual mode (at least partly), that is, activate both their languages (with the base language being more strongly activated). This is also true of readers, whether they are reading a continuous text or look-ing at individual lexical items interspersed with items from the other language. Simply knowing that there is a possibility that elements from the other language will be presented (in an experiment, for example) will probably move the bilingual away from the monolingual endpoint of the continuum. Just one guest word in a stream of base-language words may well increase this displacement. Third, the minimum and maximum possible levels of activation of the other language (language B) are still not totally clear and remain an empirical issue. Currently, and as can be seen at the two extremes of the continuum in Figure 4.1, it is proposed that the other language is probably never totally deactivated at the monolingual end and that it very rarely reaches the same level of activation as the base language at the bilingual end (except, of course, when there is a change of base language). As concerns the lack of total deactivation, there is considerable evidence in the literature that bilinguals make dynamic interferences (ephemeral deviations due to the influence of the other deactivated language) even in the most monolingual of situations. This can only happen if the other language is active to some extent at least. As for the unequal activation of the two languages in the bilingual language mode, linguists working on code-switching and borrowing have often reported that the base language usually governs the language production process (it is the "host" or "matrix" language) and hence it is used much more than the other. Of course, one can think of exceptions where the two languages could share the same level of complete activation. This may be the case, for example, in an experiment where the participants are told, or find out, that the stimuli presented belong to either of the two languages. More interestingly, simultaneous interpreters need both languages to the same extent: input is in one language and output in the other (this special case will be evoked later in this chapter). Finally, the case of non-accommodation in language choice should be mentioned, that is, when bilingual X speaks language A and bilingual Y speaks language B. Here both languages may be activated to the same level, unless one chooses to talk in terms of input and output processing systems being activated to different extents. These exceptions aside, the base language is normally more active than the other language.

4.2 Evidence for language mode

Even though the concept of language mode has been alluded to by several researchers over the years, it has not been the object of systematic study until quite recently. However, if one combines earlier research in which language mode is varied in an indirect, non-explicit way with more recent research that manipulates it explicitly, one can find strong evidence for the phenomenon. In what follows, research that pertains to language production, language perception, language acquisition, and language pathology will be surveyed.

4.2.1 Language production

In one of her first publications, Poplack (1981) reports on a 35-year-old member of El Barrio (a Puerto Rican neighborhood in New York) who was tape-recorded in four different sessions where the base language was English: "Formal" in which she responded orally to a questionnaire given to her by a bilingual member of her community; "Informal" in which she had a conversation concerning topics of interest to her with the same person; "Vernacular" where she was recorded while doing errands and chatting with passers-by in her neighborhood; and, finally, "Informal (non-group)" where she conversed with an English-Spanish bilingual who was not a member of her community. Although language mode was not manipulated directly, the informant was probably at the bilingual end of the language mode continuum in the "Informal" and "Vernacular" sessions (she was with members of her community with whom she code-switched frequently) whereas she was in an intermediate mode in the other two sessions. In the "Formal" session she probably felt that the formality of responding to a questionnaire was not conducive to code-switching, and in the "Informal (non-group)" session, she felt she did not know the other interviewer well enough to code-switch as much with her as with an in-group member. In both these cases, therefore, she probably deactivated her Spanish to some extent and was in an intermediate mode. The code-switching patterns reported by the author confirm the impact of language mode on language production: there were about four times more code-switches per minute in the "Informal" and "Vernacular" sessions than in the "Formal" and "Informal (non-group)" sessions.

More recently, Treffers-Daller (1998) has examined explicitly the effect of a speaker's position on the language mode continuum in terms of language choice and code-switching. She placed the same speaker, a Turkish-German bilingual, in three different positions by changing the context and the interlocutors, and she found quite different results. In the first context, which corresponds to a position to the right of the monolingual mode endpoint, the bilingual was speaking to members of a German-speaking family in Turkey who knew some Turkish. As a consequence, about three-quarters of the speaker's utterances were in German and not much language mixing occurred (they mainly concerned borrowings). In the second context, which corresponds to an intermediate mode, the same bilingual, in Germany this time, was speaking to a Turkish-German bilingual he did not know very well. The author noted more changes of base language than in the first context and, although the amount of mixed utterances was not much greater, these were quite different. They consisted of peripheral switches that filled a pragmatic function and that contained various types of pauses (this behavior has been called flagged switching). As for the third context, which corresponds to the bilingual end of the language mode continuum, the same bilingual interacted with a very close bilingual friend in Turkey. Here most utterances were in Turkish and there was much more language mixing than in the other two contexts. In addition, the code-switches were both intra- and intersentential and they were produced without hesitations or special highlighting (these have been called fluent switches). Based on these results, Treffers-Daller concludes that the language mode continuum concept may offer a new approach to studying variable code-switching patterns within and between communities (e.g. Poplack 1985; Bentahila and Davies 1991) because it can help predict the frequency and type of switching that takes place.

In a laboratory based study, Grosjean (1997a) manipulated the language mode French-English bilinguals were in when retelling French stories that contained English code-switches. The participants were told they were taking part in a "telephone chain" experiment whose aim was to examine the amount of information that could be conveyed from one person to another. The three French interlocutors they had to retell the stories to were described to the participants before the experiment started by means of short biographical sketches. The first interlocutor induced a monolingual mode, the second an intermediary mode, and the third a bilingual mode. The three dependent measures obtained during the retellings (number of guest language syllables, number of base language syllables, and number of hesitations produced) were all affected by the language mode the speakers were in. The number of guest language syllables (code-switches, borrowings) increased significantly as the participants moved from a monolingual to a bilingual mode whereas the number of base language syllables decreased, as did the number of hesitations.[5]

---

[5] See Chapter 5 for more details on this study and a description of other studies of the same kind.

4.2.2 Language perception

There has been far less (if any) systematic research on language mode in the domain of perception. Consequently, evidence for its impact in this modality has to come from studies that have manipulated the variable inadvertently. One example comes from two studies in the domain of speech perception. Caramazza *et al.* (1973) tested English-French bilinguals on voice onset time (VOT) continua (ba-pa; da-ta; ga-ka) and obtained identification curves in an English and in a French language set. The language sets were obtained by changing the experimenters (one English speaking, one French speaking), the settings, the language of the instructions, and the initial production task. (We should note that manipulations of this type determine what the base language will be, English or French in this case, but do not necessarily deactivate the other language.) Although the authors expected the bilinguals to behave like French listeners when in a French language set and like English listeners in an English language set (i.e. to show a perceptual boundary shift), they obtained similar functions for the two languages. These were situated in an intermediate position between the functions obtained with monolingual speakers of each language set. The authors concluded that the bilingual participants were responding to the stimuli themselves and were not influenced by language set. A few years later, Elman *et al.* (1977) decided to investigate this question further but this time to make sure that the language set was firmly established. Thus, in addition to using naturally produced stimuli, the test tapes contained an assortment of one or two syllable filler words along with the stimuli. In addition, each item was preceded by a sentence in the appropriate language (in this case, English and Spanish). This time, the authors did find a boundary shift, with ambiguous stimuli perceived significantly more as English or as Spanish depending on the language set the listeners were in. How can these contradictory results be interpreted in terms of language mode? It is proposed that, in the first study, the language set manipulation undertaken at the beginning of testing was not sufficient to keep the bilingual listeners at the monolingual endpoint of the continuum. In effect, they were probably in, or they quickly moved to, a bilingual mode when asked to identify the experimental stimuli (especially as the latter were language-neutral synthetic speech). Hence the bilingual participants produced compromise (bilingual) results that were intermediate between those of the two monolingual groups. However, in the second study, there was constant language specific information (through the natural stimuli, the carrier sentence, and the filler words) which activated one language much more than the other and hence kept the bilinguals at the monolingual end of the continuum. The stimuli were thus processed more "monolingually" in Spanish or English and this led to a boundary shift.

Language mode was manipulated by both top-down and bottom-up information in the two speech perception studies we have just seen, whereas in a lexical access study conducted some years later by Grainger and Beauvillain (1987), it depended on bottom-up information only. In this study, French-English bilinguals were asked to do a lexical decision task on two types of lists: "pure" lists which contained words from one language only and "mixed" lists which contained words from both languages. The authors found that the participants were some 36 ms faster in the pure list condition than in the other condition. We can interpret this result in the following way. In the pure list condition, the bilinguals were close to the monolingual end of the continuum (they didn't attain it though, as they knew the study dealt with bilingualism) and hence their lexical search/look-up task was made easier as one lexicon was much more active than the other. In the mixed condition, however, the bilinguals were at the bilingual end of the continuum. Both lexicons were active as words could come from either and hence the lexical decision took more time. It should be noted that in a second experiment, the authors found that the list condition effect was significant only in the absence of language specific orthographic cues. This in no way weakens the explanation just given as language mode is just one of many variables that will account for the time it takes to recognize a word.

Finally, in a 1998 study, Dijkstra *et al.* bring further, albeit indirect, evidence for the effect of language mode during perception. They tested Dutch-English bilinguals (dominant in Dutch) in three experiments and manipulated word type, language intermixing, and task. In what follows, only the first and third experiments will be examined as they pertain more directly to the language mode issue. In the first, the participants saw English/Dutch homographs and cognates, English control words, and English nonwords. They were asked to do an English lexical decision on the items presented, that is, to indicate whether the items were English words or not, and they were tested in an English language set. Although cognates were responded to significantly faster than control words (570 and 595 ms respectively), no difference was found between homographs and their controls (580 ms in both cases). In the third experiment, participants once again saw homographs (no cognates though) as well as English and Dutch control words and English and Dutch nonwords. On this occasion they were asked to do a general lexical decision, that is indicate whether the items were words in English or in Dutch. This time, the authors did find a homograph effect in English: participants reacted to homographs faster than to English control words (554 and 592 ms respectively) but not to Dutch words (554 ms). A language mode account of these results is as follows. In Experiment 1, the participants were positioned towards the monolingual end of the continuum without reaching it totally as they knew they were being tested as bilinguals. They only heard English words and nonwords (although some words were homographs and cognates) and they were asked to decide whether the items were English words or not. Thus, although their Dutch was partly active (which would explain the cognate effect), it was not sufficiently active to create a homograph effect. However, in Experiment 3, the participants were definitely at the bilingual end of the continuum. Not only were the words and nonwords both English and Dutch but the participants were asked to do general lexical decision, that is search/look-up both their lexicons to accomplish the task. As both lexicons were active, they probably considered homographs as Dutch words and hence reacted to them as quickly as to regular Dutch words. This would explain the lack of difference between homographs and Dutch control words but the significant difference between homographs and English control words. The latter, it should be recalled, belonged to their weaker language and hence were reacted to more slowly.[6]

4.2.3 Language acquisition

As will be seen later, language mode has rarely been controlled for in bilingual acquisition research. However, more recent studies have started to manipulate this variable and they have produced converging evidence for its importance. In one such study, Lanza (1992) recorded a 2-year-old Norwegian-English bilingual child (Siri) interacting either with her American mother or her Norwegian father, both of whom were bilingual. What is interesting is that the mother frequently feigned the role of a monolingual and did not mix languages with Siri. The father, on the other hand, accepted Siri's language mixing and responded to it. Lanza studied the interactions between Siri and her parents in terms of a monolingual–bilingual

---

[6] For two recent studies in the domain of language perception, see Chapter 5.

discourse context continuum on which she placed various parental strategies. For example, "Minimal grasp" and "Expressed guess" are at the monolingual end (they were precisely the strategies used by the mother) and "Move on" and "Code-switching" strategies are at the bilingual end (they were the ones used by Siri's father). These strategies produced very different results: Siri did much more content word mixing with her father (who was open to code-switching) than with her mother (who did not respond to it), and this over the whole period of study (from age 2;0 to 2;7). What this means in terms of language mode is that Siri was herself probably in different modes with her two parents—she leaned towards the monolingual end with her mother (but never reached it as she did switch with her sometimes) and she was at the bilingual end with her father.

Although Nicoladis and Genesee (1998) have not managed to repli-cate Lanza's finding with English-French bilingual children in Mon-treal, they do not seem to question the parental discourse strategies proposed by Lanza nor the results she obtained. Instead they offer other reasons for finding different results such as the different sociolinguistic context, the fact that the Montreal children may not have understood the parental strategies, or the difference in language proficiency of the children in the two studies. In fact, Genesee et al. (1996) have published some rather compelling evidence that bilingual children are very sensi-tive to the language behavior of the adults they are with. They recorded four English-French bilingual children (average age 2;2) as they spoke to their mother, to their father, or to a stranger who only spoke their weaker language. On the level of language choice, they found that each child used more of the mother's language (be it French or English) with the mother than with the father, more of the father's language with the father than with the mother, and that they accommodated to the stranger as best they could by adopting the stranger's language as the base language, at least in part, or by mixing more. As concerns language mode, it would seem that only two of the four children had enough competence in the two languages to benefit fully from movement along the language mode continuum (Jessica and Leila). If, for these children, one takes the amount of weaker language used by the parent (e.g. the amount of English spoken by a French dominant parent) to which one adds the amount of mixed utterances, and one then correlates this value with the equivalent amount obtained from the child when speaking with that parent, one obtains a very high 0.85 correlation. This indicates that the more a parent switches over to the other language during communication, the more the child does so too. This finding is very similar to Lanza's (1992). In terms of language mode, children are more in a monolingual mode with parents who do not mix language much (all other things being equal) whereas they are more in a bilingual mode with parents who mix languages to a greater extent (or at least accept language mixing).

4.2.4 Language pathology

Studies that have examined bilinguals who suffer from some form of language pathology (aphasia, dementia, etc.) have also rarely manipulated language mode or controlled for it. Thus claims that language mixing is due to the patient's pathology may have to be revised if language mode is a confounding factor (as it often is; see the next section). Just recently, Marty and Grosjean (1998) manipulated language mode in a study that examined spoken language production in eight French-German aphasic bilinguals. The patients were asked to undertake various language tasks: place one of several cards in a specified position on a board, describe a postcard in enough detail so that it can be found among several similar postcards, take part in a topic constrained interaction, and, finally, talk freely about any topic which comes to mind. The critical independent variable was the patient's interlocutor. The first was a totally monolingual French speaker who did not know any German whatsoever (unlike in many other studies where the interlocutor knew the other language but pretended not to) and the second was a French-German bilingual. The patients were told about their interlocutors' language background prior to testing and they interacted with them a bit at that time. The results clearly differentiated pathological from non-pathological mixing. Five of the eight aphasics did not mix their languages with the monolingual interlocutor (they only used her native language) and one did so extremely seldom (it was probably due to stress or fatigue) whereas two did so quite extensively. It was concluded that of the eight aphasics, six patients could still control their language mode and adapt it to the interlocutor whereas two could no longer do so.

In sum, there is increasing evidence, direct and indirect, that language mode plays an important role in language processing as well as in language acquisition and language pathology.

4.3 Language mode as a confounding and a control variable

Given that language mode plays an important role in all types of bilingual language behavior, it is important that it be controlled for if it is not the main variable being studied. Unfortunately, this has not been the case in many past studies. The consequence is that the data obtained are both very variable, due to the fact that participants are probably situated at various points along the continuum, and at times ambiguous given the confound between this factor and the variable under study. In this section, issues in bilingualism research that are affected by language mode will be presented and examples of how the variable can influence them inadvertently will be discussed. Ways of controlling language mode will then be proposed.[7]

4.3.1 Language mode as a confounding variable

One issue influenced by language mode concerns the type of data obtained in descriptive studies. For example, researchers who have examined bilingual language production have often reported instances of interference. The problem is that it is not always clear what is meant by this term (also called transfer or transference). As indicated earlier, for Weinreich (1966), interferences are instances of deviation from the norms of either language which occur in the speech of bilinguals as a result of their familiarity with more than one language. Haugen (1956) refers to interference as the overlapping of two languages, Mackey (1968) talks of the use of features belonging to one language while speaking or writing another, and for Clyne (1967) transference is the adoption of any elements or features from the other language (he uses the term as a cover term for language contact phenomena). A direct result of this broad view is that the interferences observed in linguistic studies correspond not only to interferences but also often to borrowings and even code-switches. As stated in Grosjean (1998b), we will never get to the bottom of this terminological problem, and we will never isolate interferences from code-switches and borrowings in bilingual speech, if we do not take into account (and do not control for) the language mode bilinguals and language learners are in when they are being studied (i.e. observed, recorded, tested, etc.). Very often the bilinguals' interlocutors know the language not being spoken (the one causing the interference) and hence bilinguals are in an intermediate

---

[7] For a more extensive discussion of these topics, see Grosjean (1998a) or Chapter 14.

mode if not in a bilingual mode when being recorded. When interferences occur in the bilingual mode, which they also do, they are very difficult to separate from other forms of language mixing, especially borrowings. What might appear to be an interference could also be a guest element or structure produced by the speaker who is aware that his or her interlocutor can understand mixed language.[8] (The same point is made by Poplack 1985.)

A similar problem concerns "intentional" and "unintentional" switches in second language production. Poulisse and Bongaerts (1994), for example, define unintentional switches as cases which were not preceded by any signs of hesitation and did not stand out from the rest of the utterance by a marked intonation. The problem is that it is not clear what language mode their second language learners were in when they tested them. If they were not in a monolingual mode, then their switches may not have been unintentional (at least not all of them). In fact, we are told that these switches contained a large proportion of editing terms which the speakers used to comment on an error made or on an inappropriate word used, and/or to warn the listener that what followed should be interpreted as a repair of what preceded. This would seem to indicate that the interviewers could indeed understand the other language and that the learners were at least partly in a bilingual mode. The same argument can be made about "fluent" and "flagged" switches. Poplack (1985) defines the former as switches with smooth transitions and no hesitations, whereas the latter are switches that draw attention to themselves through repetition, hesitation, intonational highlighting, and metalinguistic commentary. Poplack compares the fluent switches found in the Puerto Rican community in New York and the flagged switches obtained in Ottawa-Hull and recognizes that the difference in type could be due, in part at least, to the data collection technique used in each case—an informal participant observation technique in New York and a more formal random sampling technique in the Ottawa-Hull region. In terms of language mode, participants were probably in a totally bilingual mode in New York and in an intermediate language mode in Ottawa-Hull.

Another issue that is affected by language mode concerns whether bilinguals have an integrated semantic memory for their two languages (also called a shared or a common store) or whether they have two separate, independent semantic systems. Several studies have addressed this question and some (e.g. Schwanenflugel and Rey 1986; Fox 1996;

---

[8] See Chapter 14 (Section 14.2.2) for an example of this.

etc.) come to the conclusion that bilinguals have a shared representational system. The problem is that it is difficult to tease apart in their results what is due to the representational issue and what is caused by the language mode variable. The bilingual participants were probably not in a monolingual mode when they took part in the studies. They knew they were being tested as bilinguals and they saw words in the two languages. Because of this, they had probably activated both their languages (consciously or unconsciously) and were thus in a bilingual mode. This would invariably lead to results indicating a shared system.[9] A related issue concerns the presence or absence of language-selective access during visual word perception. Beauvillain and Grainger (1987), for example, found evidence for non-selective access when bilinguals were shown interlexical homographs. The problem, however, is that the bilingual participants in their experiment needed their two languages to do the task: they had to read a context word in one language and then decide whether the next word, always in the other language, was a word or not in that language. In order to do this, they had to activate both their languages and hence were in a bilingual language mode. (As they were tested as bilinguals, they were probably already in a bilingual mode before the experiment even started.) It is no surprise, therefore, that a result indicating non-selective processing was obtained (the same comment can be made about another well known study which examined the same question, that of Altenberg and Cairns 1983). In sum, if one is interested in such issues as the independence or the interdependence of the bilingual's language systems, selective versus non-selective processing, one versus two lexicons, etc., one should be careful not to activate the other language with the stimuli or the procedure used. When this occurs, it becomes difficult to disentangle what is due to bilingual representation and processing, and what is due to the bilingual language mode the participants are in. In addition, strict dichotomies such as selective versus non-selective processing probably have little psychological reality if one thinks of the bilingual moving along the language mode continuum in his/her everyday life. Processing may be selective (or very close to it) when the bilingual is in a monolingual mode, partly selective when the mode is intermediate and non-selective when the mode is bilingual.

---

[9] Additional details concerning the Schwanenflugel and Rey (1986) and Fox (1996) studies are given in Chapter 14 (Section 14.2.2).

A last issue pertains to the amount of language mixing that is produced by certain types of bilinguals. For example, in the bilingual language development literature, it has been proposed that children who acquire two languages simultaneously go through an early fusion stage in which the languages are in fact one system (one lexicon, one grammar, etc.). They then slowly differentiate their languages, first separating their lexicons and then their grammars. Evidence for this has come from the observation of language mixing in very young bilingual children and from the fact that there is a gradual reduction of mixing as the child grows older. However, this position has been criticized by a number of researchers (e.g. Meisel 1989; Genesee 1989; among others) and one of the points made each time (in addition to the fact that translation equivalents may not be known in the other language) is that the children were often in a bilingual mode, that is the caretakers were usually bilingual themselves and they were probably overheard using both languages, separately or in a mixed form, by the children, if not actually mixing their languages with them (see Goodz 1989). In addition, the context in which the recordings were made for the studies probably induced language mixing as it was rarely (if ever) monolingual (see e.g. Redlinger and Park 1980 and Vihman 1985).[10] The children in these studies were thus probably in a bilingual context which induced a bilingual mode and hence language mixing. In another domain, the amount of language mixing produced by bilingual patients suffering from some type of language pathology (e.g. aphasia, dementia) has been used as an indication of their pathology (e.g. Perecman 1984; Hyltenstam 1991; Ludérus 1995).[11] However, as argued in Grosjean (1998a), most of the patients recorded were at least partially in a bilingual mode when being recorded (and sometimes even in a fully bilingual mode). It is no surprise therefore that they switched to the other language, if this improved communication between the interviewer and themselves.

4.3.2 Language mode as a control variable

Until more is known about language mode (see next section), it is safer to control it by putting bilinguals in a monolingual mode or in a bilingual mode in preference to an intermediate mode (Grosjean 1998a). As

[10] Additional details concerning these two latter studies are given in Chapter 14 (Section 14.2.2).

[11] The studies by Perecman (1984) and Hylstenstam (1991) are discussed in Chapter 14 (Section 14.2.2).

concerns the monolingual mode, two inappropriate approaches must be avoided. The first is to simply put the participants in a "language set" (also called erroneously by some a "language mode") by giving them instructions in one language, getting them to do preliminary tasks in that language, occasionally presenting reminders in that language, etc. What this does is activate a particular base language (the variable depicted on the vertical axis in Figure 4.1) but it does not guarantee a particular position on the monolingual–bilingual mode continuum. A second inappropriate approach, which has been used a lot with bilingual children, second language learners, and aphasic or demented patients, has been to hide the experimenter's or interviewer's bilingualism. This is a very dangerous strategy as subtle cues such as facial expression and body language can give away the interlocutor's comprehension of the other language. In addition, it will not prevent occasional slip-ups such as responding in the "wrong" language or showing in one's response that what has been said in that language has been understood. The solution to positioning the bilingual at the monolingual end point of the continuum is unfortunately not quite as easy as one would like it to be. For interview situations, if the researcher is interested in observing how a bilingual can produce just one language (something a bilingual often has to do), then the interviewer must be completely monolingual in that language (and not feign to be so). In addition, the situation must be monolingual and there must not be any other person present who knows the other language. For more experimental situations, the difficulty is how to prevent the bilingual from activating, to some extent at least, the other language. If interest is shown in the participant's bilingualism, if he or she is tested in a laboratory that works on bilingualism, if the experimenter is bilingual, if the participant sees or hears stimuli from both languages, and if the task requires both languages (e.g. the bilingual Stroop test, bilingual word priming, bilingual association production, bilingual category matching, word translation, etc.), then any one of these factors is sufficient to put the participant in a bilingual mode, in part at least, and hence activate the two languages, albeit to differing degrees. One solution that comes to mind is to intermix bilingual participants with monolingual participants in a monolingual experiment (for example, a study that is part of a course requirement) and once the experiment is done—and after the fact only so as to avoid the Rosenthal effect—to go back to the list of participants and extract the bilinguals. As concerns the bilingual endpoint of the language mode continuum, care will have to be taken that the participants are totally comfortable producing, or listening to, mixed language. This can be done by having bilingual experimenters or interviewers who belong to the same bilingual community as the participants and, if possible, who know them well. They should interact with the participants in mixed language and the situation should be conducive to mixed language (no monolinguals present, a relaxed non-normative atmosphere, etc.).[12]

4.4 Further research on language mode

In this last section, several aspects of language mode that need to be investigated further will be mentioned briefly. They concern the assessment of language mode, the bilingual's processing systems, the case of highly language dominant bilinguals, and modeling.

4.4.1 Assessing language mode

As we have seen in this chapter, many different factors influence language mode. They range from factors that concern participants (language proficiency, language mixing habits and attitudes, usual mode of interaction), to situational factors (physical location, presence of monolinguals, formality), to factors that deal with form and content (language used, topic, amount of mixed language) and with the language act (to communicate information, create a social distance, etc.), all the way to specific research factors (aims of the study taking place, type and organization of the stimuli, task used, instructions, etc.). Future research will have to isolate these factors, determine their importance, and ascertain how they interact with one another to activate or deactivate the bilingual's languages to varying degrees and hence change the bilingual's position on the language mode continuum. Researchers will also have to examine the maximum movement possible on the continuum for various types of bilinguals. As we saw above, bilinguals differ among themselves as to the extent they travel along the language mode continuum; some rarely find themselves at the bilingual end (the other language is never very active) whereas others rarely leave this end (the other language is always very active). And within a bilingual, the minimum and maximum possible levels of activation of the other language can also vary. Another issue concerns a hypothetical resting mode for any

---

[12] See Chapter 5 for further consideration of the problem.

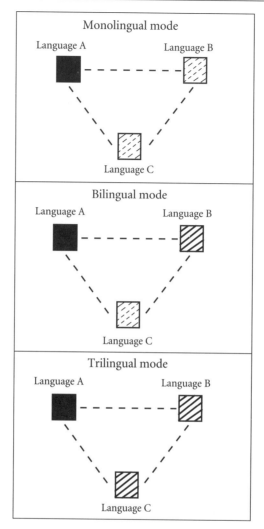

FIGURE 4.2 Visual representation of a trilingual in a monolingual mode (top part), bilingual mode (middle part), and trilingual mode (bottom part). The level of activation of a language is indicated by the degree of darkness of the squares (black is active and white is inactive). Language A is the base language in each case

bilingual individual, that is the language mode the bilingual returns to in-between language activities. Does this notion have any reality or is the bilingual constantly traveling along the continuum? Finally, to complicate things further, people who use three or more languages in their everyday lives will need to be accounted for. For example, one can certainly imagine a trilingual in a monolingual, a bilingual, or a trilingual mode. Figure 4.2 depicts each of these three modes. In the top part of the figure, the trilingual is in a monolingual mode;

language A is active and the other two languages are only very slightly active. In the middle part of the figure, the trilingual is in a bilingual mode; language A remains the base language, language B is active (but less so than language A), and language C is very slightly active. Finally, in the bottom part of the figure, the same trilingual is in a trilingual mode where language A is the base language and languages B and C are also active. What has just been said about trilinguals is true of quadrilinguals. For example, a quadrilingual can be in a language B monolingual mode where language B is being used (it is the base language) and languages A, C, and D are very slightly active. This same person, in another situation, can be in a quadrilingual mode where, for example, language B is the base language and languages A, C, and D are also active. If all this is possible, which it probably is, the language mode concept will have to be extended and its various man-ifestations in these kinds of multilinguals will have to be investigated. This said, it would be a mistake to put the language mode variable aside in bilingualism studies as long as it has not been described fully and a metric has not been developed for it (as a continuous variable affected by a host of factors, one may never be). Language mode is a variable that is constantly present, whatever the bilingual research question being studied, and it therefore needs to be taken into account at all times.

4.4.2 Language mode and the processing mechanisms

So far language mode has been defined as a state of activation of the bilingual's languages and language processing mechanisms at any given point in time. To simplify things, no difference has been made in terms of mode between language knowledge and language processing, and, in the latter case, between the input and output mechanisms. However, it could be that one will need to differentiate these three components at some time. For example, as concerns processing, a bilingual can be speaking one language and listening to another (such as when two interlocutors do not accommodate to a common base language). A simple account of this is that the language mode is the same in the input and output systems but that the base language is different. But things become more complex if the interlocutor's input is monolingual in nature (it contains no language mixing) but the speaker's output involves language mixing (or vice versa). In this case, different language modes will have to be attributed to the input and output systems. The case of simultaneous interpreters is akin to this situation. What language mode are interpreters in when they are doing simultaneous interpretation? A suggestion made in Grosjean (1997b) is that the input and output processing mechanisms of each language are indeed separated here. First, as can be seen in Figure 4.3, the interpreter is in a bilingual mode and both languages are active. However, one language is *not* more active than the other as is normally the case in the bilingual mode. Both the source language and the target language are active to the same extent (black squares in the figure) as both are needed, for perception and production respectively. Second, input and output components have been added to each language (circles in the figure) and it is their level of activation that varies. Although the two languages are equally active, the processing mechanisms are not. In this way, the interpreter will be able to input the source language (and to a lesser extent the target language, see below) and to output the target language only. Third, the input component of the source and of the target language are both active. At least three reasons require that the input component of the target language also be active: the interpreter must be able to monitor his/her overt speech (Levelt 1989), the client's occasional use of the target language must be processed (interpreters report that this indeed takes place), and a fellow interpreter's cues must be heard. Fourth, the target language output mechanism is active whereas the source language output mechanism is not (it may be totally deactivated

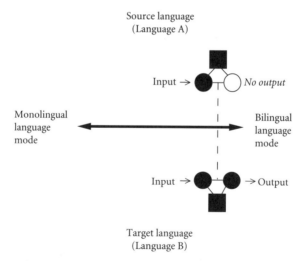

FIGURE 4.3 Visual representation of the interpreter's position on the language mode continuum when doing simultaneous interpreting. Both languages are active (black squares) but they differ as to the level of activation of their input and output mechanisms (represented by circles)

or, quite exceptionally, inhibited). In sum, the two languages are in a bilingual mode (both are active); the output mechanisms are in a monolingual mode (only one language is normally output) whereas the input mechanisms are in a bilingual mode (input takes place in the source and sometimes in the target language). How inactive the source output mechanism should be is discussed in Grosjean (1997b).

4.4.3 Highly language dominant bilinguals

Language mode will also have to be studied in bilinguals who are highly dominant in one language, such as members of minority groups who rarely use the majority language, bilingual children who are strongly dominant in one language, second language learners (on the condition that they make regular functional use of their second language),[13] etc. It has been reported repeatedly in the literature that these types of bilinguals do more language mixing when speaking their weaker language than their stronger language. Thus, Genesee *et al.* (1995) and Nicoladis and Genesee (1998) report that bilingual children code-mix more when talking with the parent who speaks their non-dominant language (irrespective of whether the parent code-mixes in return); Lanza (1992) reports that the Norwegian-English bilingual child she studied (Siri) did more function word mixing with her English-speaking mother, indicating thereby the child's dominance in Norwegian; Poulisse and Bongaerts (1994) report that the use of unintentional switches is L2 proficiency related (more proficient learners produce fewer of them); and, even in perception, Elman *et al.* (1977) report a 0.52 correlation between the degree of bilingualism and the amount of identification shift for the ambiguous VOT stimuli. This would mean that bilinguals who are highly dominant in one language may simply not be able to control language mode in the same way as less dominant or balanced bilinguals. Although they may deactivate their stronger language in a monolingual environment that requires only the weaker language (for example, it is of no use speaking Italian, one's stronger language, to an English speaker who knows absolutely no Italian), that language will simply not be developed enough or active enough to allow them to stay in a monolingual mode.[14] Future research will have to investigate the underlying mechanisms that make a stronger language "seep through"

---

[13] It is difficult to know how the language mode concept applies to "traditional" language learners who acquire their second language in a formal school environment. Those who interact in their L2 in a natural environment can be accounted for more easily.

[14] We come back to this issue in Chapter 5.

despite the fact that it has been deactivated. It will also have to isolate which part of behavior is due to competence (i.e. the representation or grammar of the weaker language) and which part is due to performance (i.e. the system's inability to activate or deactivate a language or processing mechanism at any particular point in time). Finally, attention will have to be paid to bilinguals who, through some kind of pathology (aphasia, dementia, etc.), lose their ability to move along the language mode continuum. Some can no longer leave the monolingual mode (they cannot mix languages anymore) whereas others are in a constant bilingual mode and hence mix their two languages when it is not appropriate.

4.4.4 Modeling

Models of bilingual competence, bilingual production, and perception as well as bilingual language acquisition will have to take into account language mode. For example, De Bot's (1992) global model of bilingual language production has played an important role in bilingualism research in recent years but it does not yet give a clear account of how language choice takes place (i.e. how the base language is chosen), how the language mode is set, and the impact it has on processing. Some models may have a harder time integrating language mode, in particular the bilingual language mode where both languages are active but one slightly less so than the other. For example, Green's (1998) Inhibitory Control (IC) Model supposes that a word from a chosen language is output by suppressing lemmas with the incorrect language tags. This can account for production in the monolingual mode but it is problematic when the mode is bilingual. In this case, it is often the most active word that is output, irrespective of language. Admittedly, Green does agree that code-switching would involve a cooperative rather than a competitive relationship between the word production schemas, but this needs to be spelled out. Green (p.c.) proposes that this might take place either by reducing the strength (gain) of the inhibitory relations directly or by inhibiting the inhibition. In the domain of perception, models that contain interlanguage inhibition will have a problem accounting for the perception of code-switches and borrowings in the bilingual language mode. Thus, in the Bilingual Interactive Activation (BIA) model (Dijkstra and Van Heuven 1998), one language is normally deactivated during the word recognition process by means of top-down inhibition from the other language node and lateral interlanguage word level inhibition. This will produce satisfactory results for word recognition in the monolingual mode but it will be less than optimal when mixed language is being perceived. In this latter case, it would be better if both languages were active with one more active than the other (see the base-language effect described in Grosjean 1988, 1997a). BIA has the possibility of presetting a language node from external sources at the beginning of word recognition but invariably, during the actual recognition process, the built-in cross-language inhibitory mechanisms will cause one language to be inhibited unless, of course, these mechanisms are switched off. (It should be noted that Woutersen (1997) proposes a model of the bilingual lexicon that contains language nodes and where the bilingual can be in differing language modes; it is unclear, however, how the model would be implemented computationally.) To our knowledge, the only bilingual word recognition model that currently simulates language mode is the Model of Guest Word Recognition proposed by Grosjean (1988). The computational version, BIMOLA (Léwy and Grosjean, unpublished), consists of three levels of nodes which use localist representations (features, phonemes, and words), and it is characterized by various excitatory and inhibitory links within and between levels. Among its particularities we find shared phonetic features for the languages (in this case, English and French), language independent, yet parallel, processing at the higher levels (phonemes and words), as well as the absence of cross-language inhibition processes. It does not resort to the concept of a language node as proposed by the BIA model but relies instead on overall language activation as an emergent phenomenon. Both the base language setting (a discrete value) and the language mode setting (a continuous value) can be set prior to simulation.[15]

Conclusion

This chapter has examined the many facets of language mode, a concept that has received relatively little attention in bilingualism research. This is unfortunate as taking language mode into account offers many advantages. It gives a truer reflection of how bilinguals process their two languages separately or together, it helps to understand data obtained from various bilingual populations, it accounts for problematic or ambiguous findings in the literature, and it can serve

[15] For a description of BIMOLA, see Chapter 11.

as a control variable in studies examining other topics. Language mode will invariably be present in bilingual research be it as an independent variable, a control variable, or, unfortunately, a confounding variable. Giving it the importance it deserves will facilitate our work as researchers and will further our understanding of the bilingual person.

5

Manipulating Language Mode*

A number of language production and perception studies have been undertaken in which language mode is manipulated experimentally. In the first part of the chapter, the original language mode production study is summarized. It was was done with the help of Lysiane Grosjean in Boston with French-English bilinguals and it has already been referred to briefly in Chapter 4 (Section 4.2.1). Two other studies are then described: a replication with an interesting twist undertaken by Sonia Weil in Basle, Switzerland, with Swiss German-French bilinguals, and an investigation by Paulo Caixeta in Neuchâtel, Switzerland, with Brazilian Portuguese-French bilinguals. In the latter study, the fluency of the participants was also manipulated. In the second part of the chapter, the reasons why it is so difficult to control for language mode in perception experiments, in particular the monolingual mode, are discussed. The factors that move bilingual subjects towards a bilingual mode, even though every effort is made to put them in a monolingual mode, are reviewed. The difficulties encountered are illustrated with two perception studies done by others who sought to induce a monolingual mode but who failed to do so.

5.1 Production studies

5.1.1 The Boston study

In the original Boston study (described in part in Grosjean 1997a and mentioned briefly in Chapter 4), we wanted to obtain experimental evidence for the language mode continuum. In particular, we

* The first part of this chapter appeared in Grosjean, F. (1997a). "Processing mixed language: Issues, findings and models", in A. de Groot and J. Kroll (eds.) *Tutorials in Bilingualism: Psycholinguistic Perspectives*. Mahwah, NJ: Lawrence Erlbaum Associates. The author thanks the publisher for permission to reprint it here.

wished to study two factors that appear to control where the bilingual stands along the continuum—the topic of the exchange and the person addressed. We also wanted to examine the production strategies employed when language mixing is not appropriate on one factor (person addressed) but is required by the other (topic), and we wished to obtain code-switches and borrowings in good recording conditions for further analysis in the laboratory. The method used was to ask French-English bilingual subjects who lived in Boston, USA, to summarize stories they heard in French as well as to describe cartoons to persons not actually present. The subjects, fifteen in all, were told they were taking part in a "telephone chain" experiment which was being recorded and that we were interested in the amount of information that could be conveyed from one person to another. (The persons they would be speaking to, not actually present but described by us, would, in turn, convey the same information to other persons and so on.) The first factor manipulated was the topic of the stories or cartoons that were given to them. Half the stories were in French only (they were monolingual) and concerned situations found in France. As for the accompanying cartoons, they depicted typically French scenes. The other half of the stories and cartoons were bilingual. The stories, in French, concerned typical American activities and hence contained a number of English code-switches. An extract from one of the stories is given below (code-switches are in uppercase and the translation is in italics):

L'autre jour, nous sommes allés APPLE PICKING avec les enfants. Il faisait
(*The other day we went apple picking with the kids. The weather was*)
vraiment très beau et le FOLIAGE virait au rouge. Il y avait des YARD SALES
(*really beautiful and the foliage was turning red. There were some yard sales*)
un peu partout le long des routes et on s'arrêtait parfois pour voir s'il n'y avait
(*all along the roads and we stopped from time to time to see if there*)
pas de REAL BARGAINS. On a trouvé des SECOND-HAND CLOTHES pas
(*weren't any real bargains. We found some quite cheap second-hand clothes*)
chers du tout pour les enfants. Marc avait tellement envie d'une DIRT BIKE
(*for the kids. Marc wanted a dirt bike so badly*)
qu'on la lui a finalement achetée, et Eric est reparti avec un SNOWSUIT
(*that we finally bought him one, and Eric came back with a snowsuit that*)
presque neuf...
(*was practically new...*)

As for the "bilingual" cartoons, they depicted typical American scenes (e.g. Thanksgiving Day) and could not easily be described in French without reverting to code-switching and borrowing.

The second factor manipulated was the person the subjects had to speak to. The three persons were described to the subjects before the experiment started by means of a short biographical sketch. In addition, during the study itself, the main points concerning each person were on an index card in front of the speakers. The first person (referred to as "French" below) had just arrived in the United States to do a post-doc. He could read and write English quite well but still had difficulties speaking it. He was still adapting to life in America and spoke French at home. The second person (Bilingual A) had lived in the States for seven years and worked for a French government agency. He taught French and organized French cultural events. His children went to a bilingual school and he only spoke French at home although he was bilingual in French and English. As for the third person (Bilingual B), he too had been in the States for seven years. He worked for a local electronics firm, had French and American friends, and spoke both languages at home. His children went to the local school. No mention was made of the three persons' practice of language mixing but the answers to a questionnaire filled out by each subject at the end of the experiment clearly showed that they had inferred what this behavior was for each addressee. The French listener was not considered fluent in English and, as a consequence, was not seen as code-switching to a large extent. Bilingual A was considered fluent in English but was also seen as a purist who did not code-switch very much (although slightly more than the French listener). His attitude towards code-switching was seen as negative (recall that he taught French and worked for a French agency). As for Bilingual B, he was seen as being very fluent in English and having a positive attitude towards code-switching, and hence as someone who mixed language a lot.

The subjects were run individually and the summaries and descriptions were transcribed. The amount of French and English spoken (in terms of number of syllables uttered in each language) and the hesitation pauses produced were tabulated for each story and cartoon. The results show evidence for the importance of the two variables tested. As concerns the topic, bilingual stories and cartoons produced about ten times more English in the form of code-switches and borrowings than monolingual stories and cartoons. As for the second variable, the person being addressed, Figure 5.1 presents the distribution of the mean number of French, English (code-switches, borrowings), and hesitation syllables produced for the bilingual stories (i.e. the ones with code-switches) as a function of the person addressed. If one uses the

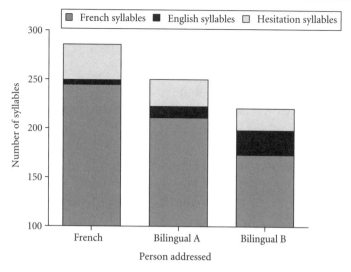

FIGURE 5.1 Distribution of the mean number of French, English (code-switches, borrowings), and hesitation syllables produced for the bilingual stories as a function of the person addressed: French, Bilingual A, and Bilingual B. Each mean is based on 30 values (15 subjects and 2 values per subject)

Source: Reprinted from Grosjean (1997a).

results obtained for Bilingual B as the bilingual standard (right hand bar), one notices, as expected, a large mean number of French syllables (173 on average; recall that the base language was French), some English syllables (25) which reflect the code-switching and borrowing taking place and a certain number of hesitation syllables (23). When one examines the results for Bilingual A (middle bar), one observes more French syllables (211 on average), fewer English syllables (12), and more hesitation syllables (27). This difference in distribution seems to be due to the fact that subjects did not feel they could code-switch as much with this person because of his purism and, in particular, his attitude towards code-switching (as we saw above, this came out strongly in their responses to the post experiment questionnaire). As a consequence, the information had to be given in French which entails hesitating more while one finds a way of conveying the information and producing rather lengthy translations. It is interesting to note that subjects did not wish to code-switch with this addressee but sometimes gave way to doing so in order not to have to find roundabout ways of conveying the information given in English in the stories. As for the French addressee who knew very little English (left hand bar), subjects had little choice but to try to say everything in French, hence the large

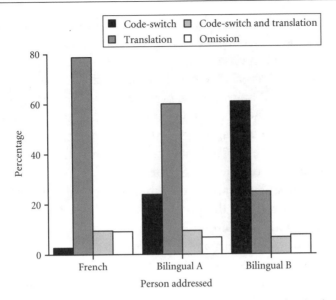

FIGURE 5.2 Strategies adopted by the 15 subjects for the code-switches in the bilingual stories as a function of the three addressees: French, Bilingual A, and Bilingual B

number of French syllables (245 on average) and hesitation syllables (36). One or two code-switches were produced (5 syllables on average) but they were invariably explained in French to the addressee. Separate one-way analyses of variance on the number of syllables (French, English, and hesitation) produced for each addressee all show main effects at the 0.01 level with all differences being significant.

Another aim of the study was to examine the production strategies employed when language mixing is not appropriate on one factor (person addressed) but is required by the other (topic). We examined in the stories what the subjects did when confronted with code-switches. We found there were four possibilities: they could reproduce the code-switch, give a translation of it, produce the code-switch followed by a translation, or simply omit the code-switch. Figure 5.2 presents the results we obtained. On examination, it is clear that as the translation bars decrease in size (from left to right, French to Bilingual B) the code-switch bars increase. These are the two preferred possibilities used by the subjects; the others (code-switching with translation, and omission) were not favored greatly. If we now examine the responses by addressee, we find the following. For the French addressee, who knew very little English, the subjects had little choice but to translate the code-switches heard: some 79 percent of the original code-switches were indeed translated. The three other possibilities played a much lesser role. For Bilingual A, who was perceived as someone who does not accept code-switching, we found that translations occupied some 60 percent of the responses. However, since his knowledge of English was good, the subjects also resorted to code-switching about a quarter of the time. As for Bilingual B, the preferred tactic was simply to reproduce the code-switches heard in the story (some 60 percent of the total responses) followed by translation (some 25 percent of the responses). Once again, the other possibilities (code-switch with translation, and omission) were not used to a large extent.

In sum, this study clearly shows that it is possible to manipulate factors that account for the point bilinguals finds themselves at on the language mode continuum and hence how much they will code-switch and borrow. In terms of a Levelt type production model (see Levelt 1989), one can suppose that both the addressee and the topic have an impact on the level of activation of the guest language (set by the Conceptualizer) and that the actual choice of lemmas is based on this level but also on the information sent to the lexicon. For Poulisse and Bongaerts (1994), lemmas are activated by conceptual information and a language cue sent by the Conceptualizer; for Myers-Scotton and Jake (1995), they are activated by language specific semantic-pragmatic feature bundles that also come from the Conceptualizer; and for de Bot and Schreuder (1993), lemmas are activated by pieces of conceptual structure sent by the Verbalizer. Whatever the origin and the nature of the information received, the system must find appropriate lemmas (in one or the other language) in order to convey as best as possible the meaning intended. This is more difficult when code-switching is either not possible or not appropriate, as in certain conditions of our study, and this produces a greater number of hesitation pauses and translations.

5.1.2 The Basle study

In this study, the aim Sonia Weil (1990) gave herself was to replicate the Boston study but with different bilinguals (Swiss German and French) who were put in a situation where a change of base language was either necessary or more appropriate. As I wrote in Chapter 4, a change of topic, of situation, of interlocutors, etc. may lead to a change in base language. This is obvious when the interlocutor does not understand all the bilingual's languages (as will be the case for one of the addressees in this study) but a bit more interesting when either language can be used and the language mode is bilingual. Since both languages are active in this mode, not only can code-switches and borrowings be produced but the base language itself can be changed; in that case, the slightly less activated language becomes the base language and vice versa. We will observe this in this study.

The speakers were twenty-four Swiss German-French bilinguals in Basle; all were university students, aged between 20 and 28. The three addressees were all linguists at the University of Zurich. They were described orally and photos of each of them, as well as short biographical sketches, were given to the subjects as they addressed them. A1 was a quasi French monolingual, originally from Paris, a specialist in French grammar. He had been living in Zurich for just one year and had minimal knowledge of Swiss German. His wife was French, they spoke French at home, and they had few Swiss German contacts. (A1 was therefore very similar to the Boston addressee named "French".) A2 was a French-Swiss German bilingual but dominant in French. He came from Lausanne in the French speaking part of Switzerland and specialized in theoretical linguistics. He had been in Zurich for three years. French was his mother tongue but he also spoke Swiss German, which he used with his friends. His wife was also from Lausanne and they spoke French with their children but also, at times, Swiss German. Finally, A3 was a balanced French-Swiss German bilingual from the bilingual city, Bienne/Biel. He was a sociolinguist and had lived in Zurich for ten years. Although French was his mother tongue, he used both languages on a daily basis. His wife came from Basle and they used the two languages with their children.

Weil only used stories (no pictures), but they were much longer than in the Boston study. They were of two types: (a) monolingual stories in Swiss German (this is important) on a topic that was familiar to a person living in Basle, and (b) bilingual stories where the base language was Swiss German and where French was the guest language. These latter stories dealt with French topics, hence the French code-switches. The approach she used was the same as in the Boston study. She welcomed her subjects in Swiss German but code-switched quite often to French during a preliminary conversation. She told them that they were part of a telephone chain experiment in which she was interested in the information that is conveyed to the next person. They were to hear stories in Swiss German and they had to retell them to one of the three persons described above; each story was to be repeated three times and they could take notes in order to recall the information given to them.

The study's result that we will concentrate on concerns the base language used by the subjects with the addressees. Recall that the stories were in Swiss German, with or without code-switches, and the question was whether the subjects would remain in Swiss German (SG) or translate the stories into French. What Weil found was that for A1, the Parisian living in Zurich, all 24 subjects used French with one exception (one of the stories with code-switches was told in SG); this means that they did indeed translate the stories into French as A1 did not know SG. For A2, 18 subjects for the stories with code-switches and 17 subjects for monolingual stories also used French. Finally, for A3, only 6 subjects used French; all 18 others used Swiss German, the language the stories had been told in. In a questionnaire given after the experiment, subjects were asked about the listeners' knowledge of Swiss German. A1 only received a mean rating of 2 (on a scale of 1 to 7), A2 was given a 4.5, and A3 a 6.5. This is definitely a variable that explains, in large part, the change over to French for A1 and, in part, for A2. Normally, and all other things being equal, if a bilingual feels comfortable with two languages and his/her listener knows one of the two better, and/or prefers it, then out of politeness, the bilingual will shift base language and speak the listener's language. Of course, there are many other factors involved (see Grosjean 1982), one of them being the language purism of the listener. The French are notorious for being proud of their language, and they make great efforts to speak and write "correct" French. When the subjects were asked about the purism of the three "listeners", A1 was given a mean rating of 5.9 (on a scale of 1 to 7), A2 3.2, and A3 2.7. This factor seems to have also played a role in the choice of the language spoken to each listener.

It is interesting to note that six subjects changed over to French for A3 even though the stories were in Swiss German and A3 was a balanced bilingual and fluent in Swiss German. Why would that be? After all, translating the stories into French was more demanding than staying in Swiss German. Weil found that personal reasons explained this behavior. Some of the six simply preferred to use French because they liked the language and some did it "out of vanity". Finally, as concerns code-switches, those speakers who stayed in Swiss German produced about three-quarters of the code-switches in the stories that contained code-switches. Of course, code-switches were not added to the stories which did not have any. As for the difference between addressees (A2 and A3; recall that all speakers changed base language when speaking to A1), there was none. Both were perceived as being sufficiently open to code-switches which were better said in the guest language.

Thus, Weil replicated the Boston study but added an interesting dimension: a change of the base language when it is appropriate. Recall that in the first study, all subjects stuck to French, the language of the stories as well as the native language of all addressees. Here, the speakers changed over to French when they felt the addressee would not understand Swiss German (A1) or might prefer the other language (A2).

5.1.3 The Neuchâtel study

In Chapter 4 (Section 4.4.3), I stated that language mode also needs to be studied in bilinguals who are dominant in one language since it is well known that they do more language mixing when speaking their weaker language than more balanced bilinguals. I cited a few studies that show a link between dominance and language mixing. Paulo Caixeta (2003) set out to study this experimentally. He wanted to assess the capability of subjects to navigate along the language mode continuum as a function of the interlocutor (monolingual or bilingual) and of their knowledge of the language being used (intermediate or advanced). He naturally expected more language mixing when the bilinguals were in a bilingual mode (already shown in the Boston and Basle studies) but he also expected more mixing by the intermediary level speakers.

Caixeta conducted his study with 32 Brazilians living in the French-speaking part of Switzerland, bilingual in Portuguese and French; 16 had an intermediate level of competence in French and 16 had an advanced level. To assess their competence in the latter language, they were given a language questionnaire, as well as two tests, a semantic association test and a naming test. The two groups were clearly different on the results obtained. Unlike the Boston and Basle studies, Caixeta used real addressees: a French monolingual who had no knowledge of Portuguese or Spanish, and a French-Portuguese bilingual, slightly dominant in French, but with excellent knowledge of Portuguese as she had lived in Brazil and went back there each year. The subjects did a number of tasks with the addressees: they talked freely, they described scenes of life in Brazil (e.g. a typical day or weekend over there, a wedding, etc.), and they described cartoons (there were some ten to twelve pictures per cartoon). The addressees had presented themselves to the subjects before the experiment started and the bilingual addressee had code-switched a bit into Portuguese to show that she knew that language. The base language during the study was French.

Caixeta obtained a number of measures but the one that interests us is the percentage of guest syllables in the subjects' productions. First, he found a greater percentage of guest syllables in the bilingual mode (with the bilingual addressee) than in the monolingual mode (with the monolingual French speaker): 4.41 percent versus 2.27 percent on average (this is significant at the 0.01 level). This result replicates those of the Boston and the Basle studies. Second, he found that the subjects who had an intermediary level of French produced a greater percentage of guest syllables than the advanced level subjects: 6.17 percent versus 0.51 percent (this too was significant at the 0.01 level). Finally, Caixeta found that the difference between the percentage of guest syllables in the monolingual and the bilingual mode was higher for the intermediary level subjects than for the advanced subjects: 3.4 percent versus 0.88 percent (this just failed to be significant; $p = 0.07$). To summarize, the more the mode is bilingual, the greater the amount of code-switching that takes place (a robust finding by now). More interesting, though, is the fact that dominant bilinguals speaking their weaker language will code-switch more than bilinguals who have good knowledge of the language, when the situation lends itself to code-switching, of course. (Note that Caixeta also found some code-switching in the monolingual mode in the intermediary level subjects, but far less.)

In Chapter 4 (Section 4.4.3), I proposed that bilinguals who are highly dominant in one language may simply not be able to control language mode when speaking their weaker language in the same way as less dominant or balanced bilinguals can. They may at first deactivate their stronger language in a monolingual environment that requires only the weaker language (e.g. it is of no use speaking Italian, one's stronger language, to an English speaker who knows absolutely no Italian). But the weaker language will simply not be developed enough to allow them to stay in a monolingual mode. Figure 5.3 is an attempt to show what takes place when dominant bilinguals, in a monolingual mode, find themselves having to speak their weaker language. In the figure, the base language, and the weaker of the two languages, is language A. This is depicted by the black triangles instead of the habitual squares. Starting off in a monolingual mode (pattern on the left), language A is the more active of the two languages; language B is much less active. But rapidly the speakers realize (consciously or unconsciously) that their competence in language A is simply not good enough and, de facto,

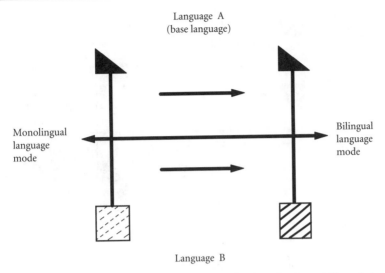

Language A
(base language)

Monolingual
language
mode

Bilingual
language
mode

Language B

FIGURE 5.3 The shift that takes place in language mode when dominant bilinguals have to speak their weaker language (language A) in a monolingual mode (pattern on the left). The shift to the bilingual mode is shown by the two arrows pointing to the right

they shift over to the bilingual mode (see the two arrows pointing to the right and the right hand pattern where language B is much more active). Language B, the bilingual's stronger language, can now be used to help out language A through the use of guest language elements in language A, the language being spoken. If the addressee knows language B, then things are not too problematic (although he/she may not like this mixing). However, if the addressee does not know language B, and the speaker does not explain the guest words or expressions, then miscommunication may occur between the two interlocutors. As stated in Chapter 4, future research will have to investigate the underlying mechanisms not depicted in the figure that make the stronger language "seep through" despite the fact that it is deactivated, at first at least. The strong grammatical and lexical links between the stronger and the weaker languages, depicted by thick continuous vertical lines in Figure 5.3, certainly play a large role in this behavior.

5.2 Perception studies

In Chapter 4 (Section 4.3.2), I stated that positioning the bilingual at the monolingual end point of the language mode continuum in a perception experiment is not quite as easy as one would like it to be. I wrote that the difficulty is how to prevent the bilingual from activating,

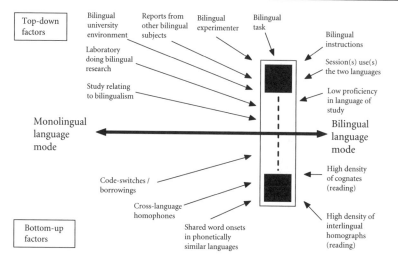

FIGURE 5.4 Top-down and bottom-up factors that can be involved in causing the language mode to move towards the bilingual end of the continuum in perception experiments

to some extent at least, the other language. I mentioned a few factors that are sufficient to push the participant towards the bilingual end point of the continuum where the two languages are activated, albeit to different degrees. In this second part of Chapter 5, I will first delve deeper into why it is so difficult to control for language mode in perception experiments, in particular the monolingual language mode. I will review a number of factors that induce a bilingual mode even though every effort is made to put subjects in a monolingual mode. I will then illustrate the problem with two perception studies done by others who failed to guarantee a monolingual mode.

Figure 5.4 represents a number of factors that can be involved in causing the mode to move towards the bilingual end of the continuum in perception experiments. I have broken them down into two categories: top-down factors (top part of the figure) and bottom-up factors (bottom part). Note that both languages, depicted by a black square, are fully active in the figure; this does not have to be case—we should keep in mind that in many bilingual situations, one language is less active than the other—but equal activation often takes place in experiments where subjects are ready to process stimuli from one or the other language. Concerning top-down factors, the following, singly or together, will ensure a shift towards the bilingual end of the continuum: knowledge that the study relates to bilingualism; a laboratory that works on bilingual research; a bilingual university environment (e.g. in most Dutch universities, both Dutch and English are used daily, at least in reading); reports from other bilingual subjects who have just been in the study or who will do it soon; an experimenter who is bilingual, even though he or she only uses one language; the task that is used (e.g. the bilingual Stroop test, bilingual word priming, bilingual naming, bilingual category matching, word translation, etc.) and/or the instructions that are bilingual; the two languages used in the experimental sessions, etc. One last factor, discussed in Section 5.1, concerns dominant bilinguals who are less proficient in the language of the study. When that is the case, then the other, stronger language may well be activated to help with the task. As for bottom-up factors, we have the presence of code-switches and borrowings in the stimuli, cross-language homophones, and shared word onsets in phonetically similar languages, as well as two factors that pertain to reading: a high density of interlingual homographs and a high density of cognates. Experiments using homographs and cognates have a tendency to make them recur frequently, very probably more so than in natural language (how many interlingual homographs do we meet when reading a newspaper, for example?). In sum, just one factor, or a combination of factors, may well move the subjects away from the monolingual end to the bilingual end of the continuum. This said, we do not know the strength of each factor, taken singly. Some are probably quite strong (e.g. the task is bilingual, or the stimuli contain code-switches and borrowings) whereas others are probably weaker (e.g. the bilingual university environment or shared words onsets). In addition, it should be recalled that several factors are probably present in any one study, making things all the more complex. In what follows, I will take two studies, from among the many that have been published, to show how difficult it is to set up a monolingual language mode.

Spivey and Marian (1999) undertook an experiment that used an innovative task to assess whether processing in bilinguals is selective (only one language processes the incoming signal) or non-selective (all the bilingual's languages are involved, to differing degrees, of course). If processing is selective, then maybe the brain is using an "input switch" (Macnamara and Kushnir 1971) to activate one language and deactivate the other, according to the authors. As they suggest, a test of the switch explanation requires that the experimental session is monolingual. They claim that in their experiment they were able to present stimuli in one language and infer the activation of lexical items in the other language "without actually compromising the monolingual speech mode" (p. 281). How did they do this? They used a headband-mounted eye tracker which allows the experimenter to see where the subject is looking at different moments during the experiment. The task was simple: Russian-English bilinguals heard pre-recorded instructions which asked them to displace objects on a board in front of them, for example, "Poloji marku nije krestika" (Put the stamp below the cross). In the distractor condition, some of the objects on the board had English names that shared initial phonetic features with the onset of the crucial Russian object (e.g. "marker" which shares onset features with "marka" ("marku" in the above sentence)). The question was whether the subjects would look at the marker on the board more often than non-distractor objects in the same place in the non-distractor condition. If so, processing could be said to be non-selective. Their finding was clear: they found that subjects were indeed more likely to make more eye movements to the interlingual distractor (31 percent of the time) than to the control distractor (13 percent). They concluded by stating that bilingual listeners do not seem to be able to deactivate the irrelevant mental lexicon when in a monolingual situation. In a word, processing is always non-selective in bilinguals.

The two authors continued their research on this question and wrote a second article (Marian and Spivey 2003) in which, much to their honor, they criticize the "monolingual mode" of their preceding study. They write that a potential confound in that study was the participants' language mode at the time of testing. They state that a number of factors may have moved the participants away from the monolingual end of the continuum, factors such as the fact that the bilinguals knew they were taking part in an experiment on bilingualism, that they were tested by bilingual experimenters fluent in both languages, and that the two languages were tested in adjacent experimental sessions. These three factors are present in Figure 5.4 as top-down factors. We could add that the bilingual subjects probably knew that the laboratory was doing bilingual research (in part, at least), that they may have received reports from other subjects who had taken part in the experiment, and, a bottom-up factor, that the word onsets of the distractors may have activated the other language. In short, there were enough factors present for the required "monolingual experimental session" (p. 281) not to be present.

Dijkstra and van Hell (2003), in a very interesting paper, discuss language mode and the factors that can modify it. They claim that one of their studies, involving Dutch-English-French trilinguals (van Hell and Dijkstra 2002) "may come closest to providing satisfactory evidence with respect to the language mode issue" (p. 8), that is having subjects in a monolingual mode. In the three experiments they conducted, they write that they aimed to bring the participants into a monolingual mode by (a) adopting a strict participant selection procedure, (b) using tasks and stimuli that did not refer to the participants' foreign language knowledge, and (c) providing an exclusive L1 communicative setting. I will first discuss (a) and (c) and then turn to (b).

Selection of participants and L1 communicative setting (a & c)

Participants in the first two experiments were chosen from a list of first-year psychology students who had taken part in university entry testing. They had listed their secondary school subjects and Dijkstra and van Hell wrote to all the students who had taken final exams in Dutch, English, and French. They were invited to take part in a memory experiment but no mention was made of the experimenters' interest in their knowledge of languages. This resulted in the selection of participants who were most fluent in Dutch (their L1), less fluent in English (their L2), and least fluent in L3 (French). As for the third experiment, the authors attempted to correct the rather low French proficiency of their trilinguals in Experiments 1 and 2 by choosing a new group with equal proficiency in L2 and L3. But here, they admit, they had to recruit students from the French Language and Literature Department; this was done by a student of French who then conducted the experiment.

If one examines the top-down factors in Figure 5.4, a number of them seem to have been involved to make the language mode less monolingual than was wished. One of them is the bilingual university environment. The authors mention a statement I had made to them in 2000 (I owe it to Marc Grosjean) that Dutch students may always be in a bilingual mode since English is used so much in their studies (not to mention in life outside the university). So, however much one tries to induce a monolingual mode, English is always activated, to some extent at least. Other potential factors involved might have been the laboratory in which the experiments were conducted (was it not known for its work on bilingualism?), the fact that participants might have talked to one another and mentioned the stimuli used (cognates; we will come to them below), and, of course, the level of proficiency in English and French of the participants in Experiments 1 and 2 (see Section 4.1 for a discussion of dominant bilinguals and the bilingual mode). As for the participants in Experiment 3, one wonders if they were not aware, in some way, that the experimenter ("a student of French"; p. 10) was interested in their various languages (the authors seem to hint at this in fact); if so, they would activate them, to some extent at least, in case they needed them. This said, choosing this new group does not do away with the lower proficiency problem (recall that this third group had lower proficiency in their L2 and L3 than in their L1); their two weaker languages might well have moved them, most probably unconsciously, toward a more bilingual mode.

Tasks and stimuli (b)

As concerns the tasks, a Dutch word association task (Experiment 1) and a Dutch lexical decision task (Experiments 2 and 3) do seem quite straightforward (and monolingual). However, both are "high processing tasks" (finding a word associate or deciding whether a word is a word or not is not akin to regular processing) and this might have interacted with the stimuli (e.g. given the participants time to "reflect" on the stimuli or, more automatically, given the stimuli time to activate the other languages). As for the stimuli themselves, they were cognates and non-cognates. Van Hell and Dijkstra (2002) define cognates as "words in different languages that have the same meaning and are spelled, and often pronounced, in the same or a similar way" (p. 780). (Note that the definition of cognates differs widely among researchers, as is discussed in Chapter 14.) There are two points one can make here. First, when the trilinguals saw Dutch-English cognates such as "adder", "bakker", "ring", "hamer", etc., wasn't there a risk that these words might activate both the Dutch and the English lexicons and hence move them away from a monolingual Dutch mode? And if the same trilinguals saw Dutch-French cognates such as "ananas", "gazon", "ceintuur", "plafond", "kado", etc., might not the same thing have happened to their Dutch and French lexicons? In this case, language activation is due to the stimuli themselves and *not* to mechanisms in the non-selective processing of languages in bilinguals. The second point relates to the density of cognates. For example, in Experiment 1, half the words presented to the participants were cognates (either Dutch-English or Dutch-French). This percentage is large and probably not what one would find if one did a Dutch corpus search and worked out the ratio of cognates to non-cognates. (But see van Hell 1998; of course, the problem is the definition one gives of a cognate). One wonders therefore if the nature of the stimuli, and their recurrence, did not "artificially" activate the languages that were not supposed to be active, that is English and French. Dijkstra and van Hell (2003) admit that this might have been a problem (p. 11). Of course, as Figure 5.4 shows, there are many other language activation factors that may add themselves to, or interact with, the one concerning the stimuli used.

In Chapter 4 (Section 4.3.2) I suggest an approach that could be used to test bilinguals in a monolingual mode. The idea would be to intermix bilingual participants with monolingual participants in a monolingual experiment (for example, a study that is part of a course requirement) and once the experiment is done, and only then, to go back to the list of participants and extract the bilinguals. Of course, one would also want to control for all the bottom-up factors given in Figure 5.4. This said, one wonders if the selective versus non-selective processing issue, at stake in many perception studies that wish to control for language mode, should be pursued without making changes to it. Would it not be more reasonable to postulate that bilinguals navigate along the language mode continuum at different moments in their everyday life (their two or more languages are therefore active and are processed to varying degrees) and that such notions as selective processing, the existence of an input switch, the presence of just one (or two) language representations, etc., simply do not do justice to the complexity of the psycholinguistics of bilingualism? Let us recall that bilinguals are speakers-hearers in their own right, with complex language representations and processing mechanisms, and not two monolinguals in one person (see Chapter 2).

PART III

The Base-language Effect

Introduction

As was seen in Chapter 4, when a bilingual is in a bilingual mode, both languages are active but one language is slightly less active than the other because it is not currently the main language of communication. In this mode, bilinguals usually first adopt a base language (also called a "host" or "matrix" language) through the process of language choice. This is governed by a number of factors such as the interlocutors involved, the situation of the interaction, the content of the discourse, and the function of the interaction (see Grosjean 1982). Once a base language has been chosen, bilinguals can bring in the other language (the guest language) in the form of code-switches and borrowings. A code-switch is a complete shift to the other language for a word, a phrase or a sentence whereas a borrowing is a morpheme, word, or short expression taken from the less activated language and adapted morphosyntactically (and sometimes phonologically) to the base language. Borrowings can involve both the form and the content of a word (these are called nonce borrowings) or simply the content (called loan shifts). Words from the guest language, whether they are code-switches or borrowings, are often called "guest words".

Over the years, "the base-language effect" has been the object of much interest. It concerns the impact the base language has on the processing of guest words (note that some 80–90 percent of an utterance is usually in the base language). In perception, the question is whether the guest language influences the perception of guest sounds and the recognition of guest words. This may lead, for example, to slower processing times for guest words just after the language switch boundary, that is the passage point from the base language to the guest language. In production, the base-language effect concerns the influence the base language might have on the actual pronunciation of guest words. Will the sounds of the latter, at least those closest to the switch boundary, be tainted by the base language? And as concerns prosody, will the base language impose its prosodic pattern on the guest language?

Chapter 6, "The Base-language Effect in Speech Perception", reviews evidence from different studies that show that the base-language effect is indeed present in perception and that it does have an impact on processing. A number of different tasks were used and, each time, the effect was shown to be present, even if momentarily.

Chapter 7, "Base-language Effect and Categorical Perception", is a reprint of a study by Judith Bürki-Cohen, Joanne Miller, and myself, which examines, by means of categorical perception experiments, the base-language effect on the identification of words in bilingual speech. It shows that the nature of the effect may depend, in part, on the acoustic-phonetic characteristics of the code-switched words.

Chapter 8 investigates whether there is a base-language effect in speech production. It contains two sections. The first is a reprint of a paper with Joanne Miller in which it is asked whether, when code-switches are produced, the phonetic momentum of the base language carries over into the guest language and hence affects the beginning of code-switches. How complete is a code-switch therefore? The second section is a very short contribution that examines the base-language effect on prosody. Here, a short pilot study with Carlos Soares is described. It produced some interesting results which showed that the suprasegmentals (prosody) of a code-switch do not always follow the same trend as that found at the segmental (sound) level.

6

The Base-language Effect in Speech Perception*

One of the earliest questions asked about language processing in bilinguals was whether switching from one language to another takes time. For example, Kolers (1966) asked French-English bilinguals to read passages of varying linguistic makeup. Some passages were monolingual in English or French, others alternated languages from sentence to sentence, and others had mixed sentences. Here the mixture of English and French was haphazard, with half the passages favoring the English word order and the other half the French order. When asked to read these passages silently, and to answer questions testing their comprehension, participants performed equally well on all three types of texts, showing that mixed passages were understood as well as monolingual passages. But when participants were asked to read the texts aloud, the type of passage had a strong effect. Kolers computed that when participants switched languages in oral reading, each switch took them between 0.3 and 0.5 seconds. A few years later, Macnamara and Kushnir (1971) studied only the perception aspect of the phenomenon since both production and perception were involved in the Kolers reading aloud experiment. First, they asked bilingual participants to read Kolers' passages silently and measured the time it took (recall that Kolers had tested comprehension in this condition). The participants read mixed passages more slowly than monolingual passages, and the researchers

* This chapter borrows elements from two publications: (1) Figure 6.1 is Figure 2 from Soares, C. and Grosjean, F. (1984). "Bilinguals in a monolingual and a bilingual speech mode: The effect of lexical access", *Memory and Cognition* 12(4): 380–6. (2) Figures 6.3 and 6.4 are Figures 7.4 and 7.5 from Grosjean, F. and Soares, C. (1986). "Processing mixed language: Some preliminary findings", in J. Vaid (ed.) *Language Processing in Bilinguals: Psycholinguistic and Neuropsychological Perspectives*. Hillsdale, NJ: Lawrence Erlbaum, 145–79. (In each case only the bottom part of the original figure is reproduced here.) The author thanks the publishers (Psychonomic Society and Lawrence Erlbaum Associates) as well as Carlos Soares for permission to reprint the figures here.

computed that each switch took about 0.17 seconds. Next, they presented unilingual and mixed sentences to participants and asked them whether their content was true or false. The authors found that as the number of switches increased, the reaction time to indicate whether the sentences were true or false also increased. Language switching took about 0.2 seconds. Macnamara and Kushnir concluded from these data that switching from one language to another—either as a listener or as a speaker—takes time, because switching runs counter to psychological "inertia". The bilingual's customary behavior is to stay within one language, and any deviation from this will take additional effort and time. They wrote: "We have certain expectations for strings of words and one such expectation is that all the words should be in a single language" (Macnamara and Kushnir 1971: 485).

Researchers criticized the Kolers and the Macnamara and Kushnir studies a few years later (see Grosjean 1982 for a review). The following were questioned: their choice of participants, the tasks they used, and especially the setting of the experiments and the materials involved. Concerning the materials, for example, many of the French segments in the sentences heard by the participants were grammatically incorrect. This led to the question: Could switching really delay the processing of language, when its very purpose in everyday life is precisely to ease the communication flow between bilinguals?

It is against this backdrop that a number of studies aimed at better understanding the processing of code-switching and the role of the base language were undertaken. Much to our surprise, a result that kept reappearing was the presence of a base-language effect. We no longer talked of "expectations" that all words should be in a single language, as did Macnamara and Kushnir (1971), but rather of the activation and/or inhibition of the languages. As we will see below, there is now good evidence that the base language being spoken (which normally makes up some 80–90 percent of the utterance) has a strong effect on perception. It is more strongly activated and hence base-language units (phonemes, syllables, words) are favored over guest-language units, at least for a short period of time.

6.1 The PTLD study

In a first study (Soares and Grosjean 1984), we investigated the lexical access of base-language words and code-switched words by means of the Phoneme Triggered Lexical Decision task (PTLD; Blank 1980).

English-Portuguese bilingual participants were presented with sentences and were asked to listen for a word or a non-word within them which began with a pre-specified phoneme. Once this word (or non-word) was found, the participants had to indicate as quickly as possible whether the item was a real word or not, that is to make a lexical decision on it. English monolingual participants were run on the English sentences only, whereas bilingual participants were tested on three separate sets of sentences (English, Portuguese, and Portuguese with code-switches). Here are examples of each type of sentence (the critical word on which a lexical decision task had to be made is underlined):

> English: "After lunch, the children asked for a piece of <u>cake</u> for dessert".
>
> Portuguese: "Depois do almoço os miudos pediram uma fatia de <u>bolo</u> para sobremesa".
>
> Code-switched: "Depois do *lunch* os miudos pediram uma fatia de *<u>cake</u>* para *dessert*".
> (Here the base language is Portuguese and the guest language is English).

Figure 6.1 presents the mean reaction times for words and non-words for the bilinguals in the three conditions: English, Portuguese, and code-switching, that is Portuguese, the base language, with English code-switches. We note that the mean reaction time to code-switched words (1,001 ms; filled bar on the right) is significantly slower than to base language words (849 ms for English words and 836 ms for Portuguese words). In the paper itself, we accounted for this result by suggesting that bilinguals always search the base-language lexicon before the less activated lexicon. This will cause a delay in the access of code-switched words as they belong to the other lexicon and are therefore only accessed after the base lexicon has been searched; hence the delay in reaction times. In a later publication (Grosjean and Soares 1986), we suggested that the longer reaction times to code-switched words may not be due, after all, to a preliminary search of the wrong lexicon but rather to a delay in the decision as to which lexicon to search. One reason for this delay could be caused by problems encountered in the mapping between the acoustic wave and the appropriate percepts (phonemes, syllables, words). Since then, we have adopted a more connectionist outlook toward lexical access in bilinguals (see Part IV) and we would now talk in terms of the levels of activation of the guest-language system (phonemes, words) being lower that those of

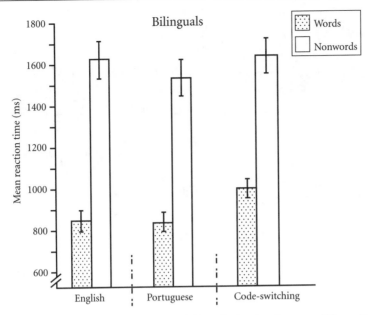

FIGURE 6.1 Mean reaction times for the bilinguals in the three conditions: English, Portuguese, and code-switching, i.e. Portuguese, the base language, with English code-switches

Note: Bars indicate +/−1 standard error of the mean.
Source: This figure first appeared in Soares and Grosjean (1984).

the base-language system. In sum, whatever the reason, a base-language effect was found in this study even though we had been careful to control for the factors that might have caused a delay in the earlier studies by Kolers and by Macnamara and Kushnir.

6.2 The gating studies

Two gating studies, one on non-words and one on words, produced additional evidence for a base-language effect. In the non-word study, Grosjean and Soares (1986) used the gating paradigm (Grosjean 1980) to determine how soon and how well the bilingual can determine the language of the item he or she is hearing. The approach entails presenting a non-word in segments, or gates, of increasing duration so that at the first gate little or no information concerning the item is given, whereas at the last gate the entire item is presented. For the sentence "I saw a <u>bive</u>", where "bive" is said as a French code-switch, the critical item ("bive") is presented by itself or preceded by the short context "I saw a". This is depicted in Figure 6.2. When presented by itself, the word

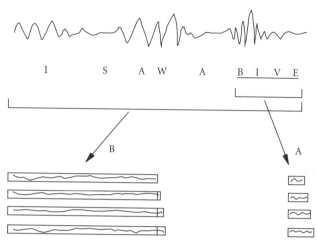

FIGURE 6.2 The gating approach. In A, the French code-switched non-word "bive" is presented in segments of increasing duration. In B, the segments are preceded by the English context "I saw a"

segments (represented by A in the figure) are very short at first and increase by steps of 30 ms until the whole non-word is presented. As for the presentation with a context (represented by B in the figure), the segments of "bive" also increase in steps of 30 ms but they are preceded by "I saw a". In such a task, the participant has to decide, after each presentation, whether the item is in French or English, and how confident he or she is on a scale of 1 to 10. The answers are used to construct language identification curves which indicate the amount of information needed to choose the appropriate language. A positive number shows that the listener has chosen the correct language and the higher the number, the more confident the participant is; conversely, negative numbers indicate the choice of the wrong language.

Below we will first examine the language identification curves obtained for the phonetically ambiguous French code-switch "bive" preceded by its English context. We will also look at the results for the more marked French code-switch "bainve" preceded by the same English context. In each case, there are two conditions, as indicated above: one in which the code-switch is presented in isolation (without the context) and one in which it is preceded by the context. If results are different for the two conditions, this would indicate a base-language effect. The participants were French/English late bilingual adults, all of French origin, who had lived in the United States for at least five years; they used both French and English in their everyday lives. They were told in French that they would be hearing segments of non-words in

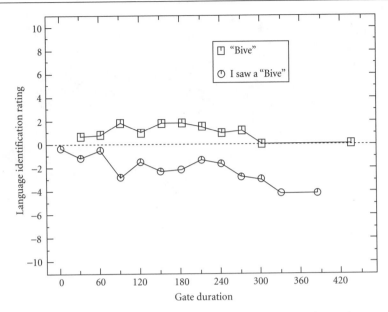

FIGURE 6.3 The language identification curves of the code-switched French non-word "bive" presented in isolation (squares) and preceded by the English carrier sentence, "I saw a" (circles). Each point (square or circle) is the mean of six ratings, one by each of six participants

Source: This figure first appeared in Grosjean and Soares 1986.

isolation, or preceded by a short sentence, and they were asked to indicate after each segment the language of the non-word being presented and to give a level of confidence. In the case of the context sets, they were told very clearly that the non-words could be in the same language as the carrier sentence or in the other language.

In Figure 6.3, we present the language identification curves obtained for the French non-word "bive" in isolation (squares) and preceded by the English carrier sentence, "I saw a" (circles). We note, first of all, that the curve of the isolated "bive" never departs very far from the language border (the dotted line) and the last two points are in fact located precisely on that border. Participants therefore had great difficulties identifying the language of "bive" and, at the last presentation, three of the six participants actually thought they heard the English version ("beeve"). One possible reason for this is that the two non-words, "bive" and "beeve" are near homophones and hence very difficult to differentiate. What is especially interesting is the identification curve of "bive" when presented in context. This is the very same phonetic sequence as the "bive" presented in isolation and yet the resulting identification curve

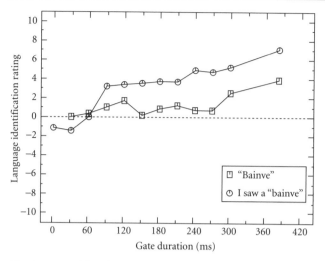

FIGURE 6.4 The language identification curves of the code-switched French non-word "bainve" presented in isolation (squares) and preceded by the English carrier sentence, "I saw a" (circles). Each point (square or circle) is the mean of six ratings, one by each of six participants

Source: This figure first appeared in Grosjean and Soares 1986.

is quite different. From the very first gate, the ratings are negative (that is, "bive" is identified as being an English item) and the ratings become progressively stronger as more of the item is heard. At the very last gate, five of the six participants feel that the item is English and the final mean rating is −4.17. The main explanation for this seems to be the base-language effect. It can be seen already in the results obtained at the first gates (0 and 30 ms) where almost no phonetic information about the word has been heard but where the ratings are already negative. As the gates increase in size, it would appear that the English carrier sentence "assimilates" the borderline "bive" so that it is now heard as a rather clear "beeve". It is a phonetically ambiguous item and it is this very ambiguity that allows the carrier sentence to pull it towards English.

We now turn to Figure 6.4, the identification curves of the code-switched non-word "bainve" containing a nasal vowel that is specific to French. When presented in isolation, "bainve" received rather low French ratings. Grosjean and Soares (1986) suggested that this could be because the initial part of the item was tinged by English (but see Chapter 8 for evidence that code-switched boundaries are usually "clean"). An interesting pattern emerges from the ratings obtained for "bainve" in context (circles). We note, first of all, the presence of negative ratings at the first two gates which signals, once again, a base-language effect. We then note a sudden change of sign in the ratings and a rather steep rise of the language identification curve which culminates in a high final rating. What is probably happening here is that the base language is now serving as a contrast for the phonetic information carried by "bainve" and is helping the participants choose the correct language. Unlike "bive", which was ambiguous and which could be assimilated into the language of the carrier sentence, "bainve" is a typically French item, and the language of the carrier sentence helps to make this even more clear. It is interesting to note, therefore, the two possible roles that the base language can have on the language identification of a code-switch: it can either help to assimilate an ambiguous item into the base language (as it did for "bive") or it can help to set up a contrast with the code-switched item so that the language of this item becomes even more clear, as in the case of "bainve".

At the beginning of this section, two gating studies were mentioned, one using non-words (we have just reviewed it) and one concerning real words (Grosjean 1988). We will present this second study in Part IV but it is important to note one result that strengthens our proposal that the base-language effect is present in bilingual speech processing. In that study, participants invariably proposed base-language (French) candidates for English guest words when presented with very short gates preceded by a base-language context. It was rare that they proposed an English candidate at the first gate (where very little, if any, information concerning the word was presented) and it was only over the following two or three gates when phonetic, phonotactic, and lexical information started arriving that they began to propose words from the other lexicon. This result is very similar to the ones above which show the importance of the base-language effect at the early gates.

6.3 The categorical perception study

The base-language effect was also investigated by Bürki-Cohen *et al.* (1989), who used a categorical perception paradigm. Since we reprint this study in Chapter 7, we will only summarize it briefly here. French-English bilinguals were asked to identify stimuli from computer-edited series that ranged from an English to a French word ("ray" to "ré", and "day" to "dé"). The results showed that sound specificity interacted with the base-language effect. The authors found that the base language had a contrastive effect on the perception of the ambiguous items when the end points of the between-language series were phonetically marked as English and French, as in "ray" and "ré", but it had no effect when the end points were phonetically less marked and thus compatible with either language, as in "day" and "dé". In sum, they found a contrastive effect with the "ray"–"ré" continuum but no assimilative effect with the "day"–"dé" continuum although this effect had been observed with other paradigms (Grosjean 1988; Soares and Grosjean 1984). To account for this loss of the assimilative effect (but keep in mind that a contrastive effect was found), the authors mention the forced choice between the two end points of the series in the experiment (participants chose "ray" or "ré", "day" or "dé"). That is, on top of the base-language context remaining constant (participants heard "Il faut qu'on catégorise..." or "We have to categorize..." with each stimulus), it is also the case that the base-language word or code-switched word remained constant. Maybe the restricted choice in a categorical perception experiment allowed participants to concentrate their attention selectively on the acoustic information contained in the stimuli while disengaging from effects of the base language. The authors propose in the end that the two effects (assimilative, contrastive) might be an indication that they arise at different stages of language processing, with different underlying mechanisms.

We should note that a few years later, Handschin (1994), using German-French bilinguals, investigated the impact of the base language (German and French) on the identification of elements taken from a between-language continuum ranging from German "Tee" to French "thé" (these are language marked end points but less so than "ray"–"ré"). Handschin found a lot of variability in the responses: nine participants did not show a base language effect (the identification curves fell one on top of the other) but seven did—four showed a contrastive effect and three showed an assimilative effect. More work is needed, therefore, on the relationship that exists between sound specificity and the base-language effect when using a categorical perception paradigm, in this case, identification.

6.4 The naming study

The last study that brings evidence for a base-language effect in the processing of mixed speech was done by Domenighetti and Caldognetto (1999) under my supervision. They had two aims: (i) to confirm that the base language delays, however slightly, the recognition of code-switches in a neutral context, and (ii) to ascertain whether the next word in the stream of speech is also delayed. This second aim is important for the understanding of the code-switching process. If the delay is carried over to the next word, then the bilingual listener will gradually fall behind the speaker, which seems quite counter-intuitive. One possibility is that the delay is momentary and is "caught up" before the code-switched word is finished and, hence, before the next word arrives.

Since it is extremely difficult to obtain "identical" sets of words from two languages, in this case French and Italian, Domenighetti and Caldognetto used a naming approach to do so. They recorded lists of words, one list in Italian and one in French, and asked bilingual participants to listen to them and repeat (name) them. An average time was then obtained for each spoken word, Italian and French, which then allowed the authors to constitute cross-language pairs. For example, French "grenouille" (frog) was paired with Italian "cena" (dinner) as both took 813 ms to be named, French "sorcière" (witch) was paired with Italian "partenza" (departure) as both took 889 ms to be named, etc. This approach exempted them from controlling numerous variables in the one and the other language (e.g. frequency, length, uniqueness point, neighborhood, etc.). The stimuli were placed in a string of French words which were preceded by a short sentence, also in French ("J'ai entendu les mots"). The words after the sentence were separated from one another by 50 ms. For example:

Sentence	Position 1	Position 2	Position 3	Position 4
J'ai entendu les mots (I heard the words)	aéroport (airport)	grenouille (frog)	sapin (fir tree)	collier (collar)
J'ai entendu les mots (I heard the words)	aéroport (airport)	cena (I) (dinner)	sapin (fir tree)	collier (collar)

In the above, the leader sentence and the words in positions 1, 3, and 4 are identical and in French. It is in position 2 that the elements of the pairs previously obtained can be found. In one case, the word also belongs to the French base language ("grenouille" in the example), and in the other, it is the other element of the pair (an Italian word) that is present. In this case, the word "cena" becomes an Italian code-switch as the base language is French (note the "I" for Italian next to it). There were twenty-four such pairs and there were also a number of filler items where the Italian word was in a different position. The question became: How long will it now take to name the elements of each pair, for example, "grenouille" and "cena", given that the base language is French? In addition, how long will it take to name "sapin" in position 3 when it is preceded by either "grenouille", a base language word, or "cena", a code-switch?

The participants were French-Italian bilinguals, aged 18 to 30, who lived in the French-speaking part of Switzerland. All had grown up with both languages and all code-switched when in a bilingual language mode. The instructions were given in French and the communication between the experimenter and the participants took place both in French and Italian. The participants were first asked to repeat the word in position 2 and they were told that it could be either a French word or an Italian word. The same procedure was then used for position 3.

The results were very clear-cut. In position 2, the base-language word (e.g. "grenouille") was named in 750 ms on average whereas the code-switched word (e.g. "cena") took 796 ms on average to be named (this result was significant at the 0.05 level). Thus, Domenighetti and Caldognetto once again found evidence for a base-language effect. As for position 3, the base-language word (e.g. "sapin") preceded by a base-language word (e.g. "grenouille") took 759 ms on average to be named. As for the same base-language word ("sapin" again) preceded by a code-switched word (e.g. "cena"), it was named in 757 ms on average. Naturally, the 2 ms difference was not significant. In sum, even if a code-switched word may take longer to process (in a neutral context), the processing delay is made up by the time the listener reaches the following word.

We should note that the authors found a 0.47 correlation between the subjective frequency of the Italian words and the difference between the naming time in the lists and the naming time in the main study. This makes sense: a frequent word in Italian will take less time to be named, whether it be a base-language word or a guest-language word. And this points to the fact that the base-language effect, for which we have produced a lot of evidence in this chapter, can be decreased to the point of being neutralized if other factors intervene (see Part IV). This said, the Kolers and the Macnamara and Kushnir studies, however much one criticizes their material, procedure, or participants, did open the way to a better understanding of the role played by base-language and guest language elements in bilingual speech processing.

7

Base-language Effect and Categorical Perception*

Speech perception involves extracting from the environment acoustic information that can be mapped onto linguistic information represented in our minds. As complex as this task is for monolingual listeners, it may be even more complex for bilingual listeners. This is because bilinguals talking among themselves, although they usually agree on one "base language" carrying the bulk of their conversation, have a tendency to switch occasionally to their other shared language—or "code"—for a word, a phrase, or even an entire sentence (see Grosjean 1982 for a discussion of linguistic and cultural constraints on code-switching).

The perception of code-switched words by bilinguals has been investigated using a variety of experimental paradigms. Soares and Grosjean (1984) used the phoneme-triggered lexical decision task (Blank 1980) to study lexical access by bilinguals in both a monolingual situation (where only one language is used) and a bilingual situation (where two languages are used, that is, where code-switching occurs). They found that bilinguals in a monolingual situation responded to word targets in both their languages as fast as monolinguals. However, their response times to code-switched words in a bilingual situation were significantly slower. Moreover, in both situations, the bilingual subjects took longer to respond to nonwords than did the monolingual subjects. These results suggest that during lexical access bilinguals use a general strategy of first searching the base-language lexicon and, only if no entry is found, then searching the lexicon of their alternate language.

* This chapter first appeared as an article: Bürki-Cohen, J., Grosjean, F., and Miller, J. (1989). "Base language effects on word identification in bilingual speech: Evidence from categorical perception experiments", *Language and Speech* 32: 355–71. The author wishes to thank Kingston Press as well as Judith Bürki-Cohen and Joanne Miller for permission to reprint it here.

This assimilative effect of the base language may also explain the results of a study by Macnamara and Kushnir (1971), who found that bilingual subjects understand monolingual passages faster than bilingual passages.

More recently, Grosjean (1988; reproduced in Chapter 10) used the gating paradigm (Grosjean 1980) to investigate the underlying process of lexical access in a bilingual situation. He presented bilingual participants with increasingly longer segments of English (and French filler) words embedded in a French sentence. In particular, he used words that were phonotactically marked as English and had no similar sounding words in French (such as "slash", with an initial consonant cluster very rare in French), and phonotactically unmarked words that had French counterparts (such as "pick", with its French counterpart "pique"). All words were monosyllabic and had the same uniqueness point, that is, the point in the left-to-right sequence of phonemes at which the word distinguishes itself from every other word (Marslen-Wilson 1984). Up to the third gate (80 ms into the word), participants guessed almost exclusively French words. Over subsequent gates, however, the number of English candidates increased. Moreover, this increase was much steeper for the words that were phonotactically marked as English than for the words with French counterparts. By the fifth gate (160 ms into the word), significantly more English candidates were proposed for the phonotactically marked than for the unmarked words. These results provide additional evidence for an assimilative effect of the base language. However, they also indicate that there may be limits to the assimilation of acoustic input to the base language. Under certain conditions, the base language may have the opposite effect, serving as a contrasting background against which conflicting acoustic information is especially conspicuous. In this case, the initial search of the base-language lexicon would be immediately aborted in favor of accessing the alternate-language lexicon. Indeed, the words that were phonotactically marked as English were recognized at earlier gates not only compared to the phonotactically unmarked words that had French counterparts, but also compared to a set of phonotactically unmarked words that had no French counterparts.

In the present study, we used the categorical perception paradigm to gain additional evidence that both base language and phonetic structure affect the perception of code-switched words. The categorical perception paradigm, which has been widely used to investigate monolingual speech perception (see Repp 1984 for an overview), was developed by Liberman and his colleagues at Haskins Laboratories (Liberman *et al.* 1957). Modifying formant transitions by means of their newly constructed pattern playback system, Liberman *et al.* synthesized an acoustic continuum ranging from [be] to [de] to [ge]. When participants were asked to identify the stimuli of the series, they divided them into three sharply defined categories, [be], [de], and [ge]. When asked to discriminate between stimuli, they discriminated best those stimuli labeled differently in the identification task, and worst those stimuli labeled as belonging to the same category.

The categorical perception paradigm has proven particularly fruitful for the study of context effects in speech perception. It has been established that the location of the category boundary, defined as the point along the series where a stimulus word is identified with equal probability as belonging to either category, is not solely based on the acoustic information contained in the stimulus, but can be influenced by information contained in the preceding sentence, such as speaking rate, syntactic structure, and semantic plausibility (see Repp and Liberman 1987 for a discussion of these findings).

In the present study, we used the categorical perception paradigm as a tool to investigate context effects in the perception of speech by bilinguals, in particular to assess whether bilinguals identify a stimulus as a member of the lexicon of one or the other language on the basis of the acoustic information contained in the stimulus alone, or whether they are influenced by the language in which the preceding words are spoken, that is, by the base language.[1] For this purpose, we constructed a stimulus series ranging from an English to a French word such that the closer a stimulus of the series was to the French endpoint of the series, the more of the French word it contained, and the closer a stimulus was to the English endpoint, the more of the English word it contained. Our first question was whether the perception of such a between-language series would be influenced by the base language in which the words were presented. While we expected that the English and French endpoints, and the near-endpoint stimuli, would be identified as the English or French word regardless of context, we hypothesized that the base language would have an effect on the identification of the stimuli in the middle of the series.

[1] In previous applications of the categorical perception paradigm to the investigation of speech perception in bilinguals, researchers were mainly interested in comparing the identification results of bilinguals with those of monolinguals (see, among others, Elman *et al.* 1977).

Our second question was whether the nature of the base-language effect, if it exists, would depend on the acoustic-phonetic makeup of the code-switched word, in particular on the compatibility of the code-switched word with the phonetic structure of the base language. We thus tested two between-language series, a "language-neutral" and a "language-selective" series. The endpoints of the "language-neutral series", English "day" and its French counterpart "dé", were chosen so that they would be similar to each other with no prominent phonetic cues marking them as either English or French. They were thus considered to be relatively compatible with either language. For this series, we expected to replicate the assimilative effect of the base language found by Grosjean with English words that sounded similar to French words (see above), so that the middle stimuli would be perceived as French in a French context and as English in an English context. On the other hand, the endpoints of the "language-selective series", English "ray" and French "ré", were chosen so that their phonetic makeup (namely, their initial consonant) would betray them immediately as English or French. They were thus compatible with only one of the two languages. Based on Grosjean's gating results with phonotactically marked English words in a French context (see above), we expected that in a French context, the middle stimuli of this series would be perceived as English, whereas in an English context, they would be perceived as French. In other words, the base language would serve as a contrasting background against which the middle stimuli would be evaluated.

In summary, then, we predicted both an effect of the base language on the perception of code-switched words and an interaction of this base-language effect with the acoustic-phonetic makeup of the code-switched items. The base language should have an assimilative effect on the perception of language-neutral stimuli and a contrastive effect on the perception of language-selective stimuli.

Before proceeding to test our two experimental questions, it was important to establish that the typical categorical perception results obtained with within-language series would generalize to our two English-French between-language series. Our first experiment, therefore, consisted of a forced-choice identification task performed on the "day–dé" and the "ray–ré" series in isolation, without base-language context. Based on the standard identification results for within-language series, we expected participants to divide both series into two discrete categories, one corresponding to the English endpoint, the other to the French endpoint. To assess further the similarities between the perception of between- and within-language series, we also asked participants to discriminate pairs of stimuli from within each series. Based on the standard results for within-language series, we expected participants to discriminate best those stimuli that they categorized differently.

7.1 Experiment 1: Identification and discrimination of between-language series in isolation

7.1.1 Materials

Two English-French series were constructed, one with language-neutral endpoints phonetically compatible with both languages and the other with language-selective endpoints compatible with only one language.

Language-neutral series

English "day" and French "dé" (thimble, dice) were chosen as endpoints that are phonetically compatible with either language. A number of tokens of each word were spoken by a bilingual speaker of British English and Parisian French (FG), who was judged by several colleagues of the authors to have no foreign accent in either language. These tokens were recorded on audiotape and subsequently digitized (sampling rate of 20 kHz, low-pass filtering at 9.8 kHz) and measured by means of a computer waveform editing program implemented on a DEC PDP 11/44 minicomputer. Two well-articulated endpoints of nearly identical duration were chosen, and the cursors at the end of the words were set so that both endpoints measured 412 ms. The spectrograms of these two endpoints are shown in Figure 7.1. As can be seen from a comparison of the formant trajectories of the two vowels, our speaker pronounced "day" with a fairly high vowel and only minimal diphthongization. The quality of the two vowels is therefore quite similar, even though their duration differs (348 ms versus 241 ms) (see Ladefoged 1975 for a discussion of the variability of the diphthong [eɪ] in different forms of English). As for the consonants, apart from the difference in place of articulation (alveolar versus dental), they also appear to be distinguished mainly by a durational property, namely, the length of their prevoicing (64 ms versus 171 ms). Differences in place of articulation (alveolar versus dental) occur in either language occasionally as a consequence of coarticulation (Ladefoged 1975), just as do variations in prevoicing and vowel length and quality. Thus the two stimuli do not contain any salient features that would exclude them from being

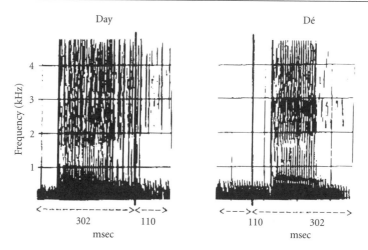

FIGURE 7.1 Spectrograms of the first and last stimulus of the series with language-neutral endpoints, ranging from the naturally produced English "day" (left) to the naturally produced French "dé" (right). The vertical lines mark the points at which the English vowel and the French prevoicing were cut back before constructing the hybrid stimuli

considered as a member of the lexicon of the other language. While still distinguishable, they are about as similar as any words taken from the two languages can be.

Apart from the two endpoints, the sixteen-member series consisted of fourteen hybrid stimuli constructed by replacing acoustic segments of the English endpoint "day" with acoustic segments of the French endpoint "dé". This was done by segmenting the digitized endpoints into parts, and then concatenating these parts. All cuts were made at zero-crossings to avoid discontinuities in the waveform. To produce the fourteen hybrid stimuli, first the English vowel was cut back by 110 ms to more closely approximate the length of the French vowel, and the French prevoicing was cut back by approximately 110 ms to more closely match the length of the English prevoicing. The cutoff points are indicated on the spectrograms in Figure 7.1. Then, increasingly longer final segments of English "day" were replaced with increasingly longer final segments of French "dé", so that the proportion of English gradually decreased, while the proportion of French gradually increased. Segments were incremented by approximately 20 ms, so that the first hybrid stimulus consisted of 282 ms or 94 percent English followed by 19 ms or 6 percent French, the second hybrid stimulus consisted of 265 ms or 87 percent English followed by 40 ms or 13 percent French, and so on, up to the fourteenth and last hybrid stimulus, which contained 18 ms or 6 percent English followed by 280 ms or 94 percent

French. Each hybrid stimulus had a total duration of 300 ms (within a few ms to allow for the fact that all cuts were made at zero-crossings). The sixteen-member series thus ranged from the original English "day" to the original French "dé", with fourteen shorter hybrid stimuli in-between. The stimuli within the series sounded remarkably natural, with no salient perceptual discontinuities within stimuli.

For the identification task, fifteen randomized blocks of the sixteen stimuli (240 stimuli in all) were recorded on audiotape, with an inter-stimulus interval (ISI) of 2 seconds and an interblock interval (IBI) of 5 seconds. The discriminability of the stimuli was assessed with a standard ABX task, using only the fourteen hybrid stimuli; that is, the endpoints (110 ms longer than the hybrids) were not used in the dis-crimination task. The twelve two-step pairs (stimulus 2 and 4, 3 and 5, and so on up to stimulus 13 and 15) were tested in four triads for each pair, ABA, ABB, BAA, and BAB, resulting in forty-eight triads. Each triad was tested four times, resulting in a total of 192 triads. The triads were randomized and recorded in four blocks of forty-eight triads each, with an ISI of 750 ms, an ITI (intertriad interval) of 3 seconds, and an IBI of 5 seconds. Each pair was thus tested sixteen times.

Language-selective series

English "ray" and French "ré" (musical note) were chosen as endpoints that are unambiguously marked by their phonetics as to the language to which they belong. A number of tokens of the two words were recorded from the same bilingual speaker who had produced the endpoints of the language-neutral series. Again, the tokens were digitized and measured. Two well-articulated English and French endpoints of almost identical duration were found and the cursors at the end of the words set so that both endpoints measured 463 ms. The spectrograms of the two endpoints are shown in Figure 7.2.

These spectrograms illustrate the distinct acoustic properties of the English semivowel [ɹ] (an alveolar approximant) and the French [ʁ] (a uvular fricative) (Ladefoged 1975). Neither of these sounds occurs in the other language. The vowel is again not very different across the two languages. As was done for the language-neutral series, the eleven hybrid stimuli of the thirteen-member language-selective series were constructed by replacing final segments of the English "ray" with final segments of the French "ré". The last 232 ms of the English vowel were replaced with the last 234 ms of the French vowel to produce the first hybrid stimulus, which consisted of 50 percent English followed

Ray

Ré

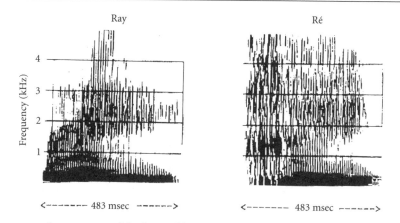

<------- 483 msec ------>   <------- 483 msec ------>

FIGURE 7.2 Spectrograms of the first and last stimulus of the series with language-selective endpoints, ranging from the naturally produced English "ray" (left) to the naturally produced French "ré" (right)

by 50 percent French. For the rest of the series, which involved the substitution of the consonantal portion, the proportion of English was decreased, and the proportion of French was increased, in steps of approximately 20 ms. The second hybrid stimulus thus contained 207 ms or 45 percent English followed by 258 ms or 55 percent French, the third hybrid stimulus 188 ms or 41 percent English followed by 274 ms or 59 percent French, and so on up to the eleventh and last hybrid stimulus, which contained 22 ms or 5 percent English followed by 441 ms or 95 percent French. The entire series, ranging from the unaltered English "ray" to the unaltered French "ré", thus contained thirteen stimuli, each measuring 463 ms (plus or minus a few ms to accommodate for zero-crossing cuts). Again, the stimuli sounded very natural, with the hybrid stimuli appearing to be somewhat unclearly pronounced, rather than artificially distorted.

The identification test tape consisted of fifteen randomized blocks of the thirteen stimuli, for a total of 195 stimuli. There was an ISI of 2 seconds and an IBI of 5 seconds. The discriminability of the stimuli was assessed in a standard ABX task. Stimulus 1 was not compared to any other stimulus because of the jump from 0 percent to 50 percent French between the first and the second stimulus. The remaining ten two-step pairs (stimulus 2 and 4, 3 and 5, and so on, up to 11 and 13) were tested in four triads per pair, ABA, ABB, BAA, and BAB, resulting in forty triads. Each triad was tested four times, resulting in a total of 160 triads. The triads were randomized and recorded in four blocks of forty triads each, with an ISI of 750 ms, an ITI of 3 seconds, and an IBI of 5 seconds. Each pair was thus tested sixteen times.

7.1.2 Participants

Eight French-English bilingual adults (six females and two males) whose first language was French served as participants. They all were very fluent in English and French and had used both languages on a daily basis for at least seven years, that is, since they had moved to the United States (Boston area). With the exception of one participant, none of them had been exposed to English as a second language before secondary school. There were individual differences in the degree of foreign accent in their spoken English. The main criteria for qualifying as a participant were daily use of both languages and membership in a bilingual community that frequently code-switches.

7.1.3 Procedure

The eight participants were run individually on both the language-neutral and the language-selective series, with the order of the two series counterbalanced across participants. Participants were tested in one session in their home environment. Oral and written instructions were given in French. Participants listened to the stimuli over binaural headphones at a comfortable listening level.

In the identification task, the participants were asked to circle the word corresponding to the perceived item on a response sheet (Dé versus Day; Ré versus Ray). They were instructed to answer on all trials, even if the words seemed to be somewhere between "day" and "dé", or "ray" and "ré". In the subsequent ABX discrimination task, they were asked to indicate, by writing down a 1 or a 2, whether they perceived the third stimulus (X) in the triad to be the same as the first (A) or the second (B) stimulus. They were instructed to answer even if the stimuli all sounded the same to them. None of the participants asked questions about the origin of the stimuli.

7.1.4 Results and discussion

The group results for the eight participants in the identification and discrimination tasks are displayed in Figure 7.3 ("day–dé") and Figure 7.4 ("ray–ré"). Percentage of identification in terms of the English endpoint ("day" or "ray") of the series and percentage of correct discrimination

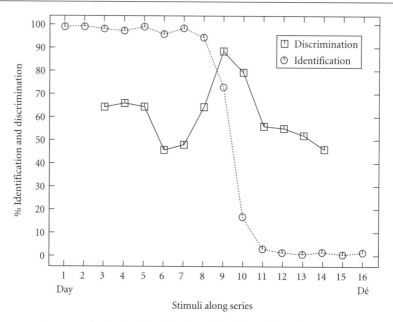

FIGURE 7.3 Group results for the identification as "day" (circles) and correct discrimination (squares) of the language-neutral series, "day–dé". Each square shows the discrimination performance for the two neighboring stimuli

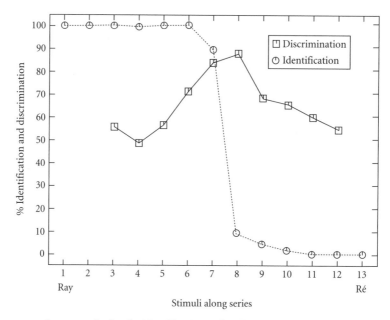

FIGURE 7.4 Group results for the identification as "ray" (circles) and the correct discrimination (squares) of the language-selective series, "ray–ré". Each square shows the discrimination performance for the two neighboring stimuli

are plotted against the stimulus number along the series. The data points in the discrimination curve refer to discrimination between the two neighboring stimuli. For example, a value of 50 percent at stimulus number 3 means that stimuli 2 and 4 were discriminated correctly half the time, which, for this task, is chance.

As can be seen, performance on the identification task was extremely orderly for both series. Furthermore, for both series, participants divided the stimuli into two rather sharply defined categories, and did not perceive the hybrid stimuli as gradually going from English to French. Nor was there any indication that they perceived any discontinuities in the construction of the stimuli. For example, despite the fact that the endpoints of the "day–dé" series were 110 ms longer than each of the hybrid stimuli, the stimuli next to the endpoints were identified virtually as often as "day" or "dé" as the endpoints themselves (virtually 100 percent of the time). Similarly, the jump from 0 percent to 50 percent French between the first and the second stimulus of the "ray–ré" series had no observable consequences as they were both identified as "ray" 100 percent of the time.

The mean category boundary[2] lies at the stimulus value of 9.37 for the "day–dé" series, where the stimulus would be approximately 55 percent French, and at 7.50 for the "ray–ré" series, where the stimulus would be approximately 75 percent French. Visual inspection of the spectrograms of the "day–dé" stimuli does not reveal any obvious reason for the specific location of the category boundary. Inspection of the spectrograms for the stimuli in the "ray–ré" series, however, reveals that the hybrid stimuli were labeled as French "ré" as soon as the characteristic uvular frication of the French [ʁ] appears, that is at stimulus 8.

Converging evidence for the location of the category boundary for each series is provided by the discrimination data. For the "day–dé" series, the best mean discrimination performance was obtained for stimuli 8–10, precisely those stimuli closest to, but on either side of, the mean category boundary (9.37). For the "ray–ré" series, the best mean discrimination performance was obtained for stimulus pair 7–9, which also straddles the mean category boundary (7.50).

---

[2] All boundary values were calculated by fitting a linear regression line to the data in the boundary region of the individual participant's identification function (i.e. excluding the data in the tails of the function) and taking as the boundary the stimulus value that corresponded to 50% identification as the English endpoint ("day" or "ray").

In summary, our results indicate that participants divide between-language series into sharply defined categories and discriminate best those stimuli that they categorize differently. Experiment 1 thus shows that the perception of a computer-edited series between monosyllabic words in two different languages is very similar to the perception of a series between two words in the same language.

7.2 Experiment 2: Identification of between-language series in English and French contexts

Experiment 1 demonstrated that a between-language series is perceived very much like a series within one language. We could thus proceed to test our two experimental questions, namely, whether categorization of the stimuli is influenced by the base-language context and, if so, whether the nature of this base-language effect depends on the acoustic-phonetic makeup of the words used to construct the series.

As we discussed in the introduction, there is evidence that bilingual participants use a general strategy of trying to map incoming acoustic information onto representations of the base language (Soares and Grosjean 1984; Grosjean 1988). In other words, the base language seems to have an assimilative effect on the perception of a code-switched word. Grosjean (1988) showed, however, that this assimilative effect of the base language may be limited to code-switched words that are phonetically compatible with the base language. In the case of words carrying distinct acoustic-phonetic cues revealing their membership in the alternate-language lexicon, the base language may have a contrastive effect. On the basis of this evidence, we made the following predictions. First, we expected the middle stimuli of our series to be perceived differently depending on the preceding base language. Second, we expected the nature of this base-language effect to vary with the nature of the series. For the language-neutral series, we expected the base language to have an assimilative effect on the middle stimuli, so that the middle stimuli would be perceived as the English endpoint in the English context and as the French endpoint in the French context. For the language-selective series, however, we expected the base language to have a contrastive effect on the middle stimuli, so that they would be perceived as the English endpoint in the French context and as the French endpoint in the English context. In other words, we expected the middle stimuli of the language-neutral series to be perceived as a base-language word but the middle stimuli of the language-selective series to be perceived as a code-switched word.

7.2.1 Materials

An English and a French context sentence similar in meaning and length were chosen. In light of the task to be performed by the participants, English "We have to categorize (ray/day)" and its French translation "Il faut qu'on catégorise (ré/dé)" seemed appropriate. It was necessary to construct new series since words spoken in context do not have exactly the same acoustic properties as the same words spoken in isolation. The accent-free French-English male bilingual who produced the endpoint stimuli in Experiment 1 also produced the stimuli for this experiment. He read ten tokens each of the English base-language sentence ending with English "day" or "ray", and ten tokens each of the French base-language sentence ending with French "dé" or "ré".

Language-neutral series

To construct the language-neutral series in context, we digitized the ten English sentences ending with "day" and the ten French sentences ending with "dé" and measured the duration of the context up to the closure before "day"/"dé", the duration of the closure, the voice-onset time (VOT) of "day"/"dé", and the total duration of "day"/ "dé". The English and French sentences closest to the average on all measures were chosen to construct the series, which was done by digital splicing. English "day" (with a VOT of 17 ms and a duration of 318 ms, cut back slightly from 324 ms to be exactly twice as long as the French endpoint) and French "dé" (with a VOT of 29 ms and a duration of 159 ms) were spliced out to provide the two endpoints. Then, increasingly longer initial segments of "day" were replaced with increasingly longer initial segments of "dé" to create the hybrid stimuli of the series. Since "day" was twice as long as "dé", the "day" segments were incremented in steps of 20 ms, whereas the "dé" segments were incremented by 10 ms (within 1 or 2 ms to allow for zero-crossing cuts). For the first hybrid stimulus, consisting of 3 percent French followed by 97 percent English, the initial 21 ms of "day" were replaced with the initial 10 ms of "dé". To construct the second hybrid stimulus, consisting of 6 percent French followed by 94 percent English, 39 ms of "day" were replaced with 18 ms of "dé" and so on, until all of "day" had been replaced with "dé" from beginning to end, and the duration of the stimuli along the series had decreased from 318 ms for the English endpoint to 159 ms for the French endpoint. The series, including the two endpoints, had 17 stimuli, which were each concatenated to the English (1,214 ms) and to the French (1,212 ms) context sentences.[3]

Language-selective series

The language-selective series in context was constructed in a similar fashion. The ten English sentences "We have to categorize ray" and the ten French sentences "Il faut qu'on catégorise ré" were digitized, and the duration of the context up to "ray"/ "ré" and the duration of "ray"/ "ré" itself were measured. One sentence in each language with contexts and stimulus words closest to the average on both measures was chosen. "Ray" (298 ms) and "ré" (224 ms) were then spliced out to create the series. The first stimulus of the series was the unaltered "ray". To produce the hybrid stimuli, increasingly longer initial segments of "ray" were replaced with increasingly longer initial segments of "ré". Since "ré" was only 75 percent of the length of "ray", roughly every 13.5 ms of "ray" were deleted and replaced with 10 ms of "ré". The second stimulus contained 13 ms of "ré" followed by 282 ms of "ray", the third stimulus contained 21 ms of "ré" followed by 272 ms of "ray", and so on. By the twelfth and last stimulus (263 ms) of the series, the initial 49 percent of English "ray" was replaced with 50 percent of French "ré". The original "ré" (39 ms shorter than the last stimulus of the series) was not included in the series. To obtain the test sentences, each stimulus was concatenated to the English (1,126 ms) and the French (1,121 ms) context sentences.

Test tapes

One English and one French test tape for both series were recorded. Each of the four tapes contained ten blocks of twelve ("ray–ré") or

---

[3] Note that in Experiment 1 we started substitution from the end of the word whereas, in this experiment, we started substitution from the beginning. The reason has to do with the acoustic-phonetic characteristics of "dé" and "day" when spoken in context, as compared to in isolation. In context the two words were spoken with no prevoicing, and the VOT value for "dé" was longer than that for "day". The consequence was that, had we started substitution from the end of the word, we would have created some stimuli that contained a sequence of burst/aspiration and the vowel of "day", followed by aspiration and the vowel of "dé". This unacceptable sequence could be avoided simply by starting substitution from the beginning of the word, as we did. The reason that substitution from the end of the word was not a problem in Experiment 1 was that both "dé" and "day" were spoken with prevoicing in isolation, so that it was possible to equate the length of the prevoicing (and vowel) before constructing the hybrid stimuli, while still keeping the release burst intact. With equally long segments of prevoicing and vowel, substitution from the end of the word never created an unacceptable sequence of the sort described above.

seventeen ("day–dé") sentences. The sentences were randomized within blocks, with an ISI of 2 seconds and an IBI of 6 seconds.

7.2.2 Participants

Twelve French-English bilinguals (ten females and two males) from the same population as in Experiment 1 served as participants. One of the participants had also participated in Experiment 1.

7.2.3 Procedure

Each participant took part in all four conditions of the experiment, with the stimuli presented in two sessions, one for each language context. Which language context and which series were tested first were counterbalanced across subjects. Participants were again tested individually in their homes. The English and French sessions were held on different days, but no longer than one week apart. During each session, written and oral instructions were given in the respective base language. The experimenter (the first author) was a multilingual speaker who naturally code-switched in all her interactions with the participants to create a setting in which code-switches do occur. Participants were told that they would be presented with repeated tokens of the context sentence followed by either the English or the French word, and that they were to circle the perceived item on a response sheet (Dé versus Day; Ré versus Ray). They were asked to respond even if they were not sure of what they had heard, that is, even if the item seemed to be somewhere between "day" and "dé", or "ray" and "ré". The test sentences were presented over binaural headphones at a comfortable listening level.

7.2.4 Results and discussion

Figure 7.5 displays the group results for the language-neutral series, "day–dé", in context. As can be seen, participants divided the language-neutral series into two well defined categories, with no significant shift of the category boundary as a function of the base language (t (11) = 0.38, p > 0.10). The mean category boundaries were located at stimulus values of 8.46 and 8.54 in the English and French conditions, respectively. This corresponds to a stimulus consisting of approximately 30 percent French followed by 70 percent English. Contrary to our prediction of an assimilative effect of the base language, the stimuli of the language-neutral series were categorized independently of the base language in which they were presented.

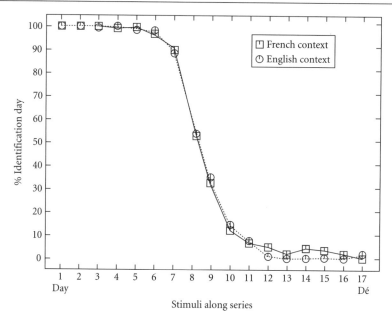

FIGURE 7.5 Group results for the identification as "day" of the "day–dé" series in English (circles) and French (squares) context

Figure 7.6 displays the group results for the language-selective series, "ray–ré". Again, participants divided the language-selective series into two well defined categories. For this series, however, there was a significant effect of the base language. In the English context, the mean category boundary was located at stimulus value 6.18 (which corresponds to a stimulus of approximately 19 percent French followed by 81 percent English), whereas in the French context, it was located at 7.14 (which corresponds to 23 percent French followed by 77 percent English). These results show that in accordance with our predictions, the middle stimuli were categorized as the English endpoint in the French condition and as the French endpoint in the English condition ($t(11) = 2.56$, $p < 0.03$). In other words, the base language had a contrastive effect on the categorization of the language-selective series.

In summary, although we did not reproduce the assimilative effect of the base language with the categorical perception paradigm, we did find affirmative answers to both our experimental questions. We found that under certain conditions, the base-language context does affect the identification of a code-switched word and, moreover, that this base-language effect interacts with the acoustic-phonetic nature of the code-switched word.

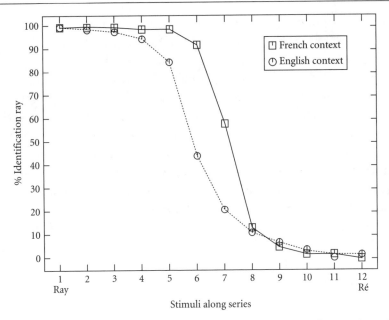

FIGURE 7.6 Group results for the identification as "ray" of the "ray–ré" series in English (circles) and French (squares) context

7.3 General discussion

Experiment 1 demonstrates that bilingual participants identify and discriminate a stimulus series ranging from a word in one of their languages to a word in their other language very much like monolingual listeners perceive a series within one language. That is, they divide the series into two discrete categories and discriminate best the stimuli they have categorized differently. The identification of a between-language series may thus serve as a tool to investigate context effects in the perception of code-switched words, that is, words that bilinguals bring in from their alternate language when talking to another bilingual.

In Experiment 2 we used this tool to find corroborating evidence for an effect of the base language on the perception of a code-switched word. Evidence for a base-language effect had been previously found in the form of delayed comprehension and lexical decision for code-switched words (Macnamara and Kushnir 1971; Soares and Grosjean 1984) and a preponderance of base-language candidates at the initial gates of both code-switched and base-language words (Grosjean 1988). In addition, we investigated the finding from Grosjean's gating study that the nature of this base-language effect might be influenced by the acoustic-phonetic makeup of the code-switched items, in particular their compatibility with the phonetic structure of the base language. To this end, we tested the effect of the base language on the identification of both a language-neutral and a language-selective series, that is, a series that was more or less compatible with both languages and a series that was compatible with only one language. And, indeed, we found an effect of the base language, but only on the language-selective series. As expected for this series, the effect was of a contrastive nature, that is, the middle stimuli of the series were identified as the alternate-language endpoint. The expected assimilative effect of the base language on the language-neutral series was not found; the middle stimuli of this series were identified as the same in both conditions.

Several possible explanations come to mind for the lack of an assimilative effect of the base language on the perception of the language-neutral series. The first is that a larger step size between the stimuli of the language-neutral compared to the language-selective series may have masked an assimilative effect. In other words, the change from English to French across the series may be too abrupt for the effect of the base language to be evident in the identification data. It is not possible to compare the step sizes of the between-language continua directly, because the stimulus dimensions of the two continua are not commensurate. However, there is an indirect way to address the issue, namely, by comparing the number of stimuli categorized inconsistently in the two series. As can be seen in Figures 7.5 and 7.6, the number of stimuli categorized inconsistently was virtually the same in the two series. Under the assumption that only inconsistently categorized stimuli are subject to base-language effects, the base language had the same number of stimuli to act upon in the two series. In other words, the category boundary had the same leeway in both series, so that the step size between the critical stimuli was at least functionally equated.

A second possible explanation is that the sentence preceding the target words was constant, so that participants knew when and where a code-switched word could occur. However, this was also the case for the language-selective series, on which the base language did have an effect, albeit a contrastive one. In addition, in Grosjean's (1988) gating experiments, target words were also always preceded by an identical string of words, and participants still proposed a preponderance of base-language words for the code-switched words with base-language counterparts even at rather late gates, that is, participants' data did show an assimilative effect of the base language.

A third possible reason for the loss of the assimilative effect of the base language is the forced choice between the two endpoints of the series in the categorical perception experiment. That is, on top of the base-language context remaining constant, it is also the case that the base-language word or code-switched word remained constant. This contrasts with Grosjean's experiment, in which the target could be one of any number of words belonging to either English or French. Maybe the restricted choice in a categorical perception experiment allowed participants to concentrate their attention selectively on the acoustic information contained in the stimuli while disengaging from effects of the base language. In view of this possibility, it is all the more interesting that we did find the predicted contrastive effect of the base language on the language-selective series. The finding of the contrastive effect and not the assimilative effect when using the categorical perception paradigm, but both effects when using the gating paradigm, might be a first indication that these two effects arise at different stages of language processing, with different underlying mechanisms (see e.g. Miller *et al.* 1984). Further experiments with different series and different languages are needed to clarify these questions. As part of this process, Grosjean is currently investigating the effect of the base language on the identification of a language-neutral series ranging from a German to a French word.

In summary, the present data, stemming from a novel use of the categorical perception paradigm, support evidence from previous experiments with different procedures that the perception of code-switched words by bilinguals does not occur solely on the basis of the acoustic-phonetic information in the code-switched word, but is influenced by the base language of the conversation. Moreover, this effect varies with the acoustic-phonetic characteristics of the code-switched words, in particular with whether they are phonetically compatible with the base language.

8

Is There a Base-language Effect in Speech Production?*

This chapter contains two main sections. The first, "The phonetics of code-switching", is a reprint of a paper (Grosjean and Miller 1994) in which it is asked whether, when code-switches are produced, the phonetic momentum of the base language carries over into the guest language and hence affects the beginning of code-switches. How complete is a code-switch therefore? The second section, "The prosody of code-switching", is a very short contribution that examines the base language effect on prosody. Here, a short pilot study which produced some interesting results is described (Grosjean and Soares 1986).

8.1 The phonetics of code-switching

Bilingualism, which can be defined as the regular use of two or more languages (or dialects), is a widespread phenomenon. It is present in practically every country of the world, in all classes of society and in all age groups; in fact, it has been estimated that half the world's population at least is bilingual. One of the most interesting aspects of bilingualism at the cognitive level is the fact that two or more languages are in contact within the same person. This phenomenon, which has led to a vast body of research (Appel and Muysken 1987; Baetens Beardsmore 1986; Grosjean 1982; Hakuta 1986; Haugen 1969;

---

* The first section of the chapter, "The phonetics of code-switching", first appeared as an article: Grosjean, F., and Miller, J. (1994). "Going in and out of languages: An example of bilingual flexibility", *Psychological Science* 5: 201–6. In the second section, "The prosody of code-switching", the three figures were originally published in Grosjean, F. and Soares, C. (1986). "Processing mixed language: Some preliminary findings", in J. Vaid (ed.) *Language Processing in Bilinguals: Psycholinguistic and Neuropsychological Perspectives*. Hillsdale, NJ: Lawrence Erlbaum Associates, 145–79. The author wishes to thank the publishers (Wiley-Blackwell Publishing and Lawrence Erlbaum Associates) as well as Joanne Miller and Carlos Soares for permission to reprint both the paper and the figures here.

Romaine 1989; Weinreich 1966), can best be understood if one examines the bilingual's various language modes.

In their everyday lives, bilinguals find themselves at various points along a situational continuum which induce different language modes. At one end of the continuum, bilinguals are in a totally monolingual mode in that they are speaking (or writing) to monolinguals of one or the other of the languages. At the other end of the continuum, they find themselves in a bilingual language mode, which means that they are communicating with bilinguals who share their two languages and with whom they normally mix languages. In this mode, bilinguals normally adopt a language to use together (the base language) and then, depending on a number of factors, mix in the other language (the guest language). One way of doing this is to borrow a lexical item from the guest language and to integrate it phonologically and morphologically into the base language (Poplack *et al.* 1988; Weinreich 1966). Thus, a French-English bilingual might say to another bilingual, "Je vais *checker* cela" (I'm going to check this). Here, English "check" is adapted to French morphology and pronounced as a French word. Another way of mixing languages, and the one that is of interest to us here, is to shift completely to the guest language—for a word, a phrase, a sentence, for example. This is known as code-switching. Thus, for example, a bilingual might say, "J'ai vu des *wild guys* à cheval" (I saw some wild guys on horseback), or "Va chercher Marc *and bribe him* avec un chocolat chaud *with cream on top*" (Go get Marc and bribe him with a hot chocolate with cream on top). Here "wild guys", "and bribe him", and "with cream on top" are said in English.

Although there has been a recent flurry of activity in the psycholinguistics of bilingualism (Harris 1992; Schreuder and Weltens 1993), less work has been done on the processing of code-switches (exceptions are de Bot 1992; Grosjean 1988; and Myers-Scotton 1993, among others). In the domain of perception, researchers have examined how the bilingual listener processes mixed language online and have studied, among other things, the base-language effect. This effect, originally proposed by Macnamara and Kushnir (1971), concerns the impact that the base language has on the guest language during the perception of code-switches. It has been shown repeatedly that there is a momentary dominance of base-language units (phonemes, syllables, words) at code-switch boundaries (at the onset of "wild", "and", and "with" in the examples above). This increased activation can in turn delay slightly the perception of units in the guest language (Grosjean 1988; Grosjean and

Soares 1986; Soares and Grosjean 1984). This effect is influenced by a number of factors, including the acoustic makeup of the code-switched item (Bürki-Cohen *et al.* 1989), its phonotactics (Grosjean 1988) and the presence or absence of a base-language homophone (Grosjean 1988). It is not yet clear how best to account for this effect nor at what level of processing it occurs.

The question asked in this study is whether there is also a base-language effect in production. Could it be that, in speaking, the phonetic momentum of the base language carries over into the guest language and hence affects at least the beginning of code-switches? How complete is a code-switch, therefore? On the one hand, the results of the perception studies reported above, and the fact that 80–90 percent of linguistic units normally belong to the base language in a mixed utterance, could lead to the expectation of some base-language influence at code-switch onset (during the first phoneme or the first syllable). On the other hand, because of the inherent differences between perception and production, there could well be no clear equivalent of the base-language effect in production. Given the flexibility of the production mechanism, a switch between languages might involve a total change, not only at the lexical but also at the phonetic level. In order to test these alternatives, we measured the onsets of code-switches by means of a well-established variable, voice onset time (VOT; Lisker and Abramson 1964), and compared the results with those obtained when the same bilinguals were speaking only one language or the other.

8.1.1 Experiment 1

Method

Participants
Five French-English bilingual adults with no reported speech or hearing disorders served individually in a session lasting 45 minutes. Membership in a bilingual community (the European French speaking community in Boston), daily use of English and French, and a regular habit of code-switching with other bilinguals (including the bilingual experimenter) were critical variables in choosing these subjects.[1]

---

[1] All participants had the following characteristics. They were native speakers of French and had started learning English in primary or secondary school; they had moved to the United States as adults and had lived in the Boston region for at least four years; they spoke English with hardly any French accent; they used their two languages on a daily basis; they code-switched when speaking French to bilingual friends and family members; and they had served previously as participants in experiments on bilingualism. No effort was made

Materials

Three stories were written in English for this study and another study involving the prosody of code-switching. The stories ranged from 270 to 300 words long, and each contained a number of words beginning with the three unvoiced stop consonants, /p/, /t/, and /k/. Each story involved three characters, a woman, a man, and a pet, with names that could be said in English and in French (Concordia, Paul, and their dog, Tito; Pepita, Tom, and their monkey, Coco; Tatiana, Carl, and their dog, Pipo). The stories were written in such a way that the names of the characters appeared a number of times (between seven and nine times each). In addition, at least fifteen words (mainly common nouns) that begin with unvoiced stops and whose French translations begin with the same consonant were included in the stories. Thus, for example, in one story, the /t/ onset was represented by the following five words (the French translations are in parentheses): temperature (température), taxi (taxi), tourist (tourist), telephone (téléphone), and Texas (Texas). The other unvoiced stops (/p/ and /k/) were represented by ten other words in this particular story.

Once the three English stories had been written, they were translated into French. Three different "full" versions of each story were typed on separate pages: English, French with English code-switches, and French. The latter two were identical except that the names of the three main characters were typed in capital letters in the version with English code-switches. Three key-word versions of each story were then prepared on separate pages, one for each full version. These contained the important words in the stories (nouns, verbs, etc.) and few if any function words. The key-word version for French with English code-switches was again the same as the French key-word version except that the names of the main characters appeared in capital letters.

Procedure

Before the experiment, participants chatted in French with the bilingual experimenter, whom they knew personally, for about fifteen minutes. Care was taken to involve code-switching into English by raising appropriate topics (work, sports, etc.). Participants were then seated in a soundproof booth with the experimenter. They were told

to test the participants' proficiency in English and French nor to use "balanced" bilinguals (see Grosjean 1982, 1985c for a discussion of the problems linked with proficiency tests and the use of balanced bilinguals).

that their task would be to read a number of stories silently and retell them to the experimenter, and that to help them during the retelling they would be given a shortened, key-word version of each story.

The participants were then asked to read out loud, in English, the names of the main characters in the three stories. Following this, the English stories were presented one at a time and, after each reading, the participants retold the story in English with the help of the English key-word version. The participants were then presented with the three versions in French with English code-switches and were asked to follow the same procedure. They were reminded that the characters were the same as in the English stories and that they would have to say the characters' names in English (i.e. code-switch over to English). To help them with the task, they were given the key-word versions in French with English code-switches.

Finally, the participants were asked again to read the names of the main characters in the three stories out loud, but in French this time. They were then given the three French stories and were told that this time they were to pronounce the names of the characters in French. During this third retelling, they used the French key-word versions of the stories.

All retellings (three in English, three in French with code-switches, and three in French only) were recorded with a lapel mike (Sony ECM-16T) and a cassette recorder (Marantz PMD 360).

Data analysis

The recordings were digitized (sampling rate of 20 kHz, low-pass filtering at 9.8 kHz) and analyzed by means of a computer editing program implemented on a DEC PDP 11/44. Given the differences in word stress in English and French, only monosyllabic words beginning with an unvoiced stop consonant were analyzed. These included the three monosyllabic test words (Paul, Tom, and Carl, henceforth called the stimulus words) in their three versions (English, English code-switch, and French) and a number of other words in their two versions (English and French). For each word, we measured the VOT of the initial consonant, that is the interval of time between the release of the stop and the onset of voicing (Lisker and Abramson 1964). For each participant and each story, the first six occurrences of each stimulus word were measured, in each of their three versions, as were as many

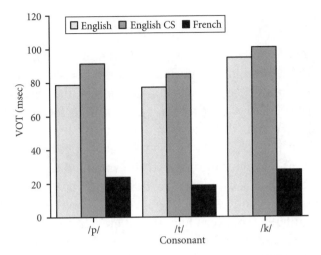

FIGURE 8.1 Mean VOT durations for the stop consonants /p/, /t/, and /k/ at the onset of the stimulus words (Paul, Tom, and Carl) in the retelling task. Each consonant is represented by three bars depicting the values obtained in the three conditions: English monolingual (English), French with English code-switches (English CS), and French monolingual (French). Each bar is the mean of 30 values (5 participants and 6 values per participant)

of the other monosyllabic words with initial unvoiced stop consonants as were produced.[2]

Results and discussion

Figure 8.1 presents the mean VOT durations for the three stop consonants /p/, /t/, and /k/ at the onset of the stimulus words. Each consonant is represented by three bars depicting the mean values obtained in the three conditions: English, French with English code-switches (henceforth English CS), and French. An examination of the English and French values reveals an expected VOT difference between the two languages (79 versus 24 ms for /p/, 77 versus 19 ms for /t/, and 95 versus 28 ms for /k/). We should note that these values are not specific to proper nouns. When these VOT values were compared with those at the onset of the other monosyllabic words in the English and French monolingual versions of the stories, no difference reached significance in the six tests conducted (two languages and three consonants).[3]

[2] Three research assistants with good knowledge of English and French undertook the measurements. On an interjudge reliability test involving eighteen measurements from the reading task in Experiment 2, the mean VOT values were 38, 39, and 39 ms ($F_{(2, 34)} = 2.70$, $p > .05$).

[3] The means over subjects for each language and each consonant, and the t values, are as follows (the first figure is for the stimulus words, the second for the other monosyllabic

Given that the participants showed a clear difference between English and French VOT values, we can address the question asked at the beginning of the study: Is there a base-language effect in the production of code-switches and, more specifically, at their onset? As can be seen in Figure 8.1 (middle bar of each consonant set), the answer is clearly negative. The English CS values (91, 85, and 101 ms for /p/, /t/, and /k/, respectively) are quite different from the French values and are similar to the English values. A one-way analysis of variance based on the participant means for each consonant set shows a main effect in each case: for /p/, F (2, 8) = 18.8, p < .001; for /t/, F (2, 8) = 17.8, p < .01; for /k/, F (2, 8) = 55.9, p < .001. A Scheffé post hoc test reveals, in each case, a significant difference between English and French, and between English CS and French, but no difference between English and English CS.[4]

These results suggest that in bilingual speech production, no phonetic momentum of the base language carries over into the guest language. Switching from one language to another appears to involve a total change, not only at the lexical but also at the phonetic level. The question that remains, however, is how immediate the change is. Bilinguals might plan their code-switches ahead of time and start changing over to the phonetics of the guest language before reaching the onset of the code-switch, that is, the shift could take place one or two words before. As for going back to the base language, this might be done after the code-switch, during the word or words that follow. In order to examine the time course of code-switching, we tracked the phonetic shift from one language to another by means of a reading task.

8.1.2 Experiment 2

Method

Participants
The same five bilingual participants took part in this experiment, which lasted twenty minutes.

words): English /p/, 79 and 71, t = 1.72, p = .16; English /t/, 77 and 74, t = 0.27, p = .80; English /k/, 95 and 97, t = 0.36, p = .74; French /p/, 24 and 19, t = 1.09, p = .34; French /t/, 19 and 22, t = 0.92, p = .41; French /k/, 28 and 37, t = 2.07, p = .11. It should be noted that the results of 29 out of 30 individual tests (5 participants, 2 languages, 3 consonants) are also non-significant.

[4] Individual analyses of variance for each participant and each consonant set confirm these general results. All 15 differences (5 participants and 3 stimulus words) between English and French and between English CS and French are significant, whereas 12 out of 15 differences between English and English CS are not significant.

Materials

The three stimulus words were embedded in two versions of an English sentence. "Tom" and "Carl" were inserted in "During the first few days, we'll tell him to copy —— constantly" and "Paul" was inserted in "During the last few days, we'll tell him to copy —— constantly". The two versions, which differed only in the presence of "first" or "last", were included so as to allow a bit of diversity in the reading and to make sure that participants remained attentive throughout the study. The two versions of the sentence were then adapted into French in such a way that the number of syllables and the last part of each sentence were similar in the two languages: "Pendant les premiers (derniers) jours, il faudra qu'il copie —— constamment".

Three reading sets were constructed from these sentences and typed on different pages. The English set contained nine tokens, three for each of the three stimulus words. The tokens were grouped by stimulus words within the set. The French set contained nine tokens of the French sentences, with the same internal organization. Finally, the code-switching set was identical to the French set except that the stimulus words were typed in capital letters.

Procedure

As in the first experiment, participants chatted in French and code-switched with the bilingual experimenter before undertaking the reading task. They were then seated in a soundproof booth, and the experimenter asked them to read out loud, at a normal rate, the sentences presented to them. They were instructed to read each sentence silently before reading it aloud, and they were explicitly told to code-switch for the proper nouns in the code-switching set of sentences (i.e. to pronounce Paul, Tom, or Carl in English). The order of the sets was English, English CS, and French. After a first pass through the three sets, the participants were given a short break and were then asked to read the sets a second time. Thus, each stimulus word was read six times in each of the three conditions. The recordings were made as in Experiment 1.

Data analysis

The sentences were analyzed as in the first study. This time, however, three measures were obtained for each sentence: the VOT of /k/ at the beginning of "copy/copie", the VOT at the onset of the stimulus words (Paul, Tom, and Carl) and, finally, the VOT of /k/ at the beginning of "constantly/constamment".

Results and discussion

Figure 8.2 presents the mean VOT durations obtained at the three measurement locations. The middle panel of the figure is the reading counterpart of the retelling data presented in Figure 8.1. As can be seen, the pattern of results is very similar. There are large differences between the English and French values (78 and 17 ms respectively for /p/; 90 and 20 ms for /t/; and 97 and 27 for /k/), whereas the English CS values (78, 92, and 96 ms for /p/, /t/, and /k/ respectively) are once again quite different from the French values and are similar to the English values. A one-way analysis of variance based on the participant means for each consonant set shows a main effect in each case: for /p/, $F_{(2, 8)} = 40.08$, $p < .001$; for /t/, $F_{(2, 8)} = 41.05$, $p < 0.001$; for /k/, $F_{(2, 8)} = 57.9$, $p < .001$. A Scheffé post hoc test reveals, in each case again, a significant difference between English and French, and between English CS and French, but no difference between English and English CS.[5] Thus, whether the task is retelling a story or reading a sentence, there is no apparent trace of the base language at the onset of the code-switch.

In order to obtain some estimate of the time course of the code-switch, that is, how early it occurs and how late it disappears, one needs to turn to the two other panels in Figure 8.2. In the top panel, which represents the VOT values of the /k/ of "copy/copie", one observes an expected difference between English /k/ and French /k/, but no difference between English CS /k/ and French /k/ (the language at this point in the English CS sentence was meant to be French and clearly is French). A one-way analysis of variance based on the participant means for each consonant set confirms this finding. A main effect is found in each case: for the Paul sentence, $F_{(2, 8)} = 12.2$, $p < .01$; for the Tom sentence, $F_{(2, 8)} = 18.7$, $p < .001$; for the Carl sentence, $F_{(2, 8)} = 19.8$, $p < .001$. A Scheffé post hoc test reveals, in each case, a significant difference between English and French, and between English and English CS, but no difference between English CS and French.[6]

An identical pattern of results is found for the /k/ in "constantly/constamment", as can be seen in the bottom panel in Figure 8.2.

[5] Individual analyses of variance for each participant and each consonant produce similar results. All 15 differences (5 subjects and 3 stimulus words) between English and French and between English CS and French are significant, whereas 13 out of 15 differences between English and English CS are not significant.

[6] Individual analyses of variance for each participant and each consonant set confirm these results. All 15 differences between English and French and between English and English CS are significant, whereas 14 out of 15 differences between English CS and French are not significant.

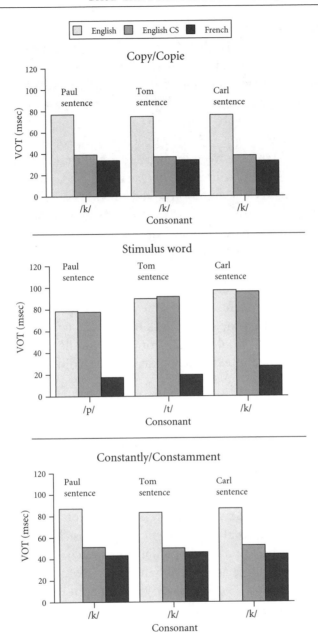

FIGURE 8.2 Mean VOT durations at three measurement locations in the reading task: the /k/ of "copy/copie" (top panel), the onset stops (/p/, /t/, and /k/) of the three stimulus words (middle panel), and the /k/ of "constantly/constamment" (bottom panel). Each panel has three sets of bars, one for each sentence (the Paul sentence on the left, the Tom sentence in the middle, and the Carl sentence on the right). Each set contains three bars, depicting the values obtained in the three conditions: English monolingual (English), French with English code-switches (English CS), and French monolingual (French). Each bar is the mean of 30 values (5 participants and 6 values per participant)

There exists a clear difference between English /k/ and French /k/, but no difference between English CS /k/ and French /k/ (the language of the English CS sentence at this point was meant to be French and clearly is). An analysis of variance based on the participant means for each consonant set, confirms this: for the Paul sentence, $F_{(2, 8)} = 19.1$, $p <$ .001; for the Tom sentence, $F_{(2, 8)} = 13.2$, $p < .01$; for the Carl sentence, $F_{(2, 8)} = 22.8$, $p < .001$. A Scheffé post hoc test reveals, in each case, a significant difference between English and French, and between English and English CS, but no difference between English CS and French.[7]

Thus, to answer the question asked previously, bilinguals do not start switching one or two words before the guest word and do not switch back to the base language during the words that follow. The fact that the /k/ of "copie" in the English CS sentences is still French means that the phonetic shift to the guest language probably takes place at, or very near, the onset of the guest word, and the fact that the /k/ of "constamment" in the same English CS sentences is already in French shows that the switch back to the base language takes place extremely quickly. It would appear from these results that bilinguals are both very flexible and extremely precise when going in and out of a code-switch.

8.1.3 General discussion

The results obtained in the two experiments provide strong evidence that the phonetics of the base language has no impact on the production of code-switches (in the situation studied here, at least). When bilingual speakers insert a word or phrase from the guest language into the base language, the switch usually involves a total change, not only at the lexical but also at the phonetic level. Cross-language phonetic slips may occur occasionally in spontaneous speech, especially at code-switch onset, but these are probably no more frequent than intralanguage phonetic slips. The articulatory system appears to be as flexible between languages as it is within a language.

When one considers the base-language effect in perception, the present result is a happy one for bilingual communication. Given that bilingual listeners favor the base language at the onset of code-switches, it is fortunate that the phonetic information at that point is

---

[7] Individual analyses of variance for each participant and each consonant produce similar results. A total of 14 differences (out of 15) between English and French are significant; 12 differences between English and English CS are also significant; however, 12 differences between French and English CS are not significant.

unambiguous. If the contrary were the case, the listener would be doubly handicapped—by a perceptual preference for the base language and by an ambiguous signal. A clearly marked code-switch onset undoubtedly counterbalances, at least to some extent, the perceptual base-language effect and hence reduces the duration of the ambiguity. Evidence for this was obtained in a study (Grosjean 1988) that examined the recognition of code-switches and borrowings. It was found that the language in which a guest word was pronounced affected the nature of the candidates proposed; there were more candidates from the guest language when the word was said as a code-switch (pronounced in the guest language) than as a borrowing (pronounced in the base language).

A possible explanation for our findings, in terms of a model inspired in large part by de Bot (1992), Levelt (1989), and Myers-Scotton (1993), is the following. When a bilingual is speaking only one language, the surface structure of the monolingual utterance is elaborated with lemmas (the semantic and syntactic components of words that are accessed in the mental lexicon) as well as with specific grammatical rules. Once this has been done, phonological encoding can take place. This process entails retrieving from the lexicon the phonological forms of the lemmas previously chosen (i.e. the lexemes) and building a phonetic plan, that is, an internal representation of how the utterance should be articulated. Several levels of processing are involved in generating a plan: a morphological and metrical level, which retrieves a word's morphemes and metrical structure; a segmental level, which specifies the word's syllables and segments; and a phonetic level, which retrieves the stored plans of the syllables and segments in terms of sequences of phones.

When the bilingual is mixing languages, that is, speaking a base language and bringing in, from time to time, elements of the guest language, the phonological forms of the guest words are accessed in the guest lexicon (or in the guest-language part of the general lexicon, depending on one's view as to the bilingual's lexicons). The guest forms are then inserted into the utterance alongside base-language forms that are, by definition, more numerous. If there are no linguistic or psycholinguistic reasons to integrate the guest forms morphologically or phonologically into the base language and hence make them into borrowings (Myers-Scotton 1993; Poplack et al. 1988), then each form's phonetic plan remains a string of guest-language phones (e.g. English word initial /t/, English word medial /a/, and English word final /m/ for the English code-switch "Tom"). These are transformed into articulatory commands, and production can proceed normally.

According to this view, pronouncing a code-switch is no different from pronouncing another word within the same base language (a position that Paradis 1977, 1986 has maintained for a long time). Of course, when a code-switch is longer and makes up its own syntactic constituent, the planning that occurs during grammatical and phonological encoding will result in differences not only at the segmental level (as in our study) but also at the prosodic level (Grosjean and Soares 1986, and next section). Future studies are needed to examine these kinds of code-switches both in reading and in more spontaneous speech as produced by different types of bilinguals.

8.2 The prosody of code-switching

We have just seen that the base language has no impact on the phonetics of code-switches, at least in the kinds of situations we examined. When bilinguals insert a word or a phrase from the guest language into the base language, the change is total. The question becomes whether this is also true at the level of prosody. Grosjean and Soares (1986) undertook a short pilot study involving a French-English bilingual. By chance, French and English have very different prosodies and this allowed us to have a glimpse at the impact of prosody on guest elements. Delattre (1965, 1966), among others, studied the many differences that exist between English and French. Using extracts of interviews of Margaret Mead for American English and Simone de Beauvoir for French, he noted the following: (a) the prevalence of falling intonation in English and of rising intonation in French; (b) the falling or fall–rise patterns at the end of English phrases and sentences, and the rising continuation contours in French; and (c) the reversed S shape of the final sentence fall in English and the convex shape of the fall in French (a fall which starts on the first syllable of the final phrase). With such vastly differing prosodic patterns, to which we should add the basically stress timed characteristics of English and the primarily syllable timed aspects of French, it is natural that we should ask ourselves how prosody is modified when a bilingual code-switches.

The pilot data that we obtained by means of a VisiPitch recorder from one French-English bilingual with a native-like accent in each language are shown in Figures 8.3 to 8.5. In Figure 8.3, we present the fundamental frequency (Fo) contour of a sentence read by the

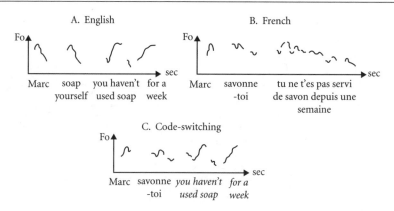

FIGURE 8.3 The fundamental frequency (Fo) contours of the English (A), French (B), and code-switched (C) versions of a sentence read by a French-English bilingual. Here the code-switched element is an independent clause

bilingual: in its English version ("Marc; soap yourself; you haven't used soap for a week"); French version ("Marc; savonne-toi; tu ne t'es pas servi de savon depuis une semaine"); and code-switched version ("Marc; savonne-toi; *you haven't used soap for a week*"). The English version (top left) shows the characteristic high fall contours of the commands ("Marc" and "soap yourself") and the final rise at the end of the surprise comment ("you haven't used soap for a week"). The French version (top right) is quite different. The commands are less marked, and the comment has a long falling contour. As for the code-switched version (bottom representation), the commands in French respect the monolingual French contours, whereas the comment in English is identical to that in the English monolingual version. Thus, it would appear that when a code-switch occurs at an independent clause break, the prosody changes along with the segmental aspects. Is this also the case when a code-switched clause is coordinated with the preceding clause? Figure 8.4 shows the sentence "Go get Marc and bribe him with a hot chocolate with cream on top", in its different versions. The top left and top right contours show the characteristic intonation patterns of English and French respectively: the falling pattern on each clause or phrase in English; the rising pattern in French when there is a continuation, and the final fall on the last phrase. In the code-switched version, the interesting clause is "*and bribe him*" because it is surrounded by French and is not in a sentence final position. A comparison of this code-switch with the two monolingual versions ("and bribe him" in the English version and "et tente le" in the French

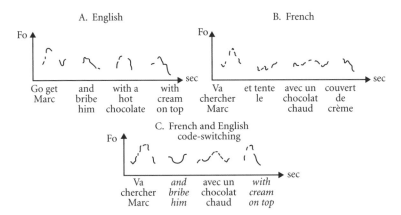

FIGURE 8.4 The fundamental frequency (Fo) contours of the English (A), French (B), and code-switched (C) versions of a sentence read by a French-English bilingual. Here the code-switched elements are a conjoined clause and a phrase

version) shows that the prosody of the code-switch does not take on the English contour—as one might have expected—but remains characteristically French (note in particular the rise on "*him*"). So, unlike what happens in Figure 8.3, here the base language's prosodic pattern imposes itself. In sum, the prosody of a code-switch does not always follow the segmental changes that occur in a switch. This is confirmed in Figure 8.5 where we present the prosodic contour of a one-word code-switch (the word "soap"). Once again, the English monolingual version ("We must soap Marc") and the French monolingual version ("Il faut savonner Marc") are quite characteristic: a falling contour on "soap" in English and a rising contour on "savonner" in French. As for the code-switch *soap* in "Il faut *soap* Marc", we note that it has a rising French contour instead of an English falling contour. This shows once again that the prosody of the base language can impose itself in certain situations. The bottom pattern shows that by integrating "soap" both morphologically and phonetically into the sentence (thus making it the borrowing SOAPER) the base-language pattern is confirmed—its contour is practically identical to "savonner" in the French version.

These pilot data need to be confirmed, but they are extremely intriguing in that they indicate that, unlike what is found at the segmental level, the prosody of code-switches does not always follow the pattern of the guest language. We saw in Section 8.1 that, when bilinguals insert a word or a phrase from the guest language into the base language, the segmental change appears to be total. But this is not always the case for prosody. If the code-switch is short and is a minor

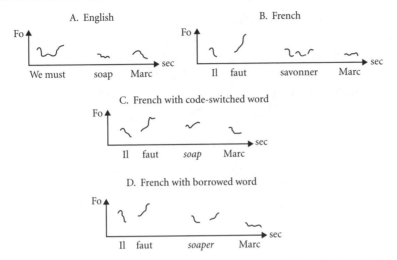

FIGURE 8.5 The fundamental frequency (Fo) contours of the English (A), French (B), and code-switched (C) versions of a sentence where the code-switched element is a word. The French version is also represented with a speech borrowing in contour D

syntactic unit, then it might well be integrated into the base language (see Figures 8.4 and 8.5). If, on the contrary, it is longer and is a more important syntactic unit, then it will carry over the prosodic pattern from the guest language (see Figure 8.3). More work is needed on the prosody of code-switching as a function of the syntactic status of the switch (sentence, clause, phrase, word), its language environment (which language precedes and follows it), and the length of the switch. Based on the pilot data we have obtained, we expect that all of these factors will affect the prosody of code-switching.

Conclusion

The results presented in Sections 8.1 and 8.2 raise some interesting issues. The first concerns the perception of code-switches and, more specifically, what it is that the listener receives from the speaker. We commented in Section 8.1 that it is rather fortunate that the phonetic information at the code-switch onset is unambiguous given that bilingual listeners favor the base language (see Chapter 6). If the information were ambiguous, the listener would be doubly handicapped—by a perceptual preference for the base language and by an ambiguous signal. We stated that a clearly marked code-switch onset undoubtedly counterbalances, at least to some extent, the perceptual base-language effect and hence reduces the duration of the ambiguity. This said, and as we have just seen in Section 8.2, when the speaker has no accent in either language and the code-switch is clearly marked phonetically as belonging to the guest language, the listener may *still* receive ambiguous information but this time from the prosody. The sounds may be clearly marked as belonging to the guest language but the prosody, as we saw, sometimes reflects the base language. Thus, the segmental information heard by the listener may point one way, that is to the guest language, but the suprasegmental information may point the other way, that is towards the base language. This contradiction in the signal, added to the basic base-language effect, may delay the processing of code-switches. To compound things, we should remember that many bilinguals have an accent in their second language (and in their other languages, if they are multilingual). Thus, when they bring guest words or phrases from their second language into their first language, for example, they are code-switching "with an accent", and this can make the task of the listener even more difficult.

A second issue pertains to the very definition of a code-switch. So far, researchers have talked of a complete shift to the other language for a word, a phrase, a sentence. This seems to be true at the segmental level (at least for someone with no accent in either language) but we saw that this may not always be true at the prosodic level. One definitional solution could be to talk of "a complete *segmental* shift to the other language" so as to take into account the lack of a prosodic shift in certain situations.

This said, more research on the phonetics and prosody of code-switching is needed. Phoneticians who wish to measure the segmental and the suprasegmental changes that take place when code-switching occurs will have to compare adequately the base-language form and the code-switched form. The solution we adopted, that is using bilinguals who had little or no "foreign" accent in either of their languages, is a first step but we should now move on to study those bilinguals (the majority?) who do have an accent in at least one of their languages. This is where the challenge lies.

PART IV
Spoken Word Recognition in Bilinguals

Introduction

This fourth part deals with research on spoken word recognition in bilinguals. Figure IV.A presents a number of factors that play a role when bilinguals are processing speech which contains no guest words (i.e. only base-language words; top part of the figure) and when it contains guest words (bottom part of the figure). The horizontal lines in the figure represent continuous speech, the empty rectangle (top part) is a base language word in the speech stream, and the black rectangle (bottom part) is a guest word. As concerns factors in speech devoid of guest words, we find a number of well-known word properties that affect their recognition: their frequency of use, their uniqueness point, their neighborhood size and frequency (although the evidence is still being debated here), their prosodic saliency, etc. We also know that when words are presented in context, as is illustrated in the figure, these lexical properties interact with various sources of knowledge (morphology, syntax, semantics, pragmatics) to speed up or slow down the recognition process. In this area of research—the study of factors that are common to both monolinguals and bilinguals—a paper with Delphine Guillelmon that examined the role of gender marking in the recognition of French nouns is presented in Chapter 9. Auditory

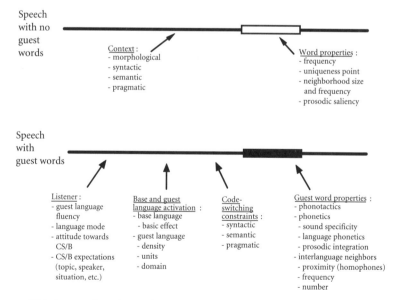

FIGURE IV.A Factors that play a role when bilinguals are processing speech which contains no guest words (top part of figure) and which contains guest words (bottom part of figure). The horizontal lines represent continuous speech, the empty rectangle is a base language word, and the black rectangle is a guest word

naming was used to examine how early English-French bilinguals (who make no gender errors in production) and late English-French bilinguals (who make such errors) react to gender marking when processing French. The question asked was whether perception would parallel production, that is, whether early bilinguals are sensitive to gender marking in perception whereas late bilinguals are less sensitive to it. Alternatively, the perception and production of gender marking might behave differently in the sense that, irrespective of what happens in production, both types of bilinguals are sensitive to gender to the same extent in perception. In fact, a difference was found between the two groups. This opens up interesting questions about the "critical period" for particular processing phenomena such as the use of gender marking in word recognition.

As concerns recognition factors in speech that contains guest words, four main categories are presented in the bottom part of Figure IV.A: factors that pertain to the listener (guest-language fluency, language mode, attitude towards code-switching and borrowing, and expectations related to these behaviors), factors that concern the level of activation of the base and the guest language (the base-language effect studied in Part III as well as certain aspects of the guest language, for example, the density of guest words), factors that involve various code-switching constraints (syntactic, semantic, and pragmatic), and, finally, factors that concern the properties of the guest word being heard (its phonotactics; its phonetics such as sound specificity, language phonetics, and prosodic integration; and the presence or absence of interlanguage neighbors such as homophones, their frequency, their number, etc.). A 1988 gating study, reproduced in Chapter 10, examined a number of guest word properties either by manipulating them as independent variables or by studying them in subanalyses. The exploration revolved around the role of three variables: phonotactics, interlanguage neighbor proximity, and language phonetics. As concerns phonotactics, the question asked was whether guest words that are marked phonotactically as belonging to the guest-language lexicon would be recognized sooner and with more ease than words not marked in this way. Concerning interlanguage neighbor proximity, would guest words that have near homophones in the base language be recognized with more difficulty than other guest-language words? Finally, as concerns language phonetics, the following question was examined: Would guest words which retain a phonetic cue as to which lexicon they belong to (by being pronounced clearly in the guest language) be easier to process than words which are integrated phonetically into the base language (that is, by being pronounced in the phonetics of the base language)? In other words, would code-switched words, which normally retain a phonetic cue as to the lexicon they are a part of, be accessed more easily than borrowings, which are usually integrated into the base language and hence have lost some of their cues pertaining to their lexicon of origin? In addition to showing the impact of phonotactics, the proximity of interlanguage neighbors, and language phonetics on guest word recognition, the study examined two other variables—sound specificity and interlanguage neighbor frequency.

At the end the study, an interactive activation model of word recognition in bilinguals is proposed; it is strongly inspired by TRACE and is governed by two basic assumptions. First, it is assumed that bilinguals have two language networks (features, phonemes, words, etc.) which are both independent and interconnected. They are independent in the sense that they allow a bilingual to speak just one language, but they are also interconnected in that the monolingual speech of bilinguals often shows the active interference of the other language, and in that bilinguals can code-switch and borrow quite readily when they speak to other bilinguals. The second assumption is that in the monolingual language mode, one language network is strongly activated while the other is activated very weakly (the resting activation level of the units of this other network is therefore very low). However, in the bilingual language mode, both language networks are activated but one more than the other (that of the base language). A number of activation characteristics are presented which can account for some of the effects found when bilinguals are in a bilingual language mode.

This "verbal" model inspired to a large extent the Léwy and Grosjean computational model of bilingual lexical access which is now known as BIMOLA. In Chapter 11, a short unpublished account of it written by Nicolas Léwy and myself is presented. After having discussed how such a model needs to take into account the bilingual's language modes, a general overview of the model is presented along with a number of its characteristics. Among these are shared phonetic features for the two languages (in this case, English and French) but a language independent organization at the higher levels (phonemes and words). The model is also characterized by various excitation links within and between levels and by one type of inhibition link. The chapter ends with an assessment of the model as it stood when the document was written; it is shown that it can account for a number of effects found in the literature on bilingual spoken word recognition.

9

The Gender Marking Effect in Bilinguals*

There is increasing evidence that, in languages that have gender agreement, a congruent gender marking usually speeds up the processing of the following noun relative to an incongruent marking (or no marking). This effect is now well established in monolinguals, but little is known about how bilinguals react to gender agreement. In this paper, we ask whether bilinguals show the same effect and whether it depends on when they acquired and started using the gender marking language on a regular basis.

In what is fast becoming a classic, Corbett (1991) states that gender is the most puzzling of the grammatical categories that interests non-linguists as well as linguists, and that it becomes more fascinating the more it is investigated. Gender can be defined as follows: "A subclass within a grammatical class (as noun, pronoun, adjective, or verb) of a language that is partly arbitrary but also partly based on distinguishable characteristics (as shape, social rank, manner of existence, or sex) and that determines agreement with and selection of other words or grammatical forms." (*Webster's Ninth New Collegiate Dictionary* 1991). Depending on the language, words (nouns usually) carry any number of genders; from two in such languages as Italian, Spanish, and French, all the way to six for Swahili. Of particular interest here is that other word classes in a language which has gender, such as adjectives, verbs, articles, pronouns, and so on, do not have a gender per se but can reflect, in their inflectional morphology, the gender of the words that do. Thus, depending on the language, a gender agreement marking can appear before or after a noun on a determiner, adjective, pronoun, and

* This chapter first appeared as an article: Guillelmon, D. and Grosjean, F. (2001). "The gender marking effect in spoken word recognition: The case of bilinguals", *Memory and Cognition* 29: 503–11. The author wishes to thank the Psychonomic Society and Delphine Guillelmon for permission to reprint it here.

so on. In the case of French, for example, "voiture" is feminine, and in the phrase "leur petite voiture" (their small car), the adjective (petite) agrees with the noun and carries a feminine ending. In the phrase, "*le* garçon", the definite article is masculine since the noun is of that gender.

It is now well established that a congruent gender marking will speed up the processing of the following noun. This has been shown in reading, for example, by Gurjanov *et al.* (1985) in Serbo-Croatian and by Colé and Segui (1994) in French. In speech, Grosjean *et al.* (1994), working with French, showed with a gating task that participants needed less of a noun to identify it when it was preceded by a gender-congruent article (they were also more confident about the word they proposed), and, with a lexical decision task, they showed that the participants were faster at deciding that the noun was a word. Recently, Jakubowicz and Faussart (1998), also working on spoken French and using a lexical decision task, replicated a strong gender effect.

Researchers have also used a neutral or baseline condition in order to determine whether the effect is due to congruency (facilitation), incongruency (inhibition), or both. Schmidt (1986), for example, found a significant incongruency effect in German, but not a congruency effect (although there was a trend in the right direction). In the spoken modality, Bates *et al.* (1996), working with Italian, found both an incongruency (inhibition) effect and a congruency (facilitation) effect with an auditory naming task (also called cued-shadowing; Bates and Liu 1997), but only an incongruency effect with a gender-monitoring task. They concluded that the inhibitory component of gender priming is more robust than the facilitatory component.

In regard to the locus of the gender-marking effect, Grosjean *et al.* (1994) mentioned two possibilities. On the one hand, the process could be internal to the lexicon in that when a word carrying a gender marking is identified, it activates all the nouns in the lexicon that share the same gender. A variant of this first possibility is that it is the gender feature of the word that activates all the nouns with that same feature. Whatever the variant, this first explanation could account for faster processing in the congruent condition (i.e. when the preceding word and the noun share the same gender) and slower processing in the incongruent condition, whatever the task used. An alternative explanation involves both the lexical and syntactic processing modules.[1] The

[1] It should be recalled that the lexical processing module is used to recognize words and to ensure that all the information needed for further processing is extracted from the mental lexicon, whereas the syntactic processing module identifies and structures the constituents.

lexical module undertakes the recognition of the words in question (e.g. an article and a noun), and the syntactic module checks that gender agreement is respected (for a similar proposal, see, among others, Gollan and Frost 2001; Van Berkum 1996). Along this line, Jakubowicz and Faussart (1998) state that the gender-marking word "sets" the feature value for the entire phrase, and the congruency and incongruency effects are the result of an automatic post-access check of the grammatical agreement between the words that have a gender marking. This checking mechanism will speed up the participant's task when there is congruency and slow it down when there is incongruency. Recently, in a paper dealing with another agreement phenomenon (number), Pearlmutter *et al.* (1999) further elaborated on this grammatical explanation by stating that there might be two processing possibilities: a compute-on-the-fly system where the agreement features are processed by the comprehension system as they are encountered and a backtrack mechanism where agreement is checked after the initial parsing, and only when possible (i.e. when the word in question is overtly marked for the agreement feature). Grosjean *et al.* (1994) stated that it might well turn out that the gender-marking effect is both a lexical effect *and* a syntactic effect, and they provided evidence for this. Bates *et al.* (1995) also stated that gender congruency effects may well involve a combination of lexical (they call it "prelexical") and syntactic ("postlexical") processing.

However one may explain the gender-marking effect in the end, it should be noted that it has been studied primarily with monolinguals. It is therefore normal to ask whether bilinguals will show the same effect and whether it depends on when they acquired and started using the gender-marking language in question on a regular basis. At first sight, it seems natural to predict that bilinguals should show the effect. After all, gender marking can be useful for a number of things irrespective of whether the listener is monolingual or bilingual. First, it may preactivate a class of nouns and/or be used in a post-access agreement check (as discussed above). Second, it can help regroup words into phrases (Van Berkum 1996). And third, at the level of discourse processing, gender marking can help to keep track of referents and so help disambiguate anaphoric or deictic referential constructions (Cacciari *et al.* 1997; Corbett 1991). This said, it might also be the case that the presence of a gender marking effect in bilinguals may depend on how old they were when they started acquiring and using the language(s). Second-language acquisition research seems to show that early bilinguals (i.e. those who acquired and used their gender-marking language regularly before adolescence) make no, or very few, gender-production errors, whereas late bilinguals (i.e. those who acquired their other language during adolescence or as adults) make a substantial number of gender errors (see e.g. Carroll 1989; Rogers 1987). This is reflected anecdotally in an interview given by Sir Winston Churchill on French radio in 1946. He was answering questions in fluent French accompanied by a heavy English accent. At one point he stated with humor: "Despite working so hard and coming so far with the French to help them win their freedom, I have never mastered the gender of French nouns!"

The question that one can ask is whether perception will parallel production—that is, whether early bilinguals who make no gender errors are sensitive to gender marking when processing language, whereas late bilinguals are less sensitive to it. Alternatively, the perception and production of gender marking might behave differently in the sense that, irrespective of what happens in production, both types of bilinguals are sensitive to it to the same extent in perception. This paper will report two experiments. In the first experiment, we will show how early English-French bilinguals react to gender marking when processing French, and in the second experiment we will examine how late bilinguals do so. In both cases, the results of the bilinguals will be compared to those of French monolinguals.

9.1 Experiment 1: Early bilinguals

The aim of this study was twofold. First, we wished to replicate with French monolinguals the results of the Bates *et al.* (1996) study, which showed both a congruency (facilitation) effect and an incongruency (inhibition) effect with auditory naming. Although the language used here is different (they used Italian), the gender system is highly similar in the two languages and there is no a priori reason to believe that the two effects cannot be replicated. Since a pilot study showed that the strength of the congruency effect depends, in part at least, on the grouping of the experimental conditions, we opted for two groupings: congruent and neutral, and incongruent and neutral. Participants heard short noun phrases made up of a determiner, an adjective, and a noun, and they were asked to repeat the noun.[2] Depending on the

---

[2] The reasons that led us to choose naming over lexical decision are linked to the bilinguals. First, some bilinguals (especially late bilinguals) do not always feel secure deciding

part of the study, the gender marking on the determiner was either congruent or neutral, or incongruent or neutral, with respect to the noun. Our second aim was to assess whether early bilinguals were sensitive to gender marking. They had acquired English and French in their early childhood and so it was expected that their behavior would be similar to that of their monolingual counterparts.

9.1.1 Method

Participants

Two groups of participants were used in this study. The first was made up of thirty-two native monolingual French-speaking students of the University of Neuchâtel (Switzerland), with no reported speech or hearing defects, who served individually in the experiment. They were assigned at random to one of two experimental subgroups of sixteen. The second group was made up of an equal number of early English-French bilingual students, with no reported speech or hearing defects, who also served individually in the experiment. To be included in this "early bilingual" group, a participant had to report having started using both languages on a regular basis in childhood (the maximum limit for this "onset of bilingualism" was 13 years old). Most participants were well under this limit as, on average, they started using their two languages in everyday life as early as 5;4 years. A questionnaire was filled out by the bilingual participants, and relevant biographical and language proficiency data are summarized in Table 9.1 (left columns). We can observe that the bilinguals were relatively young (24;4 years on average) and that they started speaking English about 2 years before they did French (1;11 and 4;0 years, respectively). There was a slight gap in time between starting to speak the second language (4;0 years) and using the two languages on a regular basis (i.e. age of onset of bilingualism: 5;4 years). This probably reflects the difference between episodic use and regular use of the second language. In regard to reported language proficiency obtained with a self-rating scale (1 = Very poor; 7 = Excellent), the participants reported very high levels of spoken English

---

whether an item is a word or a nonword in their second language, and this probably has an impact on their processing. Second, reaction times to nonwords are longer in bilinguals than in monolinguals as shown by Soares and Grosjean (1984). They explained this finding by suggesting that bilinguals search both lexicons when confronted with a nonword. We wanted the other language (English) to be as inactive as possible during the experiment (at least not above a residual activation level that is probably always there; Grosjean 2001) and hence we opted not to use lexical decision in this study.

TABLE 9.1 Biographical and Language Proficiency Means and Standard Deviations for the Two Groups of English-French Bilinguals (n = 32 in each group)

Biographical and language proficiency categories	Early bilinguals		Late bilinguals	
	M	SD	M	SD
Age	24;4	6;6	48;5	10;6
Age started speaking English	1;11	1;4	1;0	0;0
Age started speaking French	4;0	3;0	15;11	7;11
Age of onset of bilingualism	5;4	3;5	24;8	6;0
English oral comprehension[a]	6.4	0.6	6.8	0.4
French oral comprehension[a]	6.7	0.5	6.0	0.8
English oral production[a]	5.8	0.8	6.7	0.5
French oral production[a]	6.3	0.7	5.4	1.0

Note [a] Based on a self-rating scale (1 = Very poor; 7 = Excellent).

and spoken French comprehension (6.4 and 6.7 respectively). Their reported levels of spoken language production were practically as high (5.8 and 6.3 respectively). The bilinguals showed a slight dominance in French but it is quite small, especially in spoken comprehension, the skill that interests us here (difference of 0.3 between the two languages). The bilingual participants were also assigned at random to one of two experimental subgroups of sixteen.

Materials

Thirty-six French nouns—eighteen masculine and eighteen feminine—were chosen for the study (see the Appendix for a complete list). All of them started with a stop consonant. Half the words in each set were one syllable long and the other half two syllables long. Care was taken to make sure that the two sets of nouns had the same mean frequency of occurrence: 2,607 for the masculine words and 2,502 for the feminine words, based on the BRULEX data base (Content et al. 1990). Their uniqueness points (UPs) were also similar: eleven masculine words and twelve feminine words had a UP after the end of the word whereas seven masculine words and six feminine words had it before the end (based on Le Robert Oral-Ecrit 1989). All UPs were the same whether the words were preceded by a correct, an incorrect, or a neutral gender marking. (It should be noted that Grosjean et al. 1994, had a similar set of one- and two-syllable words, half masculine and half feminine; they showed that the gender marking effect is very robust and is not affected by differences in the length and in the gender of the words used.)

The stimuli were prepared in three stages. In the first stage, three determiners were chosen: "le" (masculine "the"), "la" (feminine "the"), and "leur" (neutral "their"). The three were read twenty times in a short context: "le coq" (the rooster), "la coque" (the hull), and "leur coq/coque" (their rooster/hull). (The pronunciation of "coq" and "coque" is identical in French despite the difference in orthography.) The recording took place in a soundproof studio, and a native speaker of French read the phrases at normal rate. The recording was then digitized on a Macintosh II at a sampling rate of 22 kHz with the Sound Designer II package. The five best exemplars of each determiner, "le", "la", and "leur", based on an evaluation by five judges, were then spliced out. These were measured and a final exemplar of each was chosen so that its duration was similar to that of the other two (173 ms for "le", 174 ms for "la", and 173 ms for "leur"). In the second stage, each of the thirty-six nouns were read by the same speaker in three contexts: "le joli——" (the nice——), "la jolie——", and "leur joli——". (It should be noted that the acoustic characteristics of "joli(e)" are not changed when preceded by a masculine, feminine, or neutral determiner.) Following this, one-third of the readings in each context was retained such that each noun appeared once. For example, if the reading "la jolie glace" (the nice mirror) was retained, the other two readings ("*le joli glace" and "leur jolie glace") were discarded. Thus, a third of the adjective + noun pairs retained came from the congruent reading context, a third from the incongruent context, and the final third from the neutral context. The determiners from each reading were then spliced out so as to leave thirty-six "joli(e) + noun" segments, one for each of the thirty-six nouns. Finally, in the last stage, each experimental determiner obtained in Stage 1 ("le", "la", "leur") was added to each "joli(e) + noun" segment to give three experimental exemplars: "le" + "joli + noun" (where the gender marking is correct if the noun is masculine and incorrect if it is feminine), "la" + "jolie + noun" (where the gender marking is correct if the noun is feminine and incorrect if it is masculine), and "leur" + "joli(e) + noun" (where the gender marking is neutral since "leur" carries no gender information). Thus, for example, the three experimental exemplars for "bateau" (boat) were "le joli bateau" (here the gender marking is correct), "*la joli(e) bateau" (the gender marking is incorrect) and "leur joli bateau" (the gender marking is neutral). A short (1,000-Hz) tone was placed at the onset of the noun on the right channel for timing purposes, and the interstimulus interval (ISI) was set at 3.5 seconds.

Two groups of experimental stimuli were prepared: one group contained the correct and neutral stimuli (for the correct/neutral part of the study), and the other group contained the incorrect and neutral stimuli (for the incorrect/neutral part). Two sets of stimuli were then prepared for each part, each set containing eighteen correct stimuli (or incorrect stimuli, depending on the part) and eighteen neutral stimuli. A particular noun appeared only once in each set, preceded by the correct (or incorrect) gender marking or preceded by the neutral gender marking. The order of presentation of the stimuli in each set (correct or incorrect, and neutral stimuli) was the same and was quasi random.

Procedure

The experiment was run with PsyScope (Cohen *et al.* 1993) and participants were tested individually in a quiet environment. Each participant, monolingual or bilingual, was tested on only one part—either the correct/neutral part or the incorrect/neutral part—and on only one set of stimuli within each part. Participants were asked to listen to the phrases presented to them over headphones and to repeat the word after "joli(e)" as quickly as possible. Reaction times were recorded by means of a Hewlett-Packard universal counter (HP 5,315) which was started by the tone placed on the right channel (at the onset of each noun) and stopped by the participant's vocal response.[3] A short practice session took place before the experimental session and a short break occurred halfway through the experiment. French was used throughout the testing session, which was conducted by a native speaker of French (DG).

9.1.2 Results and discussion

The following data analysis procedure was applied to the reaction times obtained. First, times above a particular cutoff point (1,000 ms) were removed. Then, for each participant, an overall mean and SD was calculated, and the values above or below two SD were replaced with values that corresponded to the mean plus two SD, or to the mean minus two SD, respectively. The values that were removed because they were greater than 1,000 ms were then replaced with the new mean, as were the missing values. For the monolinguals, in the correct/neutral part, there were no times greater than 1,000 ms, 4.17 percent of the values

---

[3] When this experiment was done, some doubt existed as to the reliability of the voice-operated relay in the PsyScope button box. We therefore decided to use an external counter that we knew from past studies to be extremely reliable.

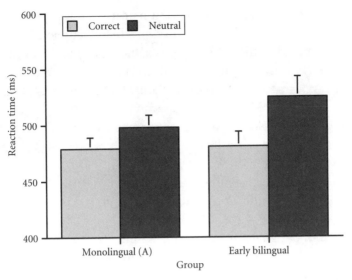

FIGURE 9.1 Mean naming times (in milliseconds) as a function of group (Monolingual (A) and Early bilingual) and gender marking (correct and neutral)

Note: Error bars represent +1 SEM.

were above or below two SD and 3.30 percent of the values were missing. In the incorrect/neutral part, 0.17 percent of the times were greater than 1,000 ms (and hence replaced by the new mean), 2.95 percent of the values were above or below two SD and 2.78 percent of the values were missing. For the early bilinguals, in the correct/neutral part, there were no times greater than 1,000 ms, 3.99 percent of the values were above or below two SD, and 2.08 percent of the values were missing. In the incorrect/neutral part, there were no times greater than 1,000 ms, 5.03 percent of the values were above or below two SD and 1.74 percent of the values were missing. Two-way analyses of variance (ANOVAs), over participants and over items, were conducted for each part: correct and neutral, and incorrect and neutral. For all of these analyses, alpha was set at 0.05.

Figure 9.1 presents the results of the correct/neutral part of the study. Mean naming times (in milliseconds) are plotted as a function of group—the monolingual group (labeled "Monolingual (A)") and the early bilingual group—and gender marking—correct and neutral. Henceforth, the neutral condition will always appear as a black bar. As can be seen, a congruency effect was present for both the monolinguals and the early bilinguals, but it was larger for the latter. When a noun was preceded by a determiner that marks the gender, monolingual participants needed 479 ms on average to name a noun preceded by a correct gender marking (e.g. "le joli bateau") and 498 ms to name it preceded by a neutral gender marking (e.g. "leur joli bateau"), a 19-ms difference. For the early bilinguals, the corresponding times were 481 ms and 525 ms, a 44-ms difference. The larger difference for the bilinguals appears to be due to their slightly longer mean reaction times in the neutral condition: 525 ms as compared with 498 ms for the monolinguals. Two-way ANOVAs confirmed these results. There was a strong congruency effect that was significant by participants and by items ($F_1(1, 30) = 60.16$, MSe = 270.76; $F_2(1, 35) = 48.54$, MSe = 749.56), a marginal group effect significant by items only ($F_2(1, 35) = 21.18$, MSe = 364.94), and a significant interaction ($F_1(1, 30) = 9.19$, MSe = 270.76; $F_2(1, 35) = 15.83$, MSe = 354.56). A Tukey HSD post hoc test shows that both the monolinguals' 19-ms and the bilinguals' 44-ms congruency differences (neutral/correct) were significant at the .01 level. Thus we have replicated a congruency effect with monolinguals using naming, and we have shown that early bilinguals, like their monolingual counterparts, are sensitive to congruent gender marking. Will monolinguals also show an incongruency effect, and will early bilinguals be sensitive to incongruent marking? The answer can be observed in Figure 9.2.

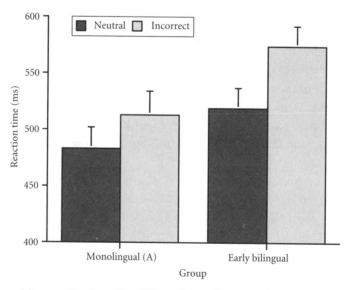

FIGURE 9.2 Mean naming times (in milliseconds) as a function of group (Monolingual (A) and Early bilingual) and gender marking (neutral and incorrect)

Note: Error bars represent +1 SEM.

Figure 9.2 presents the results of the incorrect/neutral part of the study. Mean naming times (in milliseconds) are plotted as a function of group (monolingual and early bilingual) and gender marking (neutral and incorrect). As can be seen, the incongruency effect was large for both groups: monolinguals took on average 483 ms to name items preceded by a neutral gender marking, but 513 ms when they were preceded by an incongruent gender marking, a difference of 30 ms. The corresponding values for the early bilinguals were 519 and 574 ms, a difference of 55 ms. This larger difference is in part due to the bilinguals' longer mean reaction times in the incongruent condition. The two ANOVAs showed that there was a strong incongruency effect significant by participants and by items ($F_1(1, 30) = 102.59$, MSe $= 280.06$; $F_2(1, 35) = 202.45$, MSe $= 320.15$), a marginal group effect by items only ($F_2(1, 35) = 240.22$, MSe $= 353.12$), and a significant interaction ($F_1(1, 30) = 10.03$, MSe $= 280.06$; $F_2(1, 35) = 20.46$, MSe $= 305.76$). A Tukey HSD post hoc test shows that both the monolinguals' 30-ms and the bilinguals' 55-ms incongruency differences (incorrect/neutral) were significant at the .01 level.

We have therefore been able to replicate both a congruency (or facilitation) effect and an incongruency (or inhibition) effect with monolinguals in French by means of a naming task. To do this we divided up the three conditions (correct, neutral, and incorrect) into two groups of two (correct and neutral, incorrect and neutral). In addition, we have shown that bilinguals who acquired and started using a gender-agreement language, along with another language, at age 5;4 on average, demonstrated strong congruency and incongruency effects. They have become sensitive to gender early in life and they appear to use gender marking in perception the way monolinguals do. The only apparent difference with monolinguals is that they appear to be even more sensitive to gender congruency and incongruency, as can be seen by the larger differences between the neutral and the other two conditions. It is unclear why this occurred and only future studies will be able to assess its importance.

The crucial question now becomes: Will late bilinguals show the same effects as early bilinguals? If gender marking is indeed important during language processing, then they should become sensitive to it. However, if there is a "critical period" for taking into account gender marking (in perception at least), and if late bilinguals acquired, and started using on a regular basis, their gender-marking language after this period, then they should show little if any effect.

9.2 Experiment 2: Late bilinguals

In this experiment, we examined the behavior of late English-French bilinguals and we compared it with that of French monolinguals. Since the late bilinguals were in their late 40s on average, we made sure that the monolinguals were of a comparable age.

9.2.1 Method

Participants

Two groups of participants were used in this study. The first was made up of thirty-two French monolinguals (randomly assigned to two groups of sixteen) who were matched on age with the late bilinguals (46;6 and 48;5 years respectively). The monolinguals reported no speech or hearing defects, and they served individually in the experiment. The second group of participants was made up of thirty-two late English-French bilinguals (assigned randomly to one of two groups of sixteen) who reported no speech or hearing defects and who also served individually in the study. Their first language was English and they had started learning French in school. They became regular users of both languages only when they moved to a French-speaking country as adults (the mean age of onset of their bilingualism was 24;8). Table 9.1 (right columns) presents the group's biographical and language proficiency data. We note that the late bilinguals reported starting to speak English at age 1;0, on average, and French at age 15;11 (the early bilinguals had means of 1;11 and 4;0, respectively). The large gap between starting to speak French and the onset of bilingualism (some 9 years later) is due to the fact that at first French was simply a language being learned at school and not a language of everyday interaction. It started being so only when they moved to a French-speaking country. In regard to reported language proficiency, the late bilinguals reported near-perfect English oral comprehension (mean of 6.8) and a slightly lower level of French comprehension (6.0). Their reported level of oral language production favors English (6.7) over French (5.4). It is clear that the late bilinguals were dominant in English, but what is important for our purpose is that they rated their oral comprehension in French as being very good (6.0 on a 7-point scale). This is not surprising since they had been active bilinguals for up to 24 years on average (their mean age was 48;5 years).

Materials and procedure

Exactly the same materials and procedure were used as in the first experiment. Once again, French was used throughout the testing session, which was conducted by a native speaker of French (DG).

9.2.2 Results and discussion

The data obtained from the two groups (late bilinguals and monolingual controls) were analyzed in the same way as the data in the first study. For the late bilinguals, in the correct/neutral part of the study, 1.56 percent of the times were greater than 1,000 ms, 3.65 percent of the values were above or below two SD and 3.13 percent of the values were missing. In the incorrect/neutral part, 1.74 percent of the times were greater than 1,000 ms, 4.17 percent of the values were above or below two SD and 1.56 percent of the values were missing. For the monolingual controls, in the correct/neutral part of the study, 0.17 percent of the times were greater than 1,000 ms, 3.99 percent of the values were above or below two SD and 2.60 percent of the values were missing. In the incorrect/neutral part, 0.17 percent of the times were greater than 1,000 ms, 2.60 percent of the values were above or below two SD and 2.43 percent of the values were missing. The data replacement procedures were the same as in the first experiment.

Figure 9.3 presents mean naming times (in milliseconds) as a function of group—the monolingual control group, labeled "Monolingual (B)", and the late bilingual group—and gender marking (correct and neutral). First, we can see that the monolingual group showed a congruency effect: mean naming times for the correct and the neutral conditions were 521 and 545 ms respectively (a 24-ms congruency difference). Second, we note that the late bilinguals have longer reaction times than the controls, but we are struck especially by the fact that they show absolutely no naming time difference between the correct and neutral conditions: both took 620 ms on average. The two-way ANOVAs confirm these results. There was a congruency effect ($F_1(1, 30) = 20.89$, $MSe = 120.88$; $F_2(1, 35) = 10.51$, $MSe = 542.35$), a group effect ($F_1(1, 30) = 4.94$, $MSe = 24603.92$; $F_2(1, 35) = 375.02$, $MSe = 729.83$), and an interaction ($F_1(1, 30) = 19.66$, $MSe = 120.88$; $F_2(1, 35) = 9.00$, $MSe = 594.78$). A Tukey HSD post hoc test shows that the monolinguals' 24-ms congruency difference (neutral/correct) is significant at the .01 level. Although the late bilinguals showed no congruency effect, we can wonder whether they might not be sensitive to gender incongruity.

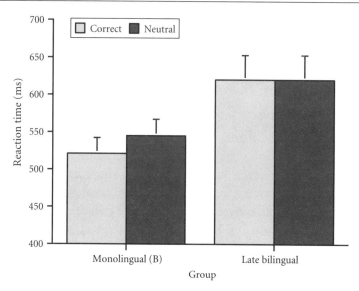

FIGURE 9.3 Mean naming times (in milliseconds) as a function of group (Monolingual (B) and Late bilingual) and gender marking (correct and neutral)

Note: Error bars represent +1 SEM.

After all, it is a phenomenon that often reaches consciousness, as can be seen when native speakers react sometimes quite strongly to gender-production errors (see Grosjean *et al*. 1994). The answer is in Figure 9.4.

Figure 9.4 presents mean naming times (in milliseconds) as a function of group (monolingual and late bilingual) and gender marking (neutral and incorrect). As can be seen, the monolinguals showed a large incongruency effect: their mean naming times were 547 ms in the neutral condition and 594 ms in the incorrect condition, a difference of 47 ms. The late bilinguals responded a bit more slowly than the monolinguals but above all they showed no apparent difference between the two conditions: Their mean naming times were 632 ms in the neutral condition and 626 ms in the incorrect condition, a 6-ms difference in the opposite direction! An ANOVA shows a marginal incongruency effect by participants only ($F_1(1, 30) = 43.09$, $MSe = 161.83$), a marginal group effect by items only ($F_2(1, 35) = 131.44$, $MSe = 937.29$), but a strong interaction ($F_1(1, 30) = 68.13$, $MSe = 161.83$; $F_2(1, 35) = 22.32$, $MSe = 1108.95$). A Tukey HSD post hoc test shows that the monolinguals' 47-ms incongruency difference (incorrect/neutral) is significant at the .01 level, whereas the bilinguals' 6-ms difference in the opposite direction is not significant.

It is clear from both these sets of results that late bilinguals are insensitive to both gender congruency and gender incongruency. It

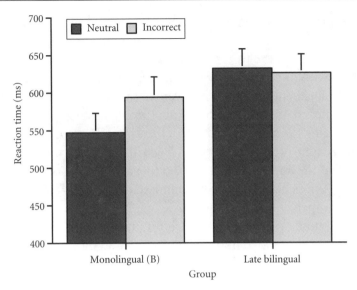

FIGURE 9.4 Mean naming times (in milliseconds) as a function of group (Monolingual (B) and Late bilingual) and gender marking (neutral and incorrect)

Note: Error bars represent +1 SEM.

is as if they just cannot use the masculine "le" cue or the feminine "la" cue during the processing of the noun phrase. In order to make sure that this absence of an effect is not simply due to overall speed of response (the bilinguals were somewhat slower than the controls, and this might have neutralized the gender-marking effect), we took the participants' mean reaction times to the neutral stimuli, in each condition and in each group, and used them to divide the participants into two subgroups: the slowest eight and the fastest eight. We then obtained subgroup means and tested them for a difference. Whereas the monolinguals showed both a congruency and an incongruency effect, whatever subgroup they belonged to, the bilinguals showed no effect, even though the bilinguals in the fast subgroups were faster than the monolinguals in the slow subgroups. We concluded that overall speed of response cannot account for the late bilinguals' absence of a gender-marking effect.

A second question we asked was whether the total lack of a congruency and incongruency effect could be linked, to some extent at least, to the late bilinguals' inability to use gender agreement when speaking French. Could the problem be linked to production, at least in part? The fact that the late bilinguals cannot always produce the correct gender when speaking might explain why they could not use gender marking during perception. In order to assess this, one month after finishing the second experiment, we phoned fifteen participants from each of the two bilingual groups, late bilinguals and early bilinguals, and asked them to repeat back each of the thirty-six nouns used in the studies but to precede them with the appropriate determiner "le" or "la". Thus, for example, if we gave them "bateau", they were to say "le bateau". (A few practice examples at the start resolved any problems they may have had understanding the task.) As expected, the early bilinguals did not make a single gender-production error (mean of 0 errors on 36 possible errors), and the late bilinguals made only very few errors (mean of 3.5 errors on 36 possible errors, with a standard deviation of 3.2). With a bit less than 10 percent errors, therefore, one can conclude that the late bilinguals know the gender of French nouns (at least that of common nouns such as those used in the experiment), and they can produce the appropriate determiner when asked to. The processing problem they had in perception, therefore, is not linked to one in production, at least not directly.

Two anonymous reviewers proposed factors related to language proficiency to explain the lack of any effects in the late bilinguals. The first factor relates to the discriminability of the three determiners, "le", "la", and "leur", by these participants. The argument is that they simply cannot hear the difference and hence will not react any differently to the three conditions. A number of counterarguments can be proposed, however. First, great care was taken to use quality exemplars of these determiners (see the Materials section of the first experiment). Second, the phonetic difference is relatively large between the three: a central vowel for the "le", a low front vowel for the "la", and the presence of an additional consonant (/R/) for the "leur". Finally, it should be recalled that the late bilinguals had been active bilinguals for up to 24 years, listening to and speaking French on a daily basis, and hence were used to discriminating vowel sounds. The second factor put forward is that of fluency. It was proposed that fluency is driving the effect, so that the more fluent a person is in the gender-marking language, the more he/she will be sensitive to gender marking. Although further research is needed to fully assess the role of this factor, one should recall that the late bilinguals rated their oral comprehension of French as very high (mean of 6.0 on a 7-point scale). Admittedly, no objective measure of fluency was obtained, but there is no reason to believe that the late bilinguals' oral comprehension of French was not good (or that their self-ratings were erroneous). In addition to their residency of more than 20 years in a French-speaking country, many have spouses and children with whom they speak French on a daily basis.

We can conclude from the above that speed of response, production skills, and language proficiency are not clear candidates to account for the absence of a gender-marking effect in late bilinguals. Since age does not seem to be a problem either (it was controlled for by testing monolinguals of a similar age), we must conclude that the absence of the gender-marking effect is probably due to when the gender-agreement language was acquired and started to be used on a regular basis.

9.3 General discussion

In this paper, we replicated in French, and by means of a naming task, the gender congruency and incongruency effects found by Bates *et al.* (1996) in Italian.[4] We then investigated whether bilinguals process gender marking, and we found that this depends on when they acquired the gender-agreement language, and started using it on a regular basis. We first showed that early English-French bilinguals behave like monolinguals both on gender congruency and gender incongruency. The only possible difference between the two groups could be that the early bilinguals may have been more sensitive to gender marking. When we tested late bilinguals, however, we found a total insensitivity to gender marking in perception, whether the gender was congruent or incongruent, although a control group of monolinguals of the same age showed both effects. An analysis in terms of speed of response and a small follow-up production study allowed us to exclude the late bilinguals' speed of response and their gender-production skills as factors accounting for the absence of the gender-marking effect.

As we indicated at the beginning of this paper, there are two possible accounts of the gender-marking effect. On the one hand, the process could be internal to the lexicon in that when a word carrying a gender marking is identified, it activates all the nouns in the lexicon that share the same gender. A variant of this first possibility is that it is the gender feature of the word that activates all the nouns with that same feature. To account for the results obtained with late bilinguals, a first suggestion could be that they have not established any gender connections among the words sharing the same gender or that they have not given a gender feature to the nouns. However, since they did extremely well on the follow-up production task, one would probably have to conclude that they do have these connections (or features), but that they

---

[4] In an unpublished study, we have found similar congruency and incongruency effects in French with a lexical decision task. The stimuli were the same as those in this paper. The results are available upon request.

simply do not activate them during auditory processing. The alternative explanation for the gender marking effect involves both the lexical and syntactic processing modules. The lexical module undertakes the recognition of the words in question (e.g. an article and a noun), and the syntactic module checks that gender agreement is respected. In the case of late bilinguals who do not show a gender-marking effect, either they never developed (or "triggered") this mechanism or they simply cannot make use of it (in perception at least).

Whatever the account, it would seem that certain processing mechanisms in a second language will never be acquired (or only partly acquired) after a specific point. In the case of gender, Carroll (1989) has proposed a detailed account of how first- and second-language learners acquire gender. According to her, when first-language learners (which in our case would correspond to our monolinguals and our early bilinguals) figure out that determiners are distinct lexical items, the phonological representations are reduced and the morphosyntactic representations are augmented to include the feature [± masc]. Thus, the reanalysis of determiners as separate words serves as a trigger for the activation of the universally specified gender feature. If the gender feature is not needed, it atrophies and disappears. In the case of second-language learners (our late bilinguals in this case), Carroll states that the functions deriving underlying phonological representations will not chunk determiners with nouns and hence will not include a gender feature. To produce gender, second language learners must develop mnemonic strategies for pairing nouns and all gender-marked words; to do so they develop rules of thumb that correspond to preference rule systems. This might explain why our late bilinguals managed to produce 90 percent of the appropriate determiners when asked to say the nouns preceded by the appropriate definite article, "le" or "la". Carroll concludes that anglophones will have no difficulty "hearing" the words that mark gender when parsing speech because they can phonologically represent all forms and carry out lexical look-up. On this point, if hearing means processing, then Carroll's statement needs to be modulated somewhat. Words will indeed be recognized (our late bilinguals reported having very good French oral comprehension), but lexical access will not be speeded up by a congruent gender marking on the preceding word(s) or slowed down by an incongruent gender marking. In other words, late bilinguals cannot call on gender marking to facilitate (or, more rarely, impede) the word recognition process.

The current study raises many interesting questions which will need to be addressed in future work. First, it would be interesting to see whether late bilinguals recognize correct and wrong gender (using grammaticality judgments, for example) even though they are not sensitive to the phenomenon during perception. They might well do so as different, more metalinguistic, skills are required. Second, it will be important to use different word recognition tasks to see if the difference between early and late bilinguals is maintained. Even though auditory naming is not a "shallow" task (see the various effects found with the task, some quite "deep"; Bates and Liu 1997), it could be that the type of task used plays a role in some way when testing late bilinguals (hopefully a very weak one). Third, and linked to this last point, it will be important to test early bilinguals who are middle aged as it is always difficult to compare participants across age groups (a suggestion made by one of the reviewers). It should be recalled that the early bilinguals were some twenty-four years younger than the late bilinguals. Fourth, concerning the relationship between gender production and perception, one could investigate how late bilinguals behave on a speeded production task. They would probably make many more errors than in our follow-up study (we put no pressure on them to respond quickly), but they would probably not reach chance level (i.e. 50 percent errors, which would be the production equivalent of the absence of a gender-marking effect in perception). If they did not reach this error level, we would have to conclude that gender perception and production are governed by somewhat different processing mechanisms. Fifth, we should study whether late bilinguals are more sensitive to gender markings if there are more of them. In our study, only the determiner carried gender information (the following adjective "joli(e)" did not) and this might have been insufficient information for our late bilinguals. There are many instances in French where several gender markings precede the noun, such as "la belle journée" (the nice day), where both "la" and "belle" carry a feminine gender marking, and late bilinguals might just become sensitive to gender marking when there are more gender cues. Finally, we can ask whether the problem we have uncovered with our late bilinguals is a general problem of agreement or whether it is limited to gender. What would happen, for example, with number agreement such as in "les beaux arbres" (the nice trees) where "les" and "beaux" both carry a plural number marking? Of course, one would have to test pairs of languages where one language does not have overt number agreement (both English and French do), but it would nevertheless be interesting to see if the processing pattern is the same as with gender.

In sum, bilinguals do indeed use gender marking during spoken word recognition, but only if they started acquiring, and using on a regular basis, the gender-agreement language at an early age. Late bilinguals do not seem to be able to use gender marking during the recognition process. One can therefore extend Sir Winston Churchill's statement in the following way "I have never mastered the gender of French nouns... *be it in production OR perception.*"

Appendix

The thirty-six words used in the study accompanied by the translation of their most frequent meaning.

Masculine nouns

One syllable	Two syllables
camp (camp)	bateau (boat)
plat (dish)	plateau (tray)
drap (sheet)	poisson (fish)
teint (complexion)	cadeau (present)
pré (meadow)	bassin (pool)
puits (well)	bijou (jewel)
disque (record)	berceau (cradle)
clan (clan)	pinceau (brush)
tube (tube)	dessert (dessert)

Feminine nouns

One syllable	Two syllables
glace (ice)	bouteille (bottle)
plante (plant)	boutique (store)
danse (danse)	galerie (gallery)
cave (cellar)	pension (pension)
poule (hen)	barrière (fence)
cage (cage)	bougie (candle)
boucle (buckle)	balance (scales)
torche (flashlight)	trompette (trumpet)
pelle (shovel)	poupée (doll)

10

The Role of Guest-Word Properties*

This chapter is best introduced by an anecdote. Olivier, a 5-year-old French-English bilingual boy, comes up to his mother and is overheard by a bilingual onlooker as saying, "Maman, tu peux me tailler mes chaussures?" (Mummy, can you sharpen my shoes?). With no apparent hesitation, the mother kneels down and starts to *tie* his shoelaces, while the onlooker strives to understand what Olivier said: "tailler des chaussures (sharpen shoes)? No, that doesn't make sense...ah, he's asking to have his shoes tied." Any reader who knows both English and French will have understood the predicament the onlooker was in: by inserting the English "tie" into his French sentence and adapting it morphologically and phonetically, Olivier unwittingly brought the English guest word ("tier") into conflict with an existing word in French ("tailler") and led the onlooker down a word recognition garden path. The mother, used to hearing Olivier employ "tie" in French, accessed the English meaning with no problem and went about the job of lacing Olivier's shoes. In the present study we will explore the underlying processes that take place when bilinguals have to recognize different types of guest words such as the word "tie" in the above example.

Bilinguals, that is those who use two languages (or dialects) in their everyday lives, move in and out of different speech modes depending on the interlocutor they are facing and the situation they are in. They are in a monolingual speech mode when speaking to monolinguals who speak only one of their two languages, and they are in a bilingual speech mode when they are speaking to other bilinguals who share the same two languages, and with whom they normally mix languages.

* This chapter first appeared as an article: Grosjean, F. (1988). "Exploring the recognition of guest words in bilingual speech", *Language and Cognitive Processes* 3: 233–74. The author wishes to thank Taylor and Francis (www.informaworld.com) for permission to reprint it here.

(For a discussion of speech modes and the continuum they belong to, see Grosjean (1982, 1985c); Grosjean and Soares (1986); and Chapter 4 of this book.) In the monolingual speech mode, bilinguals adopt the language of the monolingual interlocutor and reduce the activation of the other language. Some researchers have proposed various mechanisms, such as a switch or a monitor, that allow this reduction in activation (Macnamara 1967; Obler and Albert 1978; Penfield 1959); but others, notably Paradis (1980), have argued that such mediating devices are not necessary. All agree, however, that bilinguals rarely manage to deactivate totally the language not being spoken. This can be seen in various types of production and perception interferences, that is, the involuntary influence of one language on the other. In production, one notes pronunciation "errors", accidental lexical borrowings, "odd" syntactic constructions, etc., and in perception the residual activation of the other language can be observed in cross-language Stroop tests (Obler and Albert 1978; Preston and Lambert 1969), word–nonword judgments (Altenberg and Cairns 1983), and comprehension tasks using the phoneme monitoring paradigm (Blair and Harris 1981).

In the bilingual speech mode, the mode that is of interest to us in this study, both languages are activated, and bilinguals often use elements of one language when speaking the other. One language usually serves as the base language (the main language of communication) and the other language—we will call it the "guest" language—is brought in at various points during the interaction when the need occurs. Note that simply speaking to another bilingual does not automatically entail the use of the other language; a number of factors account for the presence of language mixing and for how much takes place (Grosjean 1982). Bringing the other language (the "guest" language) into the base language is usually done in two different ways: by code-switching or by borrowing. In code-switching, the bilingual usually shifts completely to the other language for a word, a phrase, or a sentence. For example:

(1)   C'était des *wild guys* à cheval
      "Those were wild guys on horseback"

(2)   J'ai l'impression d'être *back in the country*
      "I've got the feeling I'm back in the country"

Code-switching is a phenomenon that has received considerable attention from researchers: linguists have studied the syntactic constraints that govern the alternation between languages within a sentence (Joshi 1985; Lipski 1978, 1982; Pfaff 1979; Poplack 1980; Timm 1975; Woolford

1983); sociolinguists have studied the factors that account for code-switching (Gal 1979; Gumperz 1970; Scotton and Ury 1977; Valdes Fallis 1976); and developmental psycholinguists have studied the development of code-switching abilities in children (e.g. McClure 1977).

The other way of bringing the guest language into the base language is by borrowing a word from that language and integrating it phonetically and morphologically into the base language. For example:

(3)   On peut SWITCHER les places?
       "Can we switch the seats?"

(4)   Il a SLASHÉ le rideau
       "He slashed the curtain"

Here the English words "switch" and "slash" are pronounced in French and are integrated morphologically into the sentence. Note that these borrowings (which are also called "speech" or "nonce" borrowings) are different from "language borrowings" (or "loan words") which are borrowings only in a historical sense (Haugen 1969). The latter are now an integral part of the base language and are used by monolinguals and bilinguals alike (e.g. "weekend", "jazz", "transistor" in French; "fiancé", "croissant" in English). The borrowings we will be concerned with here are the "speech" or "nonce" borrowings produced by bilinguals when speaking with other bilinguals in a mixed language speaking mode. These kinds of borrowings, along with code-switched words, only belong to the lexicon of the other (or guest) language.

The aim of the present study is to explore how guest words, produced as borrowings or code-switches, are processed by bilingual listeners. Although much research has been undertaken to understand the processes underlying the recognition of spoken words in monolinguals (see e.g. Cole and Jakimik 1978; Foss and Blank 1980; Grosjean 1980, 1985a; McClelland and Elman 1986; Marslen-Wilson and Welsh 1978; Morton 1969), much less is known about how guest words are processed by bilinguals in a mixed-language interaction.

Recently, though, Soares and Grosjean (1984) investigated the recognition of base language words and of code-switched words in monolingual and bilingual sentences. They used Blank's (1980) "Phoneme Triggered Lexical Decision" task and obtained two interesting results. The first was that although bilinguals, in a monolingual speech mode, accessed base-language words as quickly as monolinguals, they were substantially slower at responding to nonwords. This finding provided additional evidence for the residual activation of the other language when the bilingual is in a monolingual mode. The second result of interest was that bilinguals took longer to access code-switched words than base-language words. It seemed that such factors as the phonetic and phonotactic characteristics of the guest word, the base-language context, the amount of code-switching that has occurred up to that point, etc., can account for the delay in processing.

The object of the present study is not to study further whether code-switches take more time to process than base-language words, or to investigate how the delay is made up during the ensuing speech. Such questions are important and are currently being studied. Rather, the aim here is to explore the underlying processes that are involved in the lexical access of guest words (that is, code-switches and borrowings) when they are produced and perceived in a bilingual speech mode. We will assume that the bilingual has two lexicons, which are interconnected in some way, and that guest words are stored, and therefore have to be accessed, in the other, less activated, lexicon.[1] Our exploration will revolve around the roles of two variables in the recognition of guest words—a structural or "word type" variable, and an output or "language phonetics" variable.

Concerning word type, we wish to ask the following questions. First, will guest words that are marked phonotactically as belonging to the guest-language lexicon only (because of the initial consonant cluster, for example) be recognized sooner and with more ease than words not marked in this way? Thus, will words like "snap", "blot", and "quit", which have initial consonant clusters that are more frequent in English than in French, be accessed more easily than words that do not have such language-specific cues? Second, will guest words that belong solely to the guest lexicon be identified sooner and with more ease than words that do not belong to just one lexicon? In other words, will the access of guest words like "lead" (/lid/), "tag", and "tease" be facilitated because they are nonwords in French (although possible words)? Third, will words in the guest-language lexicon that have close homophones in the base language be processed with more difficulty than other guest-language words? Thus, will "pick", "cool", and "knot", which have base-language counterparts with different meanings—"piquer"

---

[1] Although this assumption appears to be quite categorical, it is not meant to be a defense of the independence position in the debate on the organization of the bilingual's two lexicons (see Grosjean 1982 for a review of the controversy). Our use of the word "lexicon" refers to the set of lexical items that belong to one language; we make no claim, at this point, about the independence or interdependence of the two lexicons.

(to sting, puncture, steal), "couler" (to sink), and "noter" (to note down, mark)—be accessed with more difficulty than guest words with no counterparts in the base language?

The second variable we will study, the language phonetics of a word (also called "word phonetics" in this chapter), pertains to whether the guest word is pronounced in the guest language (as a code-switch) or in the base language (as a borrowing). The question of interest is whether code-switches, which normally retain a phonetic cue as to which lexicon they belong to, are easier to process than borrowings which are integrated phonetically and morphologically into the base language and thus have lost some of the cues that can help the listener access the correct lexicon. Will the language of pronunciation of a guest word affect its recognition, especially when the word is pronounced quite differently in the two languages? And what happens to guest words, such as "pick" and "cool", that have a base-language counterpart? Will they be accessed more easily when produced as code-switches than as borrowings? Although two quite distinct versions of the same word will be compared in this study (they will be produced in unaccented French and English), we should keep in mind that the borrowing and code-switching versions of a word are not always so distinct. When a bilingual has an accent in the guest language, for example, what is meant to be a code-switch will often resemble a borrowing (at the phonological level at least). These more hybrid cases will be the object of a later study.

Because the aim of the study is to gain some insight into the underlying processes involved in the identification and recognition of guest words, and not simply to study the role of word type and word phonetics, we will use an experimental paradigm that allows us to uncover some of the underlying operations involved in word recognition, namely the gating paradigm (Grosjean 1980; see Ohman 1966 and Pollack and Pickett 1963 for earlier versions).

In this task, a spoken word is presented from left to right, in segments of increasing duration. At the first presentation, only the first 40 ms of the word are presented; at the second presentation, the first 80 ms are presented; and so on, until at the last presentation, the whole of the word is presented. The subject's task, after each presentation, is to guess the word being presented and to give a confidence rating based on the guess. The gating paradigm presents a number of advantages which make it a useful tool in the study of the word recognition process. First, it allows one to assess how much of a word is needed to be identified or "isolated" correctly. This is done by determining a word's isolation point, that point in the presentation sequence at which the listener has correctly guessed the word and does not subsequently change his or her guess. It has been proposed (Grosjean 1985a) that the "isolation point" reflects the moment, in the left to right recognition process, at which the listener has a strong candidate in mind but has not yet decided to use it in the construction of the interpretative representation of the ongoing message. This point is quite close to the word's uniqueness point as defined in Marslen-Wilson and Welsh's (1978) cohort model— some 20–80 ms according to Tyler and Wessels (1983, 1985)—and corresponds quite closely to what Bradley and Forster (1987) mean when they say that a word has been accessed.

A second advantage of the paradigm is that one can examine the confidence ratings proposed by listeners at various points in time: at the isolation point, at the end of the word, and at the end of the sentence if gating continues after the word (as in Grosjean 1985a). One can also examine where, in the left to right sequence, a perfect confidence rating is given to the word. This "total acceptance point" may be the moment in time at which the word starts being used in the construction of the interpretative representation (Grosjean 1985a). This point occurs later than the uniqueness point and corresponds quite closely to what Bradley and Forster (1987) mean by word recognition, that is, the listener's fixation of belief that he or she has indeed heard word X.

A third advantage of the paradigm is that the word candidates proposed before the isolation point give some insight into the word isolation process itself. By examining responses across subjects we can infer the path followed by the individual listener when he or she is narrowing-in on a word. Thus, in this chapter, we will study the early preference bilinguals have for the base-language lexicon (as shown by Grosjean and Soares 1986), how and when they shift their preference to the guest lexicon, the conflict that arises when both a base language word and guest-language word are possible, and how that conflict is resolved.

In addition to employing all the information provided by the gating paradigm in the exploration of the underlying processes involved in the recognition of guest words in bilingual mixed speech, we will also undertake side analyses. We will study, for example, the relationship that exists between the acoustic information given to listeners (as defined by spectrographic analysis) and the moment at which a word is guessed correctly. We will also examine the impact of the "frequency pull" of words which come into conflict in the recognition process, that is guest words and their base-language homophones. We will end the chapter with a proposal for how an interactive activation model of word recognition can be modified to take into account not only the effects found in monolingual word recognition research, but also the effects that are specific to bilingual language processing. A complete model of how spoken words are recognized in bilingual speech is still far off, but we hope that our proposal can be a first step in that direction.

10.1 Method

10.1.1 Participants

A total of twelve French-English bilingual adults, with no reported speech or hearing defects, served individually in a session lasting 90 minutes. All participants had the following common characteristics. They were native speakers of French and had only started learning English in secondary school; they had moved to the United States as adults and had lived in the Boston region for at least four years (it is on their arrival in the United States that English became a language of communication for them and stopped being a language known only formally); they used their two languages on a daily basis (French in the family and with friends; English at work, in the community, and with American friends); they code-switched and borrowed when speaking French to bilingual friends and family members; and they had served previously as participants in the bilingual research project based in the Psychology Department of Northeastern University. Note that no effort was made to test the bilingual's proficiency in English and French or to use "balanced" bilinguals (see Grosjean (1982, 1985b), for a discussion of the problems linked with proficiency tests and with the use of "balanced" bilinguals). Membership in a bilingual community (the European French speaking community in Boston) and daily use of English and French for at least four years were the critical variables in choosing the participants.

10.1.2 Materials

In total, twenty-four monosyllabic English verbs and eight French filler verbs were chosen for the study. The English verbs all had the same uniqueness point, that is, that point in the left to right sequence of phonemes at which the word distinguishes itself from every other word (Marslen-Wilson 1984). The English items belonged to one of three

TABLE 10.1 A description of the two variables used in the study. Three types of words (structural variable) were pronounced either in English as a code-switch or in French as a borrowing (output variable: language phonetics of word)

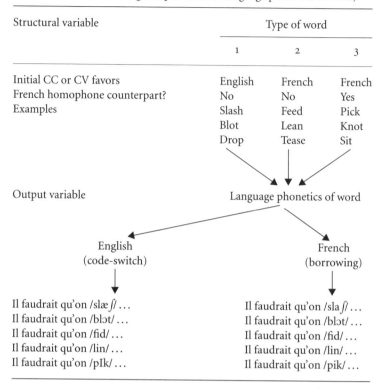

Structural variable	Type of word		
	1	2	3
Initial CC or CV favors	English	French	French
French homophone counterpart?	No	No	Yes
Examples	Slash	Feed	Pick
	Blot	Lean	Knot
	Drop	Tease	Sit

Output variable   Language phonetics of word

English   French
(code-switch)   (borrowing)

Il faudrait qu'on /slæ ʃ/ . . .   Il faudrait qu'on /sla ʃ/ . . .
Il faudrait qu'on /blɔt/ . . .   Il faudrait qu'on /blɔt/ . . .
Il faudrait qu'on /fid/ . . .   Il faudrait qu'on /fid/ . . .
Il faudrait qu'on /lin/ . . .   Il faudrait qu'on /lin/ . . .
Il faudrait qu'on /pɪk/ . . .   Il faudrait qu'on /pik/ . . .

groups, each group containing eight words (see Table 10.1). Type 1 words, like "slash", "blot", and "drop", contained initial consonant clusters (/sl/, /bl/, /dr/, etc.) that are infrequent in French but quite frequent in English. A general comparison of French and English words which have the clusters in question (accomplished by examining the *Micro Robert Dictionary* and *Webster's II New Riverside Dictionary*) showed that the English/French ratio for words with this initial consonant cluster was always in favor of English (the values ranged from 42: 1 to 2.3: 1 with a mean of 22.6). For example, twenty-six English words were found with initial /dr/ as compared to six French words, and twenty-nine English words were found with initial /sl/ but only one French word, etc. Type 2 words, such as "feed", "lean", and "tease", contained an initial CV which occurs more frequently in French than in English. The English/French ratios ranged from 0.83: 1 to 0.40: 1 with a mean of 0.59. Thus, for example, eleven French words started with French /fi/

but only five English words began with English /fi/, and sixteen French words started with French /li/ but only nine words in English began with English /li/, etc. Type 3 words, such as "pick", "knot", and "sit", were similar to Type 2 words in phonotactic configuration (the mean English/French ratio was 0.45, a non-significant difference with Type 2 words), but all had a French homophone counterpart. Thus when words like "pick", "knot", and "sit" are pronounced in French, they cannot be distinguished from their French counterparts with different meanings—"pique", "note", and "cite".

In sum, as can be seen in Table 10.1, Type 1 words were marked phonotactically as belonging to English (because of the initial cluster) and had no French counterparts; Type 2 words were not marked phonotactically as belonging to English (in fact, their phonotactics favored French) but, like Type 1 words, they had no French counterparts; and Type 3 words were phonotactically similar to Type 2 words but, unlike the first two types, they had French counterparts. The uniqueness point of all twenty-four words (with the exception of one word in each group) fell on the last consonant. Finally, the mean frequency of occurrence of the words in the three groups, as measured by Kučera and Francis (1967), was similar: 6.89, 5.10, and 8.57 respectively—$F(2,21) = 0.21$, N.S. The eight French filler verbs were one or two syllables long and began with CCs and CVs (e.g. "soulève", "pratique", "stipule", "grignote", "brosse", etc.).

Each word was embedded in a sentence that began with "Il faudrait qu'on" ("We should") and ended with a three-word NP in which each word was a monosyllable. The initial part of the sentence was chosen so that the morphological integration of the guest word, when said as a borrowing, did not necessitate an inflection and hence increase the number of syllables of the borrowing as compared to the code-switch. As for the final NP, care was taken to make sure that its last word added semantic context to the sentence. Examples of the complete sentences containing the stimulus verbs (in capitals) are:

(5) Il faudrait qu'on SLASH tous les prix
     "We should slash all the prices"

(6) If faudrait qu'on LEAN contre le mur
     "We should lean against the wall"

(7) Il faudrait qu'on KNOT ces deux cordes
     "We should knot these two ropes"

(8)   Il faudrait qu'on PICK les bons chiffres
       "We should pick the right numbers"

Two type-written versions of the twenty-four experimental sentences were then prepared for the recording of the English verbs as code-switches or borrowings. In the first, the verb was typed normally in the sentence; in the second, the verb was spelled in French. Thus, "slash" was written "slache"; "feed" was written "fide"; "knot" was written "notte"; "fool" was written "foule". The filler sentences were added to this French version. A bilingual French-English female speaker, with no apparent accent in either language, was then asked to read the two versions of the sentences. This person was chosen because she code-switches and borrows naturally when speaking to other bilinguals and has been used repeatedly to prepare experimental tapes with natural sounding code-switches. For the code-switching set, she was asked to switch naturally to English for the word in question, and for the borrowing set she was requested to read the whole sentence in French.

A waveform analysis of the code-switching and borrowing versions confirmed that all sentences were read naturally (there were no pauses before or after the stimulus words) and that the reader did in fact code-switch when requested to do so. To verify the latter, two acoustic analyses were undertaken on a subgroup of words. In the first, we measured the stop-initial voice onset time (VOT) of the code-switching and borrowing versions of the nine words that began with a stop consonant (four voiced and five unvoiced). The mean VOT value of the code-switches (English) was, as expected, longer than that of the borrowing (French): 46 and 27 ms, respectively ($t = 1.99$, $p < 0.05$). In the second analysis, we measured the duration of the high amplitude periodic portion of the waveform corresponding to the /i/ vowel in the code-switching and borrowing versions of the eight words containing that phoneme (English /i/ and French /i/). Again, as expected, the periodicity lasted longer in English than in French: 154 ms as compared to 110 ms ($t = 6.32$, $p < 0.01$). We concluded from this that the reader had indeed produced two different versions of the experimental words—a code-switching version and a borrowing version (see Table 10.1, bottom).

The recordings of the 56 sentences (24 with code-switches, 24 with borrowings, and 8 monolingual French filler sentences) were digitized at a sampling rate of 20 kHz and gated using a waveform editing program on a PDP 11/44 (see Grosjean 1980, 1985a for a general description of the procedure).[2] For each sentence, the "onset" of the stimulus word and of each of the next three words was located as best as possible by inspecting the speech waveform and by using auditory feedback. Most stimulus words began with a fricative or a stop consonant, and their "onsets" corresponded respectively to the start of the frication in the speech wave and to the end of the silence preceding the release burst.

The presentation set of each gated sentence was prepared in the following way. The first gate contained "Il faudrait qu'on" up to, but not including, the onset of the stimulus word. The second gate contained the same information plus the first 40 ms of the word. From then on, gates were incremented by 40 ms until the end of the word was reached. When the duration of the stimulus word was not an exact multiple of 40, the gate containing the full stimulus word was incremented by the amount remaining. Once the full word had been presented, three "after offset" gates were added to the presentation set. Unlike the stimulus word gates, which were incremented by 40 ms, these three gates were incremented by a whole word. The first "after offset" gate contained the carrier sentence, the stimulus word, and the first word of the following NP; the second gate contained all the previous information plus the second word of the NP; and the third gate (which was also the final presentation gate) presented the whole sentence, including the final NP.

Two experimental tapes were made from these presentation sets. Each tape contained thirty-two sets (eight for each type of word and eight fillers). The order of the fillers and of the word type exemplars was randomized. The only difference between the two tapes was that one tape presented the code-switched version of a particular word and the other tape presented, in exactly the same position, the borrowing version of the same word. Each tape contained four borrowing and four code-switch exemplars of each word type.

10.1.3 Procedure

The twelve participants were split into two groups of six, and were run individually on one of the two experimental tapes. This meant that subjects heard each of the twenty-four stimulus words either as a code-switch or as a borrowing. (As indicated above, they heard as

[2] The overall software package for speech processing was developed at Northeastern University by Thomas Erb and Ashish Tungare, and is based in part on the BLISS system developed by John Mertus at Brown University.

many code-switch exemplars as borrowing exemplars for each word type—four in each case.) The sessions were conducted in French (the usual language of communication between the experimenter, a bilingual himself, and the participants) and the instructions were written in French. The participants were told that they would be hearing English or French verbs, presented in segments of increasing duration, followed by a short three-word phrase, presented one word at a time after the stimulus word. They were also told that in the case of English verbs, the word could be pronounced in English or in French. They were asked to listen to the presentations and, after each presentation, to do three things: (1) write down the word they thought was being presented after "Il faudrait qu'on"; (2) indicate how confident they were about their guess by circling a number on a scale of 1–10 (anchored with "Incertain" (Unsure) and "Certain" (Sure)); and (3) indicate whether they thought the word was French or English (that is, belonged to the French or English language) by circling "F" (français) or "A" (anglais) on the right of the confidence rating scale. The answer sheet was arranged in such a way that the sequence of events was first to write down a word, second to give a confidence rating, and third to indicate the language of origin of the word. The participants were given 8 seconds between each presentation to accomplish these three tasks. They were asked to give a response after every presentation, however unsure they might feel about the stimulus word, and they were asked to write the English words with English orthography, even if these words were pronounced in French. A break of 15 minutes was given to the participants halfway through the 90-minute sessions.

10.1.4 Data analysis

Response sheets provided three kinds of information. The first concerned the isolation point of the word, that is, that point at which the subject correctly guessed the stimulus word and did not subsequently change his or her guess. A first analysis indicated whether this point occurred before the offset of the word, after the offset but before the end of the sentence, or never occurred at all (the participant never guessed the word). A second analysis indicated, when appropriate, at what point within the stimulus word the word was isolated (this was expressed as a percentage of the way through the word), and a third analysis indicated, again when appropriate, where during the final NP the stimulus word was isolated correctly. Note that the subjects' orthography of the words and their "A" or "F" indications always permitted one to determine whether the responses were French or English words.

The second type of information concerned confidence ratings. The total acceptance point of a word (that point at which a perfect confidence rating, i.e. 10, was given to the correct response) was located in the same way as the isolation point (before, after, never; within the stimulus word; after offset, etc.).[3] The third type of information obtained was the erroneous candidates proposed prior to the isolation point. These candidates were analyzed in terms of their language of origin and the error type they belonged to (homophone error, segmentation error, etc.). Precise indications of the measures used, and of the tests of significance that were conducted on them, are given below with the results and discussion.

10.2 Results and discussion

10.2.1 The isolation point

In this section, we will first compare the three types of words used in the study: Type 1 words which are marked phonotactically as belonging to English; Type 2 words which are not marked in this way but which only belong to English; and Type 3 words which have French homophone counterparts. We will then separate Type 1 and Type 2 words from Type 3 words, and examine the first two types of words with a measure more appropriate to them. We will end by studying two variables that account for the isolation point of Type 3 words.

The majority of words (76 percent in all) were isolated before their acoustic offset; the remainder were isolated after their offset, but before the end of the sentence (16 percent), or were never isolated at all (8 percent). Figure 10.1 presents the percentages of words that fell into each of these three categories (before, after, never) as a function of word type and language phonetics of the word. As can be seen, practically all Type 1 and Type 2 words were isolated before their ending (97 and 90 percent respectively), whereas less than half of Type 3 words (43 percent) were isolated by then. The remaining Type 1 and Type 2 words were isolated before the end of the sentence (with the exception of 4 percent of Type 2 words), but a full 20 percent of the Type 3 words were not isolated by that point. This clearly indicates that the properties of guest words, such

---

[3] Because of lack of space, the results pertaining to the confidence ratings will not be presented in this chapter. They simply confirm the isolation point data, and can be obtained from the author upon request.

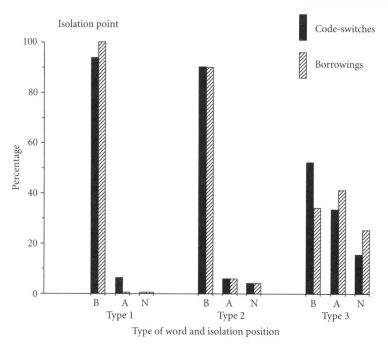

FIGURE 10.1 Percentage of words that are isolated as a function of position of isolation (before their offset (B), after their offset (A), or never isolated (N)), type of word (Types 1–3) and language phonetics of word (pronounced as a code-switch (English) or as a borrowing (French))

as their phonotactic configuration and their single lexicon membership (the English lexicon in this case), can facilitate their isolation. The presence of an initial consonant cluster in Type 1 words ("sn" in "snap", "bl" in "blot", etc.) and the presence of Type 1 and Type 2 words (such as "feed", "tag", "lean", etc.) in the English lexicon, but their absence from the French lexicon, facilitated the isolation of these words before their acoustic offset. Type 3 words, on the other hand, were difficult to isolate, not only because they are phonotactically possible in both languages, but also because they exist in both English and French ("knot" and "note", "cool" and "coule", etc.). The problem caused by these words (57 percent were either isolated late or never isolated at all) is a clear indication that in everyday interactions, bilingual listeners will have problems with such words. If the context is not constraining enough, they will mistakenly use the lexical meaning of the base-language homophone in the construction of the internal representation (the meaning of "couler" and not of "cool", for instance), and will have to backtrack later when enough contradictory information becomes available.

The second important point that emerges from Figure 10.1 is that the language phonetics of a word, that is, whether it is said as a borrowing or a code-switch, appears to play more of a role in the isolation of Type 3 words than in the identification of Type 1 and Type 2 words (at least with the present isolation measure). We note, for example, only a 6 percent difference between the number of code-switches and borrowings that were isolated before offset in Type 1 words (94 and 100 percent, respectively), no difference between them in Type 2 words (90 percent in both cases), but a 19 percent difference between code-switches and borrowings in Type 3 words (52 percent of the code-switches were isolated before offset as compared to 33 percent of the borrowings). Here the difference is in the direction predicted: code-switches, which are marked phonetically for the lexicon they belong to, were isolated sooner than borrowings. Although there were slightly more borrowings than code-switches isolated after offset (41 percent as compared to 33 percent), the deficit accrued by borrowings in the first category was not overcome before the end of the sentence, and a full 25 percent of the borrowings were never isolated, as compared to 15 percent of the code-switches. We conclude from this that pronouncing a guest word in the appropriate language may help in its identification, especially when it is not already "tagged" for the language phonotactically or lexically (as were Type 1 and 2 words).

In order to test the results obtained so far, every word response was given a position rating: a score of 1 if the word was isolated before its acoustic–phonetic offset; a score of 2 if the word was isolated after its offset but before the end of the sentence; and a score of 3 if the word was never isolated. Two analyses of variance were then conducted on these ratings, one over subjects and the other over items. A main effect was found for word type in both analyses—over items: $F(2,22) = 49.26$, $p < 0.01$; over subjects: $F(2,21) = 23.19$, $p < 0.01$. An *a posteriori* test in the over items analysis (Tukey HSD: Kirk 1967) showed that Type 1 and Type 2 words were not different from one another, but that each was different from Type 3 words ($p < 0.01$). No main effect was found for word phonetics in either analysis, but there was a significant Type × Phonetics interaction in the analysis over items: $F(2,22) = 4.32$, $p < 0.05$. An *a posteriori* test showed that only the difference between borrowings and code-switches in Type 3 words was significant ($p < 0.05$). Although the difference between Type 3 borrowings and code-switches is weakened somewhat by the fact that it was found in the over-items analysis only, further evidence will be presented throughout the chapter to show that the language phonetics of a word does indeed appear to play a role in its recognition, especially when that word has a base-language homophone.

Two findings emerge from the analysis so far, therefore. The first is that Type 1 and Type 2 words behave quite differently from Type 3 words; the former are mostly isolated before their offset, whereas the latter are difficult to isolate, and many are never isolated at all. (Note that the broad isolation measure used so far does not allow us to make any claims about the difference that may exist between Type 1 and Type 2 words.) The second finding is that the language phonetics of a word appears to play a role, especially when that word has a base-language homophone; if that word is said as a code-switch, then it will be isolated sooner than if it is said as a borrowing.

We will now examine Type 1 and Type 2 words separately from Type 3 words so as to better understand the isolation process involved in the two subsets of words.

Type 1 and Type 2 words

A within word isolation point, defined as the percentage of the way through the word needed for isolation, was computed for every response. When a particular value was missing, as when the word had been isolated after its offset, or never isolated at all, it was replaced by the mean value for the word calculated over subjects (3 percent of Type 1 values and 10 percent of Type 2 values were replaced in this way). Figure 10.2 represents the amount of a word needed to isolate it as a function of word type and word phonetics (language phonetics of the word). Two findings are apparent. The first is that Type 1 words are isolated earlier than Type 2 words: participants needed, on average, 66 percent of a Type 1 word to isolate it as compared to 78 percent of a Type 2 word. The fact that words like "blot", "slash", "snap", and "quit" are isolated sooner than words like "tag", "feed", "sip", and "beep" appears to indicate that the language specificity of the initial consonant cluster of Type 1 words helps listeners narrow-in more rapidly on the appropriate lexicon and, therefore, on the specific item within it. Note that such factors as word frequency and uniqueness point are not involved here: Type 1 and Type 2 words have similar frequencies and identical uniqueness points.

The second point of interest is that the language phonetics of Type 1 and Type 2 words appears to play little role in the time it takes to isolate them: listeners needed, on average, 70 percent of the borrowings

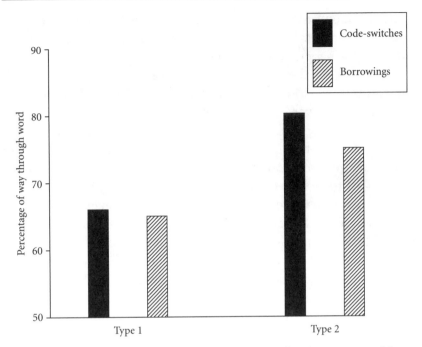

FIGURE 10.2 Amount of a word needed to isolate it (expressed as the percentage of the way through the word) as a function of type of word (Types 1 and 2) and language phonetics of word (pronounced as a code-switch (English) or as a borrowing (French)). Each point is based on 48 observations

(over both types of words) to isolate them and 73 percent of the code-switches. Thus, in this case at least, pronouncing an English word in English or in French has no effect on its identification, unless, as we saw above, it can be mistaken for a word that already exists in the base language. Two analyses of variance, one over subjects and one over items, confirm the pattern obtained. The only main effect obtained was for word type—over items: $F(1,11) = 33.60$, $p < 0.01$; over subjects: $F(1,14) = 5.09$, $p < 0.05$. No main effect was found for word phonetics, and there was no interaction.

Two aspects of the results pertaining to the language phonetics of a word are surprising. The first concerns the absence of an effect in Type 2 words which, unlike Type 1 words, do not have an initial language specific consonant cluster to indicate the appropriate lexicon. The second concerns the fact that the isolation point of borrowings (b) sometimes occurs before that of code-switches (cs). Thus, for example, participants needed 82 percent of "beep"(cs) on average to isolate it, but only 50 percent of "beep"(b); they needed 91 percent of "tag"(cs) to isolate it, but only 69 percent of "tag"(b), etc. We decided to investigate these two aspects by conducting an acoustic analysis of Type 2 word pairs (borrowings and code-switches).

We located on the speech wave form the vowel "offset" of each pair, and calculated for these items the time that elapsed between the beginning of the word and the "end" of the vowel (see Repp 1981 for a discussion of linguistic categories and their physical correlates in the speech wave). We reasoned that, by the end of the vowel, the listener would have received enough consonantal information (through co-articulation) to be able to isolate the word correctly. (The uniqueness point of these CVC words was on the final consonant.) The vowel "offset" was located in different ways depending on the words in question: (1) for the two words that ended with a voiceless stop consonant ("beep" and "sip"), the offset was defined as that point where the high amplitude periodicity associated with the vowel ended and the closure silence began; (2) for the four words that ended with a voiced stop consonant ("feed", "tag", "lead", "dab"), the offset was that point where the high amplitude periodicity ended and the closure periodicity began; (3) for the word "tease", vowel offset was that point where the periodicity ended and the aperiodic energy associated with the fricative began; and (4) for the word "lean", the offset was that point where the periodicity associated with the vowel ended and the nasal periodicity began. In each case, auditory feedback and an examination of the spectrogram was used to confirm the measurement decisions.

The vowel offset values for the sixteen Type 2 words (eight code-switches and eight borrowings) were transformed into a percentage of the way through the word and were correlated with the corresponding isolation points (also expressed as a percentage of the way through the word). The Pearson product–moment correlation obtained was 0.55 ($p < 0.05$), indicating a rather strong relationship between vowel offset and isolation point—the earlier the vowel offset, the earlier the isolation point, and vice versa. This relationship is illustrated quite clearly in Figure 10.3, where we present the spectrogram of "tag" pronounced as a borrowing (top) and as a code-switch (bottom). (For presentation purposes, the two versions are displayed without their preceding and following context.) As can be seen, the linear arrangement of the acoustic characteristics is quite different in the two languages (the initial consonant burst is longer in English, the final consonant release is longer in French, etc.) and,

"Tag" said as a borrowing (French)

t   a   g

"Tag" said as a code-switch (English)

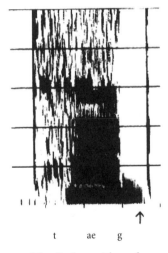

t   ae   g

FIGURE 10.3 The spectrograms of "tag" when said as a borrowing (French: top) and as a code-switch (English: bottom). The *Y*-axis goes up to 5 kHz. The vertical arrows indicate the isolation points of the two versions

therefore, the vowel offset occurs at different points in the borrowing and in the code-switch—54 and 75 percent of the way through the word, respectively. It is no surprise, therefore, that the isolation points are different for the two words—69 percent for the borrowing and

91 percent for the code-switch. What is critical, however, is that these isolation points occur at very similar informational points—during the closure preceding the release of the /g/ (see the black arrows below the spectrograms).

In order to control for other variables that may have played a role in the isolation of the words (frequency, familiarity, number of candidates after each phoneme, etc.) and which, *de facto*, would be keeping the correlation coefficient at its 0.55 level, we calculated for each word pair (borrowing, code-switch) a vowel offset difference (the difference between the end of the vowel in the code-switch and in the borrowing) and an isolation point difference (the difference between the isolation point of the code-switch and the borrowing). We then correlated these two sets of differences, and obtained a much higher coefficient of correlation: 0.82 ($p < 0.01$). Thus the greater the difference between the vowel offset of a code-switch and of a borrowing, the greater the difference between the isolation point of the two words (and vice versa). We conclude from this that the important factor in the isolation of a guest word with no base-language homophonic counterpart is whether the critical acoustic–phonetic information has been received, and not whether the word has been pronounced in the guest language or in the base language. Of course, this generalization does not include words with base-language homophones (Type 3 words) or words whose phonetic configuration changes quite drastically when pronounced in the other language—either because specific phonemes are absent in that language and close neighbors have to be used (for example, when the French /f/ replaces the English /ð/) or because the speaker has a strong accent in the guest language.

We can summarize the word isolation results so far by stating that word type (which in our case includes the phonotactic configuration of a word and its presence or absence in the base-language lexicon) is an important variable in the recognition process of guest words. The language phonetics of a word, on the other hand, plays less of a role. (Its role is more important during the narrowing-in stage, prior to word isolation, as we will see below.) Code-switches are not isolated sooner than borrowings when the words are marked phonotactically (Type 1 words) or when they belong to only one lexicon (Type 1 and Type 2 words), but only when the guest word comes into conflict with a base-language homophone. In this case, the fact that the code-switch retains some phonetic cues regarding its lexicon of origin helps in its identification.

Type 3 words

We saw in the first part of this section that Type 3 words (those with cross-language homophones) behave quite differently from Type 1 and Type 2 words: not only are they isolated later (and quite often never isolated at all), but they also appear to be the only kinds of words in which the language phonetics—whether they are pronounced in English or in French—plays a role in their isolation. In what follows, we will examine the role played by the post-offset syntactic and semantic context on the isolation of these words, and we will study how two variables—the frequency of the stimulus word and of its base-language homophone, and the specific phonetic characteristics of the guest word—can speed up or slow down the isolation of these words.

When one examines the exact isolation position of Type 3 words identified after their acoustic offset (37 percent of them in all), an interesting pattern emerges. Figure 10.4 presents the percentage of words isolated as a function of post-offset position: during the next word (+1), during the word after (+2) or during the last word of the sentence (+3). The post-offset percentages obtained for Type 1 and Type 2 words have been included for comparison. As can be seen, the narrowing-in pattern for Type 3 words is quite distinct. Whereas the few Type 1 and

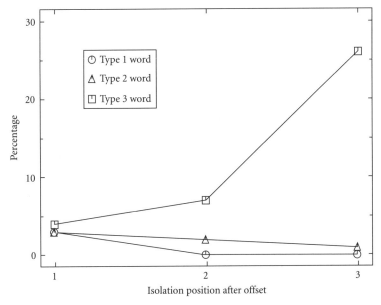

FIGURE 10.4 Percentage of words isolated as a function of word type (Types 1–3) and post-offset position: during the next word (+1), during the word after (+2), or during the last word of the sentence (+3)

Type 2 words that remain to be identified are rapidly isolated in positions +1 and +2 (where the phonetic, lexical, syntactic, and semantic information all help in the choice of the appropriate word), the isolation pattern of Type 3 words is quite different. Instead of being characterized by a slightly negative function, as in the case of Type 1 and 2 words, the isolation function is positive and rather steep between positions +2 and +3: 4 percent of the words are isolated in the first position, 8 percent are isolated in the second position, and as many as 26 percent are identified in position +3. This is a clear indication that in the case of words with base-language homophones, the isolation of the words will need to await the appropriate semantic information. This information is presented primarily in the last word of the sentence (position +3). For example, "cordes" in the sentence "knot ces deux cordes" (knot these two ropes) tells the listener that the word is not "note" (to note) but "knot". Another example involves "bières" in the sentence "cool ces deux bières" (cool these two beers); before hearing "bières" many listeners thought they were dealing with "coule" (to sink) and not "cool". It was only on hearing the last word of the sentence that a number of subjects modified their proposal. We should note that more borrowings were isolated in position +3 than code-switches (31 percent as compared to 21 percent); this is because more borrowings remained to be isolated after their acoustic offset (67 percent as compared to 48 percent) and the semantic information carried by the noun in position +3 allowed some of them to be "caught" before the end of the sentence.

A second point of interest concerning Type 3 words is the apparent role played by two variables in the isolation process: the frequency of the stimulus word and of its base-language homophone, and the specific phonetic characteristics of the word. As regards the first variable, we were struck by the rather large variability in the isolation results of Type 3 words (see Figure 10.1)—some were isolated before word offset, others were isolated during the next word or words, and some were never isolated at all. For example, when we combined the code-switching and borrowing results, we found that "peel" was isolated eleven times out of a possible twelve before its acoustic offset, and "sit" was isolated eight times before its offset. On the other hand, "knot" was always isolated after its offset (ten times during the last noun of the sentence), and "cool" failed to be isolated on five occasions. We hypothesized that this large variability in the isolation results could perhaps be explained by the frequency "pull" of the English words and of their French counterparts. If an English word is more frequent than its French homophone, then the guest word (pronounced as a borrowing or a code-switch) should be identified quite quickly. If, on the other hand, the English word is less frequent than its French homophone, then the listener should be "pulled" towards the French item, and the stimulus word should be isolated later (or maybe even never).

To test this hypothesis, we obtained subjective frequency ratings for the Type 3 English words in their infinitive form (e.g. "to peel", "to fool", "to knot", etc.) and for their homophonic counterparts (e.g. "piler", "fouler", "noter", etc.). In all, eleven French-English bilinguals were asked to rate the sixteen words on a scale of 1–10, where 1 corresponded to very infrequent words and 10 corresponded to very frequent words. This subjective estimation approach was used because there are no published frequency lists for the bilingual population we used and because Segui *et al.* (1982) have reported a very high correlation (in the order of 0.85–0.90) between subjective and observed word frequency. The ratings were averaged over participants and an "English pull index" was calculated for each word pair by subtracting the rating of the French word from the rating of the English word. The eight indices obtained in this way ranged from positive values, indicating a higher frequency for the English item, to negative values, indicating a higher frequency for the French item. Thus, for example, the pull index for "pick" was 1.18 because the estimated frequency for "pick" was 8.64 and that for "piquer" was 7.46; the index for "knot" was −3.46 because the estimated frequency for "knot" was 4.27 and that for "noter" was 7.73, etc. These eight indices were then correlated with the corresponding mean position indices of the words averaged over code-switches and borrowings (as we indicated in the first part of this section, individual indices ranged from 1 for words isolated before their acoustic–phonetic offset to 3 for words that were never isolated).

The resulting Pearson correlation coefficient was a surprisingly high −0.77 ($p < 0.05$): the stronger the pull towards the English word, the earlier the isolation point and, conversely, the stronger the pull towards the French homophone, the later the isolation. Two examples will illustrate this relationship. The pull index for "peel" was a rather high 2.45 ("to peel" is more frequent than "piler") and the position index for the word was therefore quite low (1.17; 11 of the 12 tokens of the word were isolated before offset). On the other hand, the pull index for "knot" was −3.46 ("to knot" is less frequent than "noter") and the position index for the word was therefore quite high (2.09; 11

of the 12 cases were isolated after offset). We conclude from this that the ease with which a Type 3 word is identified depends, in part, on the "frequency pull" of that word. If the word is more frequent than its base-language homophone, then it will be identified quite early on. If, on the other hand, the base-language homophone is more frequent, then the identification of the guest word will be delayed.

A second factor which appears to affect the isolation of Type 3 words, but for which we only have a small amount of evidence, is the specific phonetic characteristics of the words. A side analysis showed that code-switches that are "flagged" phonetically as being English— such as "pick"(cs) or "wrap"(cs)—are isolated relatively early, whereas their borrowing counterparts—"pick"(b) and "wrap"(b)—are isolated late. On the other hand, code-switches that are not as strongly marked phonetically, such as "knot"(cs), are isolated in the same amount of time as their borrowing counterparts, such as "knot"(b).

We can conclude this first part by stating that the two variables under examination—word type and the language phonetics of a word—both play a role in the identification of guest words. They do so, however, to different degrees. Word type is a strong variable that accounts for the different isolation points of three types of guest words: words that are marked phonotactically as belonging to the guest-language lexicon only (Type 1 words); words that are not marked in this way, but that only exist in the guest language (Type 2 words); and words that have base-language homophones (Type 3 words). The language phonetics of a word, on the other hand, is a variable that appears to take on some importance mainly when there is an ambiguity concerning the origin of the lexical item, that is, whether it belongs to the base-language or to the guest-language lexicon. And even then, other variables, such as the frequency of occurrence of the guest-language word and of its homophonic counterpart, as well as the phonetic specificity of individual sounds in the guest-language pronunciation, will intervene to increase or decrease the effect of the language phonetics variable.

10.2.2 The word isolation process

The experimental paradigm we have used in this study allows us not only to determine how much of the stimulus word is needed to isolate it, but also to better understand the word-isolation process itself. This is done by analyzing the candidates proposed prior to the isolation point. As in earlier research (Grosjean 1980, 1985a), we will assume that by

examining responses across subjects we can infer the path followed by
the individual listener. We will also assume that the candidates proposed by the subjects on the basis of gated information are similar, in
part at least, to those that would be available were we able to tap into
the word-isolation process as it takes place during online processing
of language. In what follows, we will first illustrate the narrowing-in
process of three exemplars of the guest words used in the study, one for
each of the three types of words. We will then examine in more detail
three aspects of the word isolation process.

Figure 10.5 presents the candidates proposed for the word "snap"
(vertical axis) as the length of the gate increased in duration (horizontal
axis). The top part of the figure presents the candidates proposed for the
code-switched version of the word, and the bottom part the candidates
for the borrowed version. The word offset is marked by a horizontal
dashed line, and the three gates beyond that represent the post-offset
presentations where the stimulus word is presented along with the next
word ("tous"), the next two words ("tous en"), or the next three words
("tous en rythme"). Candidates proposed at only one gate duration
are depicted by a dot; those that are proposed over two or more gates
are depicted by a line. The number of subjects proposing a particular
candidate is represented by the thickness of the line—the more subjects,
the thicker the line. English candidates are written in capitals on the vertical axis and are represented by continuous black lines or bars; French
candidates are written in lower case and are depicted by discontinuous
lines or bars.

A number of interesting points emerge from the figure. The first is
that the two versions of "snap" (which have slightly different total durations) are isolated at very similar points, and much before their offsets.
This simply illustrates what has been stressed so far about Type 1 words:
their initial consonant cluster and their single lexicon membership
allows them to be isolated very early on. A second point that emerges is
that the candidates at the very early gates are more often French words
than English words: of the twenty-four candidates proposed at the first
two gates of the two versions, thirteen are actual French words and four,
for which no actual lexical item is written (we have marked this with
a Ø), are thought to be of French origin. This is further evidence of
the base-language (assimilation) effect studied by Grosjean and Soares
(1986): when listening to a base language, the listener "expects" (or is
primed for) the next item to be in the base language, unless "warned"
otherwise. The third point is that the phonotactic (consonant cluster)

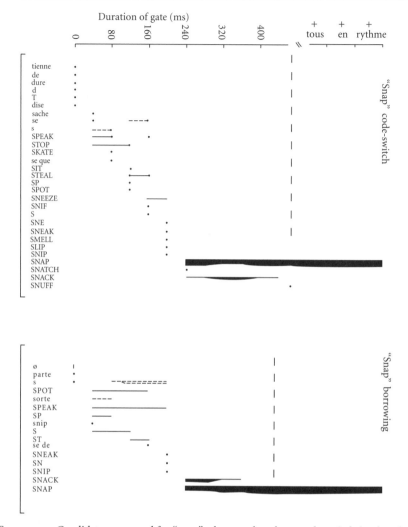

FIGURE 10.5 Candidates proposed for "snap" when produced as a code-switch (top) and as a borrowing (bottom)

Note: The candidates are listed on the vertical axis and the duration of the gates are marked along the horizontal axis (gates were incremented by 40 ms). The dashed vertical line marks the offset of the words; after that point the gates were incremented by a full word. Candidates proposed at only one presentation are depicted by a dot; those proposed over two or more presentations are depicted by a continuous line. The number of subjects proposing a particular candidate is represented by the thickness of the line—the more participants, the thicker the line. English candidates are written in capitals and are represented by continuous black lines; French candidates are written in lower case and are depicted by discontinuous white lines or bars.

information that is given in the early gates leads to a rapid decline of French candidates and a rapid increase of English candidates that begin with /s/ plus a consonant. The fourth point is that the decline of French candidates is not quite as rapid for the borrowing as for the

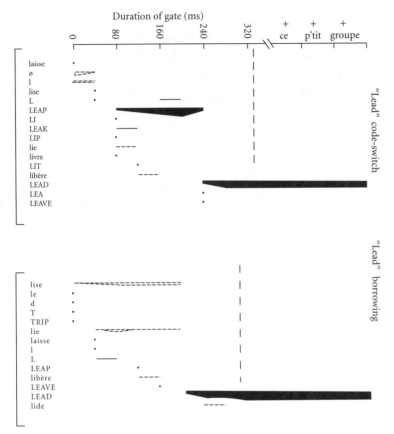

FIGURE 10.6 Candidates proposed for "lead" when produced as a code-switch (top) and as a borrowing (bottom)

Note: See the caption of Figure 10.5 for details.

code-switch: 40 percent of all erroneous candidates (tokens) are French words when the borrowing is presented, as compared to 28 percent for the code-switch. This word phonetics effect is only momentary, however, and as soon as enough acoustic–phonetic information has specified the word "snap" (whether it is pronounced in English or French), it is isolated by the majority of subjects.

Figure 10.6 presents the narrowing-in patterns for the two versions of the Type 2 word "lead". Like "snap", both versions of the word are isolated before their offset, albeit later than the Type 1 word. This early isolation is due to the fact that "lead" belongs unambiguously to the English lexicon and that, by the time the offset is reached, the listener has received enough information to isolate it correctly. The actual isolation points of the two versions are very similar (82 and 77 percent of the way through the word for the code-switch and the borrowing, respectively), but the narrowing-in patterns are quite different. What is especially striking is the rather rapid selection of English candidates in the case of the code-switch (at the third gate, four of the six candidates are already English words) as compared to the maintenance of French candidates when the borrowing is being heard. Overall, 60 percent of the erroneous candidates (tokens) for the code-switch are English words, whereas only 17 percent of the candidates for the borrowing belong to that language.

This difference between the two versions of "lead" is probably due to the distinct pronunciations of the word in the two languages. The initial /l/ in English is very different from its counterpart in French, and this difference is reinforced by the different articulations of English /i/ and French /i/. Thus, when listening to the code-switched version, listeners quickly opt for English words that start with English /li/ (note the "leap" garden path), whereas when listening to the borrowed version, listeners choose French /li/ words (note the "lise" garden path). The cue for French is so strong in the case of the borrowing that one subject actually wrote "lide?" (and circled "F" on the answer sheet). The error was not due to a problem in spelling as the listener switched her guess to "lead" and circled "A" (for "anglais") two gates later. It is interesting to note that despite the early choice of the English lexicon in the case of the code-switch, the isolation of the actual item takes place no earlier in time than when the borrowing is presented. This is because words are isolated when the sequence of sounds allows them to become unique, as we saw above, and this point is reached at about the same time in the two versions of "lead" (the closure of the final /d/ begins 82 percent of the way through the code-switch and 78 percent of the way through the borrowing).

Figure 10.7 presents the candidates proposed for the two versions of the Type 3 word "pick". As is clearly evident, very different narrowing-in patterns emerge from the presentation of the two versions. With the code-switch, after two gates of uncertainty (and hence of French candidates), listeners quickly propose English candidates and then narrow-in very rapidly on the stimulus word. The pattern for the borrowing is quite different. Although some subjects opt for the stimulus word quite early on (it is slightly more frequent than the base-language counterpart "pique"), the acoustic–phonetic cues just prior to word offset force almost all of them to switch over to the French homophone (at the offset, five of the six participants proposed "pique"). In the

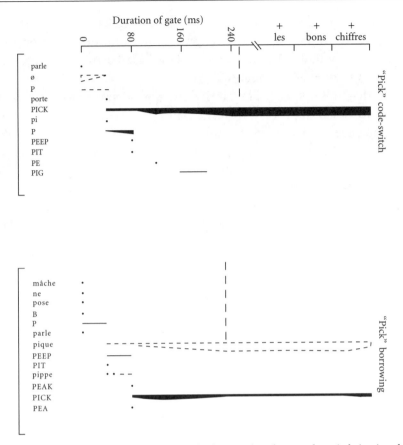

FIGURE 10.7 Candidates proposed for "pick" when produced as a code-switch (top) and as a borrowing (bottom)

Note: See the caption of Figure 10.5 for details.

post-offset presentations, the rather constraining context created by the last word of the sentence—"chiffres" in "les bons chiffres" ("the right numbers")—only made one of the five participants change over to "pick" at the last gate; the remaining four ended the gating sequence with the erroneous candidate "pique". This is a clear example of how Type 3 words can be affected by the language they are said in: if they are pronounced in the base language and neither the context nor the frequency pull is in favor of the guest language, then there is every chance that the base-language homophone will be accessed; if, on the other hand, they are pronounced in the guest language, then the listener will often opt for the correct word. This difference in access strategies will be even greater when the phonetics of the two versions of the word are clearly those of the respective languages, as was the case for "pick"

(French and English /pi/ are pronounced quite differently). Of course, not all guest words are cued so strongly for one or the other lexicon and, in that case, both the stimulus word and the base-language homophone may be proposed as candidates.

In what follows we will examine in more depth three aspects of the word isolation process: the candidates proposed at the early gates, the language of erroneous candidates before word isolation, and the erroneous candidates of Type 3 words in the post-offset presentations.

The early candidates

Figure 10.8 presents, for the three types of words used in the study, the average number of English candidates proposed during the first five gates (the results are averaged over borrowings and code-switches). Two clear patterns emerge from Figure 10.8. The first is that subjects show a strong base language effect at the beginning of the word. It is rare that they propose an English candidate at the first gate (where very little, if any, information concerning the word is presented) and it is only over the next two or three gates, as the phonetic, phonotactic, and lexical information starts arriving, that they begin to propose words from the other lexicon. This finding is very similar to the ones obtained

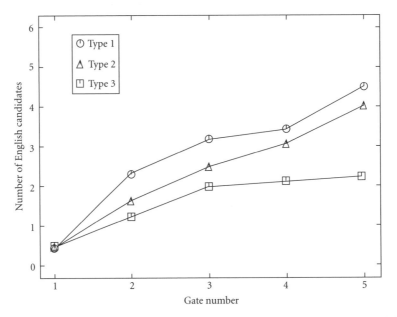

FIGURE 10.8 The average number of English candidates presented as a function of the number of the gate (from the first to the fifth) and the type of word (Types 1–3)

Note: Each point is based on 96 observations.

by Grosjean and Soares (1986), where subjects were given gated non-sense code-switched words in context and had to guess the language of these words. Invariably, during the first two or three gates, subjects thought the language of the word was the context (base) language. This base-language effect (studied in a different manner by Macnamara and Kushnir 1971, and discussed in Chapter 6) could explain why many studies have found some delay in the recognition of code-switched words as opposed to base-language words (see e.g. Soares and Grosjean 1984). In the case of code-switches, listeners may at first search the wrong lexicon, whereas in the case of base-language words they immediately search the correct lexicon.

The second pattern to emerge from Figure 10.8 is that the functions of Type 1 and Type 2 words rise more rapidly than that of Type 3 words. Whereas the early information in the first two types of words indicates that the items are probably English words, the early information of Type 3 words points towards French words (the base-language homophones). Thus, after a short rise in the number of English candidates, the Type 3 function stabilizes and remains low until further information, usually in the post-offset position, "shocks" the participant to switch over to the guest-language lexicon.

An analysis of variance over participants confirms the pattern just described. A main effect was found for position—$F(4,35) = 17.47$, $p < 0.01$—and for type—$F(2,70) = 9.23$, $p < 0.01$—and there was no significant interaction. An *a posteriori* test (Tukey HSD) showed that Type 1 and Type 2 words were not different from one another, but that each was different from Type 3 words ($p < 0.05$). In addition, a significant difference was found between both Type 1 and Type 2 words and Type 3 words at gate number 5 ($p < 0.05$).

In order to determine whether there was an effect of language phonetics over the early gates, separate analyses of variance were conducted (over subjects) for each word type. All three showed a significant main effect for position, but none produced a language phonetics main effect (all three were in the expected direction and the Type 3 analysis was close to showing an effect). We reasoned that the language phonetics effect was probably reduced by the fact that not all words were marked by "strong" phonetic cues when pronounced in English or in French. In order to assess whether this explanation was correct, we conducted a separate analysis of Type 2 words. We took the four words with "strong" phonetic cues, that is those which started with consonants that are very different in English and French (in our case, the consonants /t/ and /l/

in "tease", "lead", "lean", "tag"), and examined the candidates proposed
for these words when said as code-switches and borrowings.

We found that the number of English candidates proposed increases
as more of the word is given, but this increase is different for the
two versions. For the borrowings, the acoustic–phonetic cues at the
beginning of the words (the short VOT for the /t/ or the "clear" /l/, for
example) clearly indicate a French word and thus French candidates
are proposed. It is only at gate 5 that listeners realize that, despite the
unambiguous acoustic–phonetic cues, no French word corresponds to
the phonetic sequence; they then start proposing English candidates.
The pattern for the code-switches is quite different. The early acoustic–
phonetic cues (long VOTs, "dark" /l/) all point to English words and the
number of English candidates, therefore, increases rapidly at each gate.
The lexicon membership information that comes in later only confirms
the correct choice of lexicon made at the beginning. An analysis of
variance conducted over participants confirms these findings. There
is a main effect for position—$F(4,30) = 4.76$, $p < 0.01$—and a main
effect for word phonetics—$F(1,30) = 6.57$, $p < 0.05$—but no interaction. We conclude from this that if a guest word is pronounced very
differently as a code-switch and as a borrowing, then the choice of the
early candidates will be greatly affected. In the case of the code-switch,
listeners will propose candidates from the guest lexicon and will then
narrow-in on the appropriate candidate in that lexicon. In the case of
the borrowing, however, listeners will first start with candidates from
the base language lexicon and then revert to candidates from the guest
lexicon when they realize that no base-language words correspond to
the sequence of sounds being heard.

The language of erroneous candidates

In our examination of erroneous candidates, it appeared to us that
the language in which a guest word was pronounced affected not only
the language of the first candidates proposed in the gating sequence
(especially when the word was pronounced very differently in the two
languages), but also the language of the erroneous candidates all the
way up to the isolation point. If this proved to be correct, the language
phonetics of a word would join the phonotactic configuration of the
word and its lexicon membership in accounting for the language of the
erroneous candidates. In order to test this, we calculated for every word
the percentage of erroneous candidates that were English. To do this we
counted the number of candidate tokens (minus the correct stimulus

TABLE 10.2 Percentage of erroneous candidates that are English when each word type is presented as a code-switch (English) or as a borrowing (French)

Language phonetics of word	Type of word		
	1	2	3
English (code-switch)	51.75	45.38	27.75
French (borrowing)	44.63	31.25	14.75

word candidate tokens) that were proposed up to the last gate of the word (the gate just prior to the first post-offset gate), and calculated the percentage that were English words. (When we had doubts regarding the language identity of a word, as when it is spelled similarly in the two languages, we consulted the language identification answers given by the participants.)

Table 10.2 presents the results averaged over word exemplars. As can be seen, both the type and the language phonetics of the word appear to play a role in the proportion of guest-language candidates proposed during the isolation process. The larger percentage of English candidates is obtained with Type 1 words where both the phonotactics and the single lexicon membership are clear indications that an English word is being presented; an intermediate percentage is obtained with Type 2 words where only the absence of the words in the French lexicon is an indication that they are English words; and the lowest percentage is obtained with Type 3 words where the presence of a base-language homophone leads the listener down a base-language garden path. In addition, in each of the three cases, the percentage of English candidates is larger for the code-switches than for the borrowings, clearly indicating that the language phonetics of the word plays a role in the candidates proposed. An analysis of variance over participants confirms these results. A main effect was found for word type—$F(2,21) = 5.39$, $p < 0.01$—and for word phonetics—$F(1,21) = 4.34$, $p < 0.05$—and there was no interaction.

We conclude from this that, in the early stages of word isolation, the two variables we have been studying (word type and language phonetics) both play a role. It is only in the later stages—the actual isolation of the stimulus word and the total acceptance of the word— that word phonetics loses some of its impact (although not for Type 3 words); as for word type, it continues to play a role throughout the isolation/recognition process.

Type 3 erroneous candidates in the post-offset presentations

Unlike Type 1 and Type 2 words, which were practically all isolated before their acoustic–phonetic offset, as many as 37 percent of Type 3 words were isolated after offset. Given this result, it is interesting to examine the narrowing-in process of Type 3 words when the next word or words were given along with the stimulus word. In what follows, we will examine the erroneous candidates proposed in place of Type 3 stimulus words when the latter were presented in offset positions +1, +2, and +3 words. We classified the 114 erroneous post-offset candidates into one of three categories:

1. Phoneme error candidates, that is candidates which differed from the stimulus words by the addition, omission, or substitution of one or more phonemes (from the same or the other language). For example: "sit"(cs) → "set"; "fool"(cs) → "fourre"; "cool"(cs) → "coure".

2. Segmentation error candidates, that is bisyllabic candidates that blend information from the stimulus word and the word following it. For example: "lease(cs) ce" → "listen"; "knot(cs) ces" → "answer".

3. Homophone candidates, that is candidates that are base language homophones. For example: "knot"(cs) → "note"; "lease"(cs) → "lisse"; "pick"(b) → "pique"; "sit"(b) → "cite".

Table 10.3 presents the percentage of borrowing and code-switching candidates that fall into each of the three categories (note that these results are based on 112 errors—not 114—because two erroneous

TABLE 10.3 Percentage of types of errors made for Type 3 words in the three offset presentations as a function of the language phonetics of the guest word (English or French)

Type of error	Language phonetics of word	
	French (borrowing)	English (code-switch)
Phoneme	6	71
Segmentation	0	13
Homophone	94	16

candidates could not be classified). As can be seen, the types of errors made when listening to borrowings and code-switches in the post-offset presentations are very different. This is confirmed by a highly significant Pearson's Chi Square for proportion computed on raw frequencies—$\chi^2 = 71.7$, $p < 0.01$. As expected, the candidates proposed for a borrowing are primarily base-language homophones. A full 94 percent are the French counterpart of English words: "pile" for "peel"(b), "coule" for "cool"(b), "lisse" for "lease"(b), etc. As for the remaining candidates, 6 percent fall into the phoneme error category and none are in the segmentation error category. From this we infer that if an English cross-language homophone is borrowed into French, and thereby becomes identical to an existing French counterpart, then the listener will assume it is the French word (and will feel quite confident about it). It is only when contradictory semantic information is heard (the last noun in the sentence, in our case) that the listener will be forced to backtrack and to access the English counterpart.

The candidates proposed for Type 3 code-switches reflect a more complex narrowing-in process. Whereas listeners go down the homophone garden path quite systematically with borrowings (and are only "shocked" out of it with later occurring top-down information), such is not the case with code-switches. Only 16 percent of the Type 3 code-switch candidates are base-language homophones; the remaining 84 percent fall into the phoneme error category (71 percent) and the segmentation error category (13 percent). We hypothesize that fewer homophones are proposed with code-switches because the English phonetics of the code-switch enters into (momentary) conflict with the internal representation of the French homophone. (On hearing a Type 3 code-switch, a subject commented that the speaker had an "odd" pronunciation in French!) Given that the homophone garden path is partly closed (but not the French lexicon path—89 percent of all post-offset code-switch candidates are French words), the listener proposes candidates that are phonetically similar (phoneme error candidates) or even candidates that combine information from the stimulus word and the following word (segmentation error candidates). Phoneme substitutions in two different words account for practically all of the phoneme error candidates: in the first, subjects proposed "coure" and not "coule", when presented with "cool"(cs); in the second, they proposed "fourre" and not "foule", when given "fool" (cs). The acoustic–phonetic information of the code-switch and the internal phonological representations of several possible candidates ("cool", "coule", "coure"; "fool", "foule", "fourre") interacted in such a way that neither the stimulus word, nor the French homophone were proposed; it was, instead, a third "compromise" candidate that emerged. (Note that both words were perceived as homophones when presented as borrowings.)

We should stress, finally, that Type 3 code-switches are the only items that fall into the segmentation error category ["knot(cs) ces" → answer; "lease(cs) ce" → "listen"]. These errors, although few in number, reflect once again the difficulties listeners had with words where the language phonetics signaled one lexicon but the base-language context and the presence of a base-language homophone signaled the other lexicon.

In summary, the analysis of the word isolation process has confirmed the importance of the two variables under study. The type of word that is presented affects how early guest-language candidates are proposed and how many there are as compared to base language candidates. As for the language phonetics of the word, it too plays an important role in the early stages of the recognition process: there are proportionally more English candidates when the word is said as a code-switch than as a borrowing, and the candidates of Type 3 words differ greatly in nature depending on their language phonetics. The variable takes on even more importance when guest words are pronounced very differently in the two languages, as we saw with Type 2 initial /t/ and /l/ words. As we noted, the importance of the language phonetics variable is at its highest during the narrowing-in stage; its importance diminishes (at least for Type 1 and Type 2 words) in the isolation and total acceptance stages. Finally, additional evidence was found for the base-language effect: when listeners hear the very beginning of a guest word presented in context, they propose base-language candidates in preference to guest language candidates.

10.3 Elements of a model of guest-word recognition

The results of numerous experiments, and the outcome of much theorizing in current psycholinguistic research, have substantially increased our knowledge of how spoken words are recognized during the online processing of speech. However, this work has been conducted mainly with monolinguals, and thus little is known about how bilinguals recognize spoken words in real time, especially when they are in a bilingual speech mode. A model that can account for mixed language word recognition has yet to be developed, but in what follows we will point to a few of the main features it could have.

The model will have to account for the general effects that have been found in studies of word recognition in monolinguals as well as the effects that are specific to bilingual language processing. Among the general effects we find the following:

1. Low-frequency words take more time to recognize than high-frequency words (Foss 1969; Howes 1957; Rubenstein and Pollack 1963).
2. Words are not always recognized from left to right, from onset to offset (Nooteboom 1981; Salasoo and Pisoni 1985).
3. When words *are* recognized from onset to offset, recognition occurs close to the word's uniqueness point, that is the point in the left to right phonotactic configuration at which the word diverges from other words (Marslen-Wilson 1984).
4. Words in continuous speech are not always recognized one word at a time, that is two words can be recognized simultaneously, or a later occurring word can be recognized before an earlier occurring word (Grosjean 1985a; McClelland and Elman 1986).
5. The syntactic, semantic, and pragmatic contexts of the sentence in which a word occurs affect its recognition (Grosjean 1980; Miller and Isard 1963; Morton and Long 1976; Tyler and Wessels 1983).
6. Various sources of knowledge, such as the listener's knowledge of the world and the rules of the language, also affect the word's recognition (Cole and Jakimik 1978; Marslen-Wilson and Welsh 1978).

It should be noted that existing models of word recognition, such as those of Forster (1976), Marslen-Wilson and Welsh (1978), Morton (1969), and McClelland and Elman (1986) account for a number of these effects, but none accounts for all of them.

In addition to these general effects, the model for bilinguals will need to capture a number of effects found in this study:

1. *The base-language effect.* When a guest word is presented in a base-language context, and only its very beginning has been heard, the candidates proposed are invariably members of the base-language lexicon.

2. *The phonotactic effect.* Words marked phonotactically as belonging to the guest language only (Type 1 words) are recognized sooner and with more ease than words not marked in this way.

3. *The single lexicon effect.* Words that belong solely to the guest lexicon (Type 1 and Type 2 words) are recognized sooner and with more ease than words that do not belong to just one lexicon.

4. *The base-language homophone effect.* Words in the guest-language lexicon that have close homophones in the base language (Type 3 words) are processed with more difficulty than other guest-language words.

5. *The language phonetics effect.* (a) During the narrowing-in stage preceding the isolation of a word, the proportion of guest-language candidates is affected by the language phonetics of the word (i.e. the language it is pronounced in). (b) Strong language phonetic cues will activate the lexicon that contains words characterized by these cues, and thus affect the language of the candidates proposed and, at times, the final isolation point of the appropriate candidates (as with those with cross-language homophones). (c) Cross-language homophones pronounced in the base language (Type 3 borrowings) are isolated later than when they are pronounced in the guest language (Type 3 code-switches), and the nature of the candidates prior to isolation are quite different for the two versions of the words.

6. *The frequency effect for cross-language homophones.* The ease with which a guest language homophone is identified depends on the "frequency pull" of that word as compared to that of its base-language homophone.

Although most existing models of monolingual spoken word recognition could be extended to account for word recognition during mixed speech processing, the type of model that may have the most promise is an interactive activation model, such as the TRACE model proposed by McClelland and Elman (1986). According to this model, language processing takes place through the excitatory and inhibitory interactions of a large number of processing units, each working continuously to update its own activation on the basis of the activations of other units to which it is connected. In TRACE, the units are organized into three levels: features, phonemes, and words. Throughout the course of processing, each unit is continually receiving input from other units, continually updating its activation on the basis of these inputs and, if it is over threshold, it is continually sending excitatory and inhibitory signals to other units. Connections between levels are bidirectional and there is no between-level inhibition (inhibition only exists within one level, between units that are inconsistent with one another). Although neither word frequency nor context effects are at present accounted for by the model, these can be built in quite easily, according to the authors: word frequency can be accommodated in terms of variation in the resting activation level of word units, and contextual influences can be thought of as supplying activation to word units from even higher levels of processing.

How could an interactive activation view of word recognition be modified in order to accommodate word processing in bilinguals, be it in a monolingual or a bilingual speech mode? First, we will assume that bilinguals have two language networks (features, phonemes, syllables, words, etc.) which are both independent and interconnected. They are independent in the sense that they allow a bilingual to speak just one language; they are interconnected in the sense that the monolingual speech of bilinguals often shows the active interference of the other language and that, when bilinguals speak to other bilinguals, they can code-switch and borrow quite readily. This view has long been defended by Paradis (1981, 1986), who proposes that both languages are stored in identical ways in a single extended system, though elements of each language, because they normally appear only in different contexts, form separate networks of connections, and thus a subsystem within a larger system. According to Paradis, bilinguals have two subsets of neural connections, one for each language (each can be activated or inhibited independently because of the strong associations between elements), while at the same time they possess one larger set from which they are able to draw elements of either language at any time.[4]

---

[4] It should be noted that this proposal does not address head-on the question of whether the bilingual has one or two lexicons. The reason is that there probably exist as many experimental studies that find evidence for the one-lexicon view as studies that defend the two-lexicons hypothesis (Grosjean 1982). Unfortunately, however, these studies have often confounded the basic question (one versus two lexicons) with the task employed to examine the question; thus, many of the results obtained have reflected the experimental paradigm and not the underlying reality. In addition, the types of bilinguals used as subjects have varied from one study to another, making any definite statement problematic. The mixed model proposed by Paradis (1981, 1986) is thus not only intellectually appealing but also a nice compromise.

Other assumptions that can be made are the following. In the monolingual speech mode, one language network is strongly activated while the other is activated very weakly; the resting activation level of the units of this other network is therefore very low. In the bilingual speech mode:

1. Both networks are activated but the base-language network is more strongly activated (this accounts for the base-language effect). The resting activation level of the language not being used as the base language (the guest-language network) can be increased or decreased depending on the amount of mixed language (code-switching, borrowing) that occurs during the interaction.

2. The activation of a unit in one network and of its "counterpart" in the other depends on their degree of similarity. Thus, for example, if English /b/ is activated, French /b/ will also be activated (to some extent, at least) as the two consonants are quite similar. On the other hand, the activation of English word initial /p/ will lead to a much lower level of activation of French word initial /p/, as the two consonants are quite different. And when English /r/ is activated, its French counterpart should receive very little activation (apart from some possible top-down lexicon activation due to the fact that the two sounds have the same orthography). Cross-language activation of "counterpart" units concerns phonemes (as we have just seen), but also all other types of units (features, words, etc.).

3. The activation of units (or of a combination of units, such as consonant clusters) that are specific to one language increases the overall activation of that language network and thus speeds up the recognition of the words of that language (this accounts for the phonotactic effect and the language phonetics effect).

4. The activation of a word that is specific to just one language increases the overall activation of that network and thus speeds up the recognition of the words of that language (this accounts for the single lexicon effect).

5. The activation of words that are similar in the two lexicons will normally slow down the recognition of the guest-language word (this explains the cross-language homophone effect). But the frequency pull of the two homophones (reflected in their different resting activation levels), and the language phonetics of

the input, will interact with the recognition process of the guest word to speed up or slow down the access of that word (this accounts for the Type 3 word frequency and language phonetics effects).[5]

Much work needs to be done to refine this interactive activation view of the recognition of words in bilinguals. In particular, we need to think about which connections—between and within language networks—are inhibitory and which are excitatory. As we learn more about such models in general, and as more experiments on bilingual mixed speech are conducted, changes will be brought to the model. What is encouraging at this point though is that such a view does away with the switch or monitor mechanism that has been proposed by a number of researchers (Macnamara 1967; Obler and Albert 1978; Penfield 1959) and discussed by others (Grosjean and Soares 1986; Paradis 1980). According to proponents of the switch or monitor mechanism, its role is to tell the processing system which language is being spoken so as to direct the incoming signal to the processors of the appropriate language. The evidence for this mechanism is mainly based on studies which have shown that it takes bilinguals more time to process mixed speech than monolingual speech. But this evidence is both insubstantial and indirect. It is not because bilinguals may process code-switches more slowly than base-language words that one can conclude that there is a language switch/monitor involved in the processing; the delay could be due to numerous other factors (see Grosjean and Soares 1986). In addition, the proponents of the mechanism do not address pertinent questions such as: Is the switch/monitor an essential part of language

[5] An anonymous reviewer asks whether the results reported in the study cannot help distinguish between two models of bilingual lexical organization and access—on the one hand, two distinct lexicons, one of which is searched before the other; on the other hand, only one lexicon which contains a number of different acoustic features detectors which are abstract enough to discriminate between many of the different allophones that are distinct in the two languages. According to the reviewer, an interaction between the structural variable (word type) and the output variable (language phonetics) could be interpreted as evidence for a single system. Unfortunately, the data cannot help choose between these two views because a significant interaction was found in the isolation point results (see Figure 10.1 and the statistics that pertain to it), but none was observed in the confidence rating data (results that were obtained in the study but that are not reported here for lack of space). The reviewer asks to what extent we need to postulate truly distinct networks. We should point out that the view that we have adopted (based on Paradis 1981, 1986) does not defend the independence position; rather it proposes a mixed model—"separate" networks of connections which belong to a single extended system.

processing or does it "fall out" of the processing? If the former, at what stage does it come in—during the acoustic to phonetic mapping of the speech sounds or after this mapping? The data and the model we have presented do not prove the absence of a language switch or monitor, they simply show that the processing system can do without it, and that language decisions (e.g. was that word English or French?) can simply emerge from the process. Having heard a particular sound, syllable, or word, we can then make the metalinguistic statement that Language X or Language Y is being spoken. That the system needs to make this decision in order to process the incoming signal is highly unlikely.

We have shown in this study that the recognition of guest words is a highly complex process. Only further research using different paradigms, materials, and bilinguals with different pairs of languages will allow us to assess the validity of what we have proposed. The challenge for the psycholinguist interested in bilingual language processing will remain, for many years to come, to understand how processing in mixed language takes place so rapidly and so efficiently despite, as we have seen, many intricate underlying operations.

11

The Léwy and Grosjean BIMOLA Model*

Bilinguals, that is, those people who use two or more languages (or dialects) in their everyday lives, have been the object of much psycholinguistic research in recent years. Many studies have been concerned with representational issues, such as the internal organization of the bilingual's lexicon (Schreuder and Weltens 1993), but fewer have examined the processes which underlie the perception and production of language. In addition, it is predominantly written language that has been explored rather than speech (but see Cutler *et al.* 1992; Hernandez *et al.* 1994; etc., for studies in this modality). This state of affairs is surprising if one takes into account the fact that bilinguals spend more time speaking than they do writing and that, when speaking, they have to process both monolingual utterances in their two (or more) languages and mixed utterances that contain code-switches and borrowings. For instance, in the two sentences

(1) Ça m'étonnerait qu'on ait *pitched* autant que ça

(2) Ça m'étonnerait qu'on ait PITCHÉ autant que ça
     "I would be surprised if one had pitched that much"

the listener has to process in what is predominantly a French sentence (French is the base language) the English word "pitched". This guest word is said as a code-switch in the first sentence (it is not integrated into French) but as a borrowing in the second sentence (where it is adapted phonetically and morphologically into French).

* This chapter, written by Nicolas Léwy and François Grosjean, is a slightly revised version of, "A computational model of bilingual lexical access", which was written in 1996 and has remained unpublished. Parts of the paper are based on the first author's Master's thesis. The research was supported in part by Grant 12-33582.92 from the Swiss National Science Foundation. I wish to thank Nicolas Léwy for his permission to reproduce the document here.

A model of bilingual language processing will have to explain how bilinguals process utterances that are monolingual and bilingual (i.e. mixed). At the level of lexical access, a fair amount of experimental research has been conducted to understand how bilinguals recognize guest words (see Grosjean 1997a for a review), but the computational component of this research has been neglected. In this chapter, therefore, we will present a computational model of bilingual lexical access (BIMOLA) that is under construction and that is based on interactive activation networks. We will first discuss the kind of effects that this model has to account for. We will then present a general overview of the model and discuss a number of its characteristics. Finally, we will assess the model as it stands currently.

11.1 What does a model of bilingual lexical access have to account for?

Bilinguals are competent but specific speaker-hearers who find themselves at various points along a situational continuum which induce different language modes (Grosjean 1982). They are in a monolingual language mode when listening to monolinguals who know only one of their languages, and they are in a bilingual language mode when they are listening to other bilinguals who share the same two languages and who mix them either by code-switching or by borrowing. In this mode, it is generally assumed that one language serves as the base language and the other is the guest language. The monolingual and bilingual language modes can be regarded as two endpoints with bilinguals choosing intermediary positions on the language mode continuum depending on such factors as the speaker, the topic, the setting of the conversation, etc.

A model of bilingual lexical access will have to account for word recognition in these various language modes. In the monolingual language mode, it will need to account for well-established effects such as frequency, uniqueness point, etc. (see Frauenfelder and Tyler 1987, for a review). It will also have to explain the fact that the bilingual's inactive language may play a role in monolingual word recognition. In the bilingual language mode, in addition to these effects, the model will have to capture a number of specifically bilingual effects proposed by Grosjean (1988; see also Li 1996). Among these we find: (1) the base-language effect (the first candidates proposed for a guest word presented in a base-language context are invariably members of the base language); (2) the unit similarity effect (a unit in one language, e.g. a phoneme, which shares properties with a unit in the other language will be activated when that unit is presented); (3) the phonotactic effect (guest words marked phonotactically as belonging to the guest language are recognized with more ease than words not marked in this way); (4) the language phonetics effect (prior to the identification of a guest word, the proportion of guest-language candidates is greater for code-switches than for borrowings); (5) the base-language homophone effect (guest words that have close homophones in the base language are processed with more difficulty than other guest words); and (6) the cross-language homophone frequency pull effect (the ease with which a guest-language homophone is identified depends on the frequency of that word as compared to the frequency of its base-language homophone).

11.2 General presentation of the model

The formal framework of interactive activation networks (McClelland and Rumelhart 1981) has produced a number of models of cognitive processes (see e.g. McClelland and Elman's 1986 TRACE model of spoken word recognition). A model of bilingual lexical access, strongly inspired by TRACE, was first proposed by Grosjean (1988). We have since extended this verbal version, elaborated its computational specifications and have implemented it in Oberon (Reiser and Wirth 1992). The model is now called BIMOLA (Bilingual Model of Lexical Access) and its architecture is presented in Figure 11.1.

As can be seen, BIMOLA consists of three levels of nodes which use localist representations: features, phonemes, and words. The feature level nodes are shared by the two languages whereas the phoneme and word nodes are organized according to the subset hypothesis proposed by Paradis (1989), that is, independently (each language is represented by a subset of units) but also as one large system (both subsets are enclosed in a larger set). At both the phoneme and word levels, units can have close or distant neighbors, which are depicted in the figure by their spatial proximity and how dark they are. At the word level, frequency is accounted for by node pre-activation and is depicted by the size of the units. Phoneme nodes are duplicated over time, whereas word nodes are not. Between-level connections consist of bottom-up and top-down activation. Feature-to-phoneme activation is based on a metric space of phonemes defined by a cross-language grading system of similarity between the feature values of the target and those

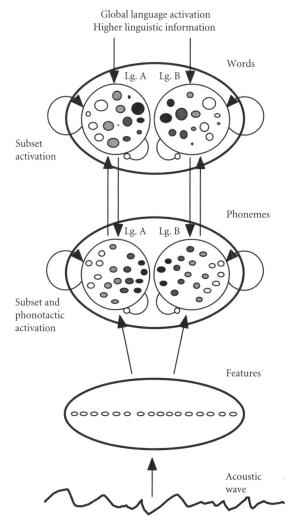

FIGURE 11.1 A visual representation of BIMOLA—a bilingual model of lexical access

of the candidate phonemes. Phoneme-to-word and word-to-phoneme activation occurs between word nodes and the phoneme nodes they are made up of. Words also receive top-down pre-activation based on external information about the listener's language mode and higher linguistic information. Within-level connections involve subset activation, phonotactic activation, and lateral inhibition. Subset activation and lateral inhibition are present at both the phoneme and word levels, and they operate within a language only. Phonotactic activation, on the other hand, is present at the phoneme level only and is based on distributional properties of word-initial segments. All connections can be turned on or off. The language pair that has been implemented is English and French, but the model is meant to be a general bilingual model and hence independent of language pair.

11.3 Specific characteristics

We will focus our attention in this section on four characteristics of the model which we consider important: shared features, metric space of phonemes, within-language excitation, and the status of inhibition.

11.3.1 Shared features

Because most feature systems are monolingual (see e.g. Chomsky and Halle's (1968) "The Sound Pattern of English" (SPE) and recent proposals such as Shillcock *et al.* 1992), we had to construct our own bilingual feature system which we based on SPE for English and Dell (1985) for French. Our combined inventory of English and French phonemes, to which we have added a number of allophonic variants, consists of 43 consonants, 26 vowels, 6 glides, and 8 diphthongs (83 sounds in total). We use three types of features: binary features (as used in traditional phonology), ternary features (with a medium value of 0.5), and multi-valued features (ranging from 0.0 to 1.0 in steps of 0.1). In addition to rearranging some of the original features in Chomsky and Halle and Dell, we propose three new features to represent length, aspiration (for consonants), and instability (for vowels and diphthongs). In all, sixteen features are included in our feature matrix.

11.3.2 Metric space of phonemes

Our bilingual feature matrix provides a measure of distance between sound pairs and hence defines a metric space of phonemes. This is an abstract space in which a phoneme can have close or distant neighbors. The following metric function is used:

$$dist = \rho(x, y) = \sum_i |x_i - y_i| w_i$$

where the distance between phonemes x and y is a linear sum of feature value differences, some of which are weighted with a correction factor ($w_i > 1$) in order to standardize the distributions of distances within vowels and consonants. Figure 11.2 presents the distances calculated between French /b/ and a number of other sounds in the two languages. Close neighbors are French /d/ (distance = 1.2), French /g/, and English

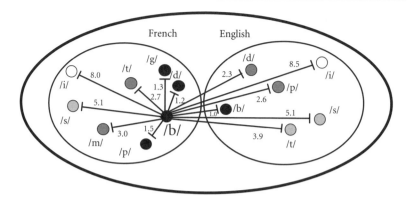

FIGURE 11.2 Distances calculated between French /b/ and a number of sounds in the two languages. Close neighbors are grouped together and are depicted with dark circles; distant neighbors are more spread out and are depicted with clearer circles

/b/, somewhat distant neighbors are English /d/ and /p/, and distant neighbors are French and English /s/ and /i/.

Like TRACE, we accept strings of phonemes as mock speech input and convert them directly to bottom-up activations based on the proximity between the phoneme that is currently being specified in the feature nodes and the candidate phonemes. The distance is converted to a feature-to-phoneme activation in the following way:

$$A = 1 - \frac{dist}{maxdist} = 1 - \frac{\rho(x, y)}{\max\limits_{(x,y)} \{\rho(x, y)\}}$$

where *maxdist* is the maximum distance over all pairs of sounds. (In our phoneme space, the maximum distance is 11.9, and corresponds to the distance between English /tʰ/ and French /ɔ̃/.) Thus, for example, whenever French /b/ is specified at the feature level, the phoneme node representing French /b/ receives a maximum activation of 1.00, French /d/ receives 0.90, English /p/ 0.78, French /s/ 0.57, English /i/ 0.29, etc.

11.3.3 Within-language excitation

The activation levels of the two language networks are set initially through top-down pre-activation and are changed thereafter by means of various dynamic mechanisms that involve within-language excitation. The initial settings correspond to a particular position on the language mode continuum. In the monolingual language mode, the base-language network is strongly activated whereas the guest-language network is only very weakly activated. In the bilingual language mode, both language networks are activated but the base language is activated

a bit more. Two types of dynamic mechanisms can change the activation level of the networks. First, between-level mechanisms allow
for bottom-up and top-down excitation. The bottom-up mechanism
maps the activation of the lower layer units onto the next layer units
which are connected to them (it projects the sensory input onto higher
levels of linguistic abstraction) and, by doing so, it also maps information about the language currently being spoken. Similarly, the top-
down mechanism maps language information to lower levels. In both
cases, language network self-excitation emerges as a by-product of these
processes. Second, there are two types of lateral, within-level, dynamic
mechanisms (these are relatively rare in IA models). One is a subset
excitatory mechanism which captures the idea that, if a word in a given
language is activated, it is probable that it is that language which is being
spoken. Thus, each word sends a small positive signal to the other words
in the same language. The more words in a language that are active,
the more these signals will be exchanged, and therefore the greater the
activation of the word subset as a whole. (This mechanism also functions at the phoneme level.) The other lateral mechanism is a phonotactic, between-phoneme, excitatory mechanism in which first-position
consonants excite second-position consonants in English more than in
French so as to reflect the statistical difference between word-initial CC
configurations in these languages (as reported by Delattre 1965, among
others). Through these various excitatory mechanisms, we can do away
with a language node as proposed by the BIA model of bilingual visual
word recognition (Grainger and Dijkstra 1992; Van Heuven *et al.* 1998).
There is no empirical evidence that such a node exists, nor do we know
how this node is created when a new language is learned. In our model,
network activation is distributed over all the nodes of a language and
hence a specific node dedicated to this purpose does not need to be
postulated.

11.3.4 The status of inhibition

As we have seen, our model has many excitatory mechanisms. Obvi-
ously, this leads to many candidates being activated, one of which will
ultimately have to win. It is generally accepted that competition plays
an important part in lexical access (see Altmann 1990) but opinions
diverge on how to instantiate it. It can be done through a decision
process (e.g. Marslen-Wilson 1987) or through lateral inhibition (e.g.
McClelland and Elman 1986; Norris 1994). Whereas computational

reasons clearly favor lateral inhibition (McQueen *et al.* 1995), little experimental proof of its psycholinguistic reality has been proposed apart from analogies being drawn with other domains of cognition where inhibitory processes play a part (Dagenbach and Carr 1994). The issue of lateral inhibition becomes even more complex when one is dealing with bilingual processing. The question is whether units (words or phonemes) should inhibit units that belong to their own subset only or whether they should inhibit all units, within and between languages. Basing our approach on the subset hypothesis which favors language specific inhibition, on TRACE, and on computational ease, we decided that units within a level would inhibit one another but only within a language. There is no cross-language inhibition in our model as compared to the BIA model. This is a parsimonious solution as only half as many links are necessary (and even less for three or more languages).

11.4 A first assessment of the model

The architecture of our model is now implemented and we are in the process of fine-tuning the connection weights and enlarging the lexicons. A first assessment can already be made based on its current status. As concerns general aspects of word recognition, the model accounts for both the frequency effect and the uniqueness point effect. In addition, like TRACE, it allows for words to be recognized from their middle or from their end. As concerns the representation of time, the model has followed a solution that is slightly different from that of TRACE. Instead of duplicating all nodes over time, it only duplicates phonemes. This preserves connectionist resources but it does have the disadvantage of not being able to deal with continuous and misaligned word recognition.

We have made sure that the model can replicate the bilingual effects proposed by Grosjean (1988). The base-language effect is obtained by means of the various within-language excitatory mechanisms (bottom-up, top-down, subset activation, etc.), which allow for the base-language network to be more strongly excited and hence for early candidates to come from the base language. The unit similarity effect is instantiated by the activation of a phoneme in one language and of its "counterpart" in the other language based on their distance in the metric space of phonemes. As concerns the phonotactic effect, we have a built-in phoneme-level mechanism which favors consonant clusters in a particular language. The language phonetic effect is made possible

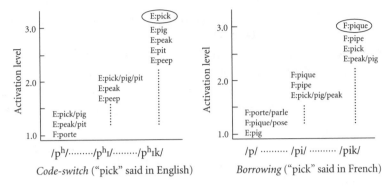

FIGURE 11.3 Candidates activated when the word "pick" is said as a code-switch (left) or as a borrowing (right). Only frequency pre-activation and bottom-up activation are on

by the bottom-up and the subset excitation mechanisms. Finally, the base-language homophone effect results in delayed identification of guest words that have a close homophone in the base language as both candidates are strongly activated. However, the differing frequency pull of the cross-language homophones (reflected in their different pre-activation levels) and the language phonetics of the input will influence the recognition process and speed up or slow down the access.

To show the behavior of the model as it stands today, Figure 11.3 presents two examples which illustrate frequency pre-activation and bottom-up activation (the other mechanisms are turned off). As can be seen, the candidates proposed are quite different for the two versions, that is when "pick" is said as a code-switch (in English therefore) and as a borrowing (in French). Note that the latter is a homophone with French "pique" (to prick). There is a larger proportion of English candidates for the code-switch and of French candidates for the borrowing as predicted by the language phonetics effect. The borrowing is processed with difficulty (the cross-language homophone "pique" is preferred) although "pick" is helped by the frequency pull effect ("pick" is more frequent than "pique" and therefore more pre-activated). The final outcome for the borrowing is the erroneous proposition of "pique" but this could be modified if the model took into account semantic information.

Conclusion

We have described in this paper a computational model of lexical access which has been strongly inspired by the interactive activation framework (TRACE in particular), and which has the task of accounting for processing in the bilingual's different language modes. Its various architectural characteristics such as its set of shared features, its metric space of phonemes, its dynamic mechanisms of within-language excitation, etc., allow it to account for a number of effects found in experimental studies of monolinguals and bilinguals. We are currently fine-tuning the free parameters and incorporating larger lexicons. In addition, we plan on comparing the model's behavior to that of the BIA model, which has been developed for visual word recognition and which is different in a number of ways from ours (e.g. the presence of a language node, many inhibitory connections, etc.). Finally, we hope to integrate our model into a larger model of bilingual language processing which would cover both perception and production.

PART V
Biculturalism, Bilingualism, and Deafness

Introduction

This part contains two chapters. Chapter 12 is a short introduction to the bicultural person and has been included to accompany the chapter that follows. First, the bicultural is characterized as someone who takes part, to varying degrees, in the life of two or more cultures, who adapts, at least in part, to these cultures, and who combines and blends aspects of the cultures. Then a number of points are discussed such as becoming bicultural, cultural dominance, and the lack of coextensiveness between bilingualism and biculturalism. The chapter ends with a discussion of how biculturals choose to identify with the cultures they belong to. Based on a number of factors, some identify with just one culture, some reject both cultures, and some identify with the two cultures.

Chapter 13, "The Bilingualism and Biculturalism of the Deaf", contains three parts. In the first, what it means to be bilingual in sign language and the oral (majority) language is explained. Similarities with hearing bilinguals are discussed (diversity, attitude towards one's bilingualism, the complementarity principle, as well as language mode) as are differences (the lack of recognition of Deaf people's bilingual status, the maintenance aspect of this kind of bilingualism, the difficulty for certain skills to be acquired fully, and the bilingual mode Deaf bilinguals find themselves in most of the time). The second part examines the biculturalism of Deaf people: like hearing biculturals, they take part, to varying degrees, in the life of two worlds (the Deaf world and the hearing word), they adapt their attitudes, behaviors, languages, etc., to each of the two worlds, and they combine and blend aspects of the two. The decisional process they go through in choosing a cultural identity is discussed and the difficulties met by some subgroups—hard-of-hearing, oral deaf, late deaf, even some hearing people who have close ties with the Deaf world—are examined. The chapter ends with a discussion of the Deaf child and why it is so important for him/her to be able to grow up bilingual in sign language and the oral language. The role of both languages is pointed out and it is argued that pursuing solely an oral approach puts the child at risk cognitively, linguistically, and personally.

12

The Bicultural Person: A Short Introduction*

Even though one sees the term "bicultural" almost as often as the word "bilingual"—in the title of educational programs, in state or federal laws, on the cover of books, etc.—one knows much less about biculturalism than about bilingualism. And yet many people are bicultural, although they are probably not as numerous as bilinguals, and many of the "advantages" or "disadvantages" of bilingualism are often linked to biculturalism and not to bilingualism.

Before attempting to define the bicultural person, it is important to explain what we mean by culture. When one examines books on ethnology, ethnography, and anthropology, one is struck by the diversity of definitions that relate to this term. Different schools of thought stress different aspects such as the behavior of individuals, their cultural knowledge (social facts and rules, customs, beliefs, etc.), their cultural identity, the organization of networks (social, economic, political), etc. For our purpose here, culture reflects all the facets of life of a group of people: its organization, its rules, its behaviors, its beliefs, its values, its traditions, etc. As humans, we belong to a number of cultures (or cultural networks): major cultures (national, linguistic, social, religious, etc.) and minor cultures (occupation, sport, hobby, etc.). Thus, we are all, in a sense, "multicultural" even if we have not come into contact with another major culture, in the same way that the monolingual speaker is in some way "multilingual" due to the fact that he/she changes language styles, repertoires, and levels when going from one situation, or one speaker, to another.

What is interesting is that some cultures, mainly minor cultures, are complementary (it is permissible to belong to several or all of these

* This short introduction to the bicultural person is based in part on Grosjean, F. (1983). "Quelques réflexions sur le biculturalisme", *Pluriel* 36: 81–91.

at the same time) whereas others, mainly major cultures, are often mutually exclusive (belonging to one and the other is not as acceptable, and thereby raises problems). Thus, it was practically impossible during the Second World War to be both Japanese and American just as it is currently difficult to be both a Kosovar Serb and a Kosovar Albanian, an Estonian and a Russian, or a Tutsi and a Hutu. In what follows, we will concentrate on people who belong to two major, often mutually exclusive, cultures but we will keep in mind that we all belong to numerous cultural networks which are complementary. Working at the level of major cultures makes isolating the characteristics of the bicultural person easier just as it is easier to examine the bilingual who knows and uses two quite distinct languages. Once this is done, one can move on to examine other cases such as what it means to belong to two or more minor cultures or what it means to be tricultural.

12.1 Characterizing the bicultural person

Biculturals are characterized by at least three traits:

1. They take part, to varying degrees, in the life of two or more cultures. An example would be young Chinese people who live in Great Britain and who take part in the life of their Chinese community as well as that of the English majority. Other examples are Cuban immigrants in the United States, and North Africans in France.

2. They adapt, at least in part, their attitudes, behaviors, values, languages, etc., to these cultures. This is a dynamic aspect whereby biculturals choose different components of life based on the cultural situation at hand. So, to take the example of the young Chinese people in Great Britain, they will adapt their language and their behavior depending on whether they are with other Chinese people or with members of the English majority.

3. They combine and blend aspects of the cultures involved. Certain characteristics (attitudes, beliefs, values, behaviors, etc.) come from the one or the other culture whereas other characteristics are blends based on these cultures. In this latter case, it becomes difficult to determine the cultural origin of a particular characteristic since it contains aspects of both cultures. An example is the body language of a bicultural, which is often a blend of the body language of culture A and of culture B. Figure 12.1 depicts both the combination and blending aspects of this third trait.

FIGURE 12.1 The bicultural's combination of two cultures (A and B) along with the blending component

We observe, therefore, in biculturals an aspect that is adaptable and controllable (which allows them to adapt to the situation, context, etc.) and an aspect that is more static; here, the blend of features from the two cultures (illustrated by the dark rectangle in the figure) is always present and cannot be adapted to given situations. This is important as it means that not all behaviors, beliefs, and attitudes can be modified according to the cultural situation the bicultural person is currently in. A French-German bicultural, for example, blends aspects of both the French and of the German culture and cannot, therefore, be 100 percent French in France and 100 percent German in Germany, however hard he or she tries. This aspect is a differentiating factor between bilingualism and biculturalism: bilinguals can usually deactivate one language and only use the other in particular situations (at least to a very great extent), whereas biculturals cannot always deactivate certain traits of their other culture when in a monocultural environment.

Other criteria have been put forward to define the bicultural person but they are questionable and we will not add them to the three characteristics given above. One relates to cultural identity and the fact that one should be able to identify fully with both cultures. But, as we will see below, many biculturals only identify with the one or the other culture, or sometimes do not identify with either, even though they are bicultural. A second criterion is accepting one's bicultural status. However, one often meets biculturals who do not do so. This is also the case for bilinguals who recognize using two languages in their everyday lives but who often do not accept being labeled as bilingual (see Chapter 2). A third criterion is the manner in which a person has become bicultural. Some maintain that one must have grown up with both cultures to be defined as bicultural when, in fact, there are many ways of becoming bicultural (see the following section). A fourth criterion concerns how well one knows the two cultures. Some maintain that one must know them perfectly to be called bicultural. But this is rarely the case, just as knowing two languages perfectly is quite rare. Biculturals develop their bicultural competency based on need and amount of contact with each of their two cultures. The balanced bicultural who is fully integrated in the one and the other culture is as rare as the balanced bilingual who is equally fluent in all skills of her two or more languages. Most biculturals have a cultural dominance due to the fact that they have greater contact with, and spend more time in, one culture than in the other, but this in no way makes them less bicultural. Among other criteria mentioned we find: feeling at ease in both cultures (it is unfortunately not always the case); being recognized as bicultural (this is even rarer); being accepted fully by the two cultures in question; etc. All of these criteria are questionable, or even wrong, which explains why we have not added them to the three defining characteristics given above.

12.2 Additional points

A number of additional points need to be made.

Becoming bicultural

People become bicultural because they are in contact with two (or more) cultures and have to live, in part at least, within these cultures. This can take place in early childhood (e.g. a child is born within a bicultural family or has daily contact with two cultures from birth) and can continue throughout life. Hence, we find children who belong to a cultural minority who come into contact with a second culture in school, adolescents anchored in a culture who pursue their studies in another culture, adults who emigrate to another country for various reasons (economical, political, religious, etc.), and even second and third generation immigrants who rediscover their home culture after having grown up in the majority culture. A psycho-ethnology of biculturalism will need to study the cognitive and social processes involved in becoming bicultural and account for similarities and differences in how one becomes bicultural depending on age, cultural origin, the causes of cultural contact (e.g. migration and schooling), and so on.

Cultural dominance

It is rare that the two cultures have the same importance in the life of the bicultural. One culture often plays a larger role than the other. One can therefore speak of "cultural dominance" just as one speaks of "language dominance" in bilinguals. This dominance is illustrated in Figure 12.2.

| Dominance of culture A | Dominance of culture B |

FIGURE 12.2 The bicultural's dominance in one of two cultures

When a person takes part in the life of three cultures—the person is thereby tricultural—the same phenomenon happens: one culture may be more important than another, as is illustrated in Figure 12.3.

Biculturalism and bilingualism

Bilingualism and biculturalism are not necessarily coextensive. Many people are bilingual without being bicultural (members of diglossic communities, inhabitants of countries that have lingua francas or different school languages, etc.) and, similarly, some people are bicultural without being bilingual (e.g. members of a minority culture who no longer know the minority language but who retain other aspects of the culture). Thus, the Egyptian who uses both dialectal Arabic and classical Arabic is bilingual but not bicultural, and the Kenyan who knows and uses a local language, Swahili, and English is trilingual but rarely bi- or tricultural. Inversely, the Jewish French person who identifies with, and participates in, the life of French culture as well as Jewish culture is not always bilingual; this is also true of many Basque people who participate in both Basque and French cultures. Different countries can have a common language without having a common culture (take Great Britain, Canada, and the United States) and hence the biculturalism that develops due to movement between these cultures is not accompanied by bilingualism.

The extensive research that has been undertaken on bilingualism can help us understand biculturalism, a topic that has been studied far less. Take, for example, the bicultural's cultural behavior: Which aspects of a culture are adaptable to a specific cultural situation and which are not?

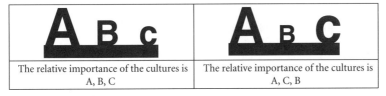

| The relative importance of the cultures is A, B, C | The relative importance of the cultures is A, C, B |

FIGURE 12.3 The relative importance of the three cultures in a tricultural

How do biculturals interact with the two (or more) cultures to which they belong? How do they switch from one culture to another, etc.? The language mode model of bilingual behavior (see Chapter 4), modified to take into account culture, may be a means of obtaining answers to these questions. Like bilinguals, bicultural people often find themselves at various points along a situational continuum that requires different types of behavior. At one end, they are in a monocultural mode and must deactivate as best they can their other culture. (Note though that the blending component in biculturals makes this practically impossible, hence the frequent presence of cultural interferences.) At the other end of the continuum, they are with other biculturals like themselves with whom they use a cultural base within which to interact (the behaviors, attitudes, beliefs, etc., of one culture) and into which they bring in the other culture in the form of cultural switches and borrowings when they choose to do so.

Rarer instances of biculturalism

We will mention two here. The first concerns biculturals who no longer take part in the life of one of their two cultures (e.g. after having migrated). Are they still bicultural? It should be noted that the same question can be asked of bilinguals who, for various reasons, no longer use one of their two languages. In fact, these biculturals remain passive biculturals because they continue to combine and blend aspects of the two cultures. It is only when the characteristics of just one culture take over completely (but do they ever?) that one could say that the person has reverted back to monoculturalism. The second case relates to people who identify with two cultures but who only participate in the life of one culture, and who do not combine and blend aspects of two cultures (e.g. third generation Ukrainian-Americans who call upon their Ukrainian origins but who do not interact with that culture and have no trace of it). This is a weak form of biculturalism which is quite common in a world that is seeking out its roots.

12.3 Identity and biculturalism

One aspect of biculturalism that is crucial, especially for bicultural children and adolescents, concerns the acceptance of one's bicultural identity. To be able to reach the point of saying, "I am bicultural, a member of culture A and of culture B", a bicultural person often has to go through a long, and sometimes trying, process. This process takes into account the perception of members of cultures A and B, and integrates a number of other factors. As concerns the perception of others, it is based on factors such as kinship, language, physical appearance, nationality, education, attitudes, etc. The outcome is in the form of a double categorization which can produce similar results (X is judged to belong solely to culture A or to culture B) or contradictory results (X is categorized as a member of culture A by members of culture B and as a member of culture B by members of culture A). Not only is this latter categorization contradictory but it is often absolute in the sense that cultures do not readily accept that a person can be part of their culture and also part of another culture. The attitude is either "You are A" or "You are B" but rarely "You are both A and B".

Faced with this double, sometimes contradictory, categorization, biculturals have to reach a decision as to their own cultural identity. To do this they take into account the perception of the two cultures and bring in other factors such as their personal history, their identity needs, their knowledge of the languages and cultures involved, etc. The outcome of this long process, shown in Figure 12.4, is a decision to identify solely with culture A, to identify solely with culture B, to identify with neither culture A nor culture B, or to identify with both culture A and culture B. Of course, the optimal solution for biculturals is to opt for the fourth alternative, that is to accept their biculturalism, but unfortunately many biculturals, influenced as they are by the

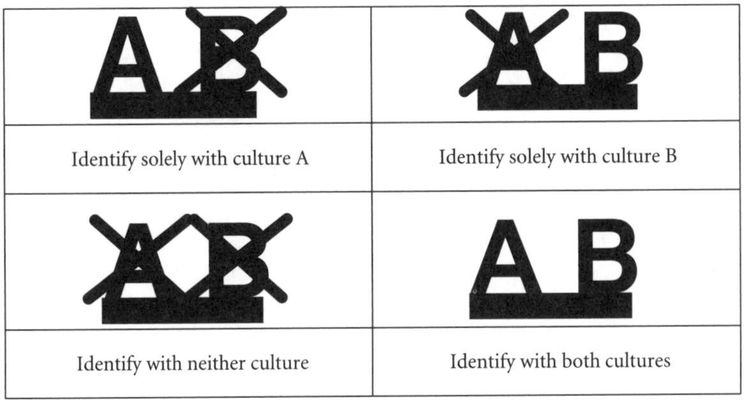

A̶B̶	X̶A B
Identify solely with culture A	Identify solely with culture B
X̶A̶B̶	A B
Identify with neither culture	Identify with both cultures

FIGURE 12.4 The four outcomes of the bicultural's identity process

categorization of the cultural groups they belong to, often choose one of the first three alternatives (A, B, neither A nor B). These solutions are seldom satisfactory as they do not truly reflect the bicultural person and they may have negative consequences later on. Those who choose either culture A or culture B (that is, turn away from one of their two cultures) are often dissatisfied with their decision, and those who reject both cultures feel uprooted, marginal, or ambivalent. With time, and after a long, sometimes arduous process, many biculturals come to terms with their biculturalism. The lucky ones can belong to a new cultural group (see the many hyphenated groups in North America) and most others, who are isolated biculturals, will ultimately navigate with a certain degree of ease between and within their two or more cultures.

13

The Bilingualism and Biculturalism of the Deaf*

This chapter contains three parts. In the first, what it means to be bilingual in sign language and the oral (majority) language is explained and similarities with hearing bilinguals and differences are discussed. The second part examines the biculturalism of Deaf people: like hearing biculturals, they take part, to varying degrees, in the life of two worlds (the Deaf world and the hearing world), they adapt their attitudes, behaviors, languages, etc., to both worlds, and they combine and blend aspects of the two. The decisional process they go through in choosing a cultural identity is then discussed and the difficulties met by some groups are examined. The chapter ends with a discussion of the Deaf child and why it is so important for him/her to be able to grow up bilingual in sign language and the oral language. The role of both languages is pointed out and it is argued that pursuing solely an oral approach puts the child at risk cognitively, linguistically, and personally.

13.1 The Deaf bilingual

It is only in recent years that the bilingualism of the Deaf has started to be studied (on this topic, see, among others, Ann 2001; Battison 1978; Bernstein *et al.* 1985; Bishop and Hicks 2005; Davis 1989; Grosjean 1986, 1992, 1996; Kannapel 1974; Kettrick and Hatfield 1986; Lee 1983; Lucas 1989; Lucas and Valli 1992; Stokoe 1969). The bilingualism present in the Deaf community, also called bimodal bilingualism, is a form of minority language bilingualism in which the members of the community acquire and use both the minority language (sign language) and the majority language in its written form and sometimes in its

* This chapter was written specifically for the book and is influenced by several papers I have written on the bilingualism and biculturalism of the Deaf. See the Appendix for references.

	Oral language		Sign language	
Modality	Production	Perception	Production	Perception
Spoken	Speaking	Listening Lip reading (+/− cued speech)	XXXXXXX	XXXXXX
Written	Writing	Reading	Writing sign language	Reading sign language
Sign	Producing a signed version	Perceiving a signed version	Signing	Perceiving Signing
Finger spelling	Producing and perceiving finger spelling			

FIGURE 13.1 The languages, skills, and modalities involved in the bilingualism of the Deaf

spoken or even signed form. (We will use the labels "sign language", and "majority language" or "oral language" throughout as we do not want to restrict ourselves to the case of one language pair, e.g. American Sign Language (ASL) or British Sign Language (BSL) and English; French Sign Language (FSL; LSF) and French; etc.) Sign language bilingualism can, of course, also involve the knowledge and use of two or more different sign languages but this form of bilingualism is less common in the Deaf community and has been the object of fewer studies. Given the definition of bilingualism used throughout this book, notably in Chapter 2, most Deaf people who sign and who use the majority language (even if only in its written form) in their everyday lives are indeed bilingual.

13.1.1 Similarities with hearing bilinguals

Deaf bilinguals share many similarities with hearing bilinguals. First, they are very diverse. Depending on their degree of hearing loss, the onset of deafness (prelingually or postlingually), the language(s) used in childhood, their education, their occupation, their social networks, etc., they have developed different knowledge and use of their languages (sign language and the majority language), as well as a diversity in the skills concerned (production and perception) in the various language modalities involved (spoken, written, signed, etc.). Figure 13.1 presents the languages, skills, and modalities present in sign-oral language bilingualism. Thus, in the spoken modality, we find the production of the oral language (speaking) and its perception (listening, lip reading); of

Modality	Oral language		Sign language	
	Production	Perception	Production	Perception
Spoken			XXXXXX	XXXXXX
Written				
Sign				
Finger spelling				

FIGURE 13.2 The configuration of a Deaf bilingual who is dominant in sign language

course, there is no spoken version of sign language, hence the crosses
in Figure 13.1. In the written modality, we find writing and reading the
oral language (in its written form), as well as writing and reading sign
language (see recent efforts to allow sign language to be written such as
Valerie Sutton's SignWriting). In the sign modality, we have the production of signs (signing) and the perception of signs (perceiving signs)—
these correspond to the two right-hand cells in the figure—as well as
the production and perception of signed versions of the oral language
(left-hand cells) which include "manually coded systems" (e.g. Seeing
Essential English in the USA, Sign Supported English in the UK) as
well as pidgin sign language (PSE), the sort of language used by hearing
people who have not fully mastered the true sign language of the Deaf.
Finally, finger spelling concerns both languages (oral language and sign
language) since it finds its source in the oral language (it is a visual
representation of the spelling of the oral language) but it is also integrated in various ways into sign language. Were we to assess different
Deaf people's competencies according to this table, we would find a lot
of diversity. Figures 13.2 and 13.3 show just two possible configurations.
The degree of knowledge and use in a language skill is shown by the
degree of shading in a cell; the lighter the shading, the less knowledge
and use, the darker the shading, the more knowledge and use. Thus, in
Figure 13.2, we have represented the configuration of a Deaf bilingual
who is dominant in sign language (both the real sign language of the
community and the PSE version used by and with hearing people). The
person has fairly good knowledge (and use) of the oral language in its
written form but less so of the same language in its spoken form. On the
other hand, the Deaf bilingual represented in Figure 13.3 is dominant
in the oral language (note the rather dark shading for the spoken and

Modality	Oral language		Sign language	
	Production	Perception	Production	Perception
Spoken			XXXXXX	XXXXXX
Written				
Sign				
Finger spelling				

FIGURE 13.3   The configuration of a Deaf bilingual who is dominant in the oral language

written modalities) whereas his/her knowledge and use of sign language is slightly less developed. In both cases, we have active sign-oral language bilinguals but with different configurations. We should note that the diversity found in Deaf bilinguals is no different in its extent to that found in hearing bilinguals with two or more oral languages; they too are very diverse in their knowledge and use of their languages.

A second similarity with hearing bilinguals is that most Deaf bilinguals do not judge themselves to be bilingual. In some countries, some Deaf people may not be aware that sign language is different from the majority language, and in general many Deaf do not think they are bilingual because they do not fully master all the skills that accompany the oral language (or, at times, the sign language). This is a well-known phenomenon found among many bilinguals, be they hearing or Deaf, who have a tendency to evaluate their language competencies as inadequate. Some criticize their mastery of language skills, others strive their hardest to reach monolingual norms, others still hide their knowledge of their "weaker" language, and most simply do not perceive themselves as being bilingual even though they use two (or more) languages regularly.

A third similarity between Deaf and hearing bilinguals is that both are governed by the complementarity principle (see Chapter 3). They use their languages for different purposes, in different domains of life, with different people. Some domains are covered by both languages but others are specific to a language.

Finally, like hearing bilinguals, Deaf bilinguals find themselves in their everyday lives at various points along the language mode continuum. When they are communicating with monolinguals, they restrict themselves to just one language and are therefore in a monolingual mode. They deactivate the other language and remain, as best they can, within the confines of the language being used (for example, a written form of the majority language). At other times, Deaf bilinguals find themselves in a bilingual mode, that is with other bilinguals who share to some extent their two languages—sign language and the majority language—and with whom they can mix their languages. Here, depending on such factors as their knowledge of the two languages, the person(s) being addressed, the situation, the topic, the function of the interaction, etc., they choose a base language—usually a form of sign language (the natural sign language of the community or a signed version of the spoken language). Then, according to various momentary needs, and by means of signing, finger spelling, mouthing, etc., they bring in the other language in the form of code-switches or borrowings. The result has been called contact signing (Lucas and Valli 1992).

13.1.2 Differences with hearing bilinguals

Although the bilingualism of the Deaf shares many characteristics with that of hearing people, a number of aspects are specific to the Deaf group. First, until recently there has been little recognition of Deaf people's bilingual status. They are still seen by many as monolingual in the majority language whereas in fact many are bilingual in that language and in sign. It is only in the last 40 years or so that sign language has been recognized as a language in an increasing number of countries, allowing thereby the recognition of the bilingual status of Deaf bilinguals. Second, Deaf bilinguals, because of their hearing loss, will remain bilingual throughout their lives and from generation to generation. They have a need for sign language as a means of communication among themselves (and with some hearing people) but also of the majority language for life outside the Deaf community (extended family, work, etc.). This maintenance of bilingualism is not always found with other minority groups who, over the years, can shift to a form of monolingualism (either in the majority language, the minority language, or in some other form of language).

A third difference, again due to hearing loss, is that certain language skills in the majority language may never be fully acquired by Deaf bilinguals. The skill that immediately comes to mind is speaking. Many Deaf people either do not speak very well (despite numerous hours spent practicing this skill) or refuse to use their voice because of the negative feedback they have received from hearing people. A fourth difference concerns language mode. Although movement takes place along the language mode continuum, Deaf bilinguals rarely find themselves at the monolingual signing end. Thus, unless they are communicating with a monolingual member of the majority language (via the written modality, for example), they will most often be with other bilinguals and will thus be in a bilingual language mode. The final difference is that the patterns of language knowledge and use appear to be somewhat different, and probably more complex, than in spoken language bilingualism. When a sign language bilingual uses sign language with one interlocutor, a form of signed spoken language with another, a mixture of the two with a third, a form of simultaneous communication (sign and speech) with a fourth, etc., the diverse behaviors are the result of a number of complex factors:

1. The bilingual's actual knowledge of the sign language and of the majority language. This competence, in terms of linguistic rules and lexical knowledge, can often be characterized in terms of how prototypical it is.

2. The channels of production: manual (sign, finger spelling), oral (speech, mouthing with or without voice), written, etc. Some of these channels are more appropriate to one of the two languages (speech or writing for the majority language) but others, such as the sign modality, can be used, to some extent at least, for one or the other language. How these modalities are combined during the interaction is of particular interest.

3. The presence of the other language in a bilingual language mode. As we saw above, either one language is chosen as the base language and the other language is called in at various points in time or a third system emerges that combines the two languages (what Lucas and Valli, 1992 call contact signing). In both cases, the languages can interact in a sequential manner (as in code-switching) or in a simultaneous manner (signing and mouthing) and can involve various modalities. Recently, Emmorey *et al.* (2003) have shown that, when in a bilingual mode, bilingual speakers who are fluent in sign language and the oral language (in their case, ASL and English), rarely code-switch, that is stop talking and switch to signing. Instead, most code-blend, that is produce signs simultaneously with English words. For example, when uttering the word "jump", they also make the corresponding sign. Nouns and verbs are the most involved in blends and the vast majority are found to be semantically equivalent in the two languages (as in the above example).

13.2 The Deaf bicultural

We noted in Chapter 12 that biculturalism has been studied far less than bilingualism and this is true also in the domain of Deafness. Several works have dealt with Deaf culture (see Padden and Humphries 1988 for the United States; Ladd 2003 for England; Delaporte 2002 for France), but they have concentrated on what it means to be a member of a Deaf community and less on the Deaf who are also members of the hearing world. And yet, Deaf biculturals are numerous since they live in, and interact with, both worlds.

13.2.1 The biculturalism of the Deaf

In Chapter 12, we used three traits to characterize biculturals:

1. They take part, to varying degrees, in the life of two or more cultures.
2. They adapt, at least in part, their attitudes, behaviors, values, languages, etc., to these cultures.
3. They combine and blend aspects of the cultures involved. Certain characteristics (attitudes, beliefs, values, behaviors, etc.) come from the one or the other culture whereas other characteristics are blends based on these cultures.

There is little doubt that many Deaf people meet these three criteria: they live in two or more cultures (their family, friends, colleagues, etc. are either members of the Deaf community or of the hearing world); they adapt, at least in part, to these cultures; and they blend aspects of these cultures. Of course, such factors as deafness in the family, age of onset of deafness, degree of hearing loss, type of education, etc., may lead some Deaf people to have fewer contacts with the hearing world while others have more (their bicultural dominance can thus differ), but it is nevertheless true that most Deaf people are not only bilingual but also bicultural.

As Ladd (2003: 225) writes, even if Deaf communities have developed *bona fide* cultures, their existence inside majority cultures, together with the large numbers of Deaf people being brought up within hearing families, has led to some degree of biculturalism. A small study by Salamin (2003) in the French speaking part of Switzerland confirms this. She interviewed sixteen Deaf people, all members of the Deaf community, and found that 75 percent of them have been in continuous contact with the hearing world since their childhood and that they share their time between the two worlds: family, work, sport, and some friends belong to the hearing world whereas other friends, associations, and some family members belong to the Deaf world. Of course, most Deaf people are Deaf dominant biculturals in that they identify primarily with the Deaf community. In Salamin's study, for example, 50 percent of the respondents indicated that the Deaf world occupied most of their time, 25 percent indicated both worlds, and the rest indicated the hearing world.

The bicultural Deaf become very adept at adapting to the two worlds. Delaporte (2002) gives an interesting example taken from French Deaf culture (it is probably no different in other Deaf cultures). When meeting hearing people, the Deaf will adapt to hearing norms. They will shake their hand, instead of greeting them with a gesture; they will introduce themselves simply, and not refer to their life history (parents, schooling, etc.) as they would with other Deaf people; to attract their attention, they will not touch them as they would do with other Deaf; they will keep a greater physical distance between them than they would with other Deaf, and they will not fixate them for too long; and, when leaving, they will shorten the farewells. According to Salamin (2003), 75 percent of the Deaf she interviewed stated that they had no difficulties adapting behavior such as this to the group with which they are interacting.

We should point out two differences between the biculturalism of the Deaf and of the hearing. First, many Deaf still acculturate into the Deaf culture—what will often become their dominant culture— relatively late (in adolescence, even adulthood). Their first years are mainly spent in the hearing world (recall that 90 percent of the Deaf have hearing parents). This is different to what normally happens in the hearing world where acculturation takes place early into the bicultural's dominant culture and then into the second culture. A second difference relates to dominance. Most Deaf biculturals are usually dominant in one culture, the Deaf culture, whereas hearing biculturals vary as to their dominance (culture A, culture B, or a balance between the two cultures).

13.2.2 Identity and biculturalism in the Deaf

We saw in Chapter 12 that biculturals choose to identify and belong to one culture only (culture A or culture B), to neither culture, or to both cultures. We also saw that it is this latter possibility which is the optimal solution for them as it truly reflects their bicultural entity. This choice between alternatives is also true of Deaf people. During the long, and sometimes arduous, process involved, Deaf people have to take into account a number of factors such as their type and degree of deafness, their ties with their family, their education, their network of friends, their competence in sign language and in the oral (majority) language, their acceptance or not by the two worlds, their own identity needs, etc. They finally arrive at a decision: to identify with just one of the two cultures, to identify with neither, or to identify with both. For example, Salamin (2003), in her study, found that a little more than half of those interviewed (56 percent) identified with both worlds whereas 38 percent identified with the Deaf world only; the rest felt they were "in-between".

The decisional process involved in choosing a cultural identity is complex and, unfortunately, not everyone manages to finally identify with the two worlds. Here are a few examples. Hard-of-hearing people usually have ties with both worlds but often feel rejected by one of the two worlds—and sometimes by both. Some decide to identify solely with the Deaf world; they learn sign language and they cut off the ties they have with their hearing past. Others do not feel welcome in the Deaf world, despite the effort they make to learn sign language and to acculturate into this world; hence they finally choose to live in the hearing world only. Others feel estranged from both worlds and manage as best they can. Another example concerns the oral deaf who discover the Deaf world and sign language later on in life. They too become bicultural but it is often done by rejecting their hearing past and taking refuge in the Deaf world. How many have symbolically switched off their hearing aids or their implants in order to mark their new identity? And yet, given their past, they ought to be able to identify with both worlds, even if they now prefer the world of the Deaf. A third example concerns the late deaf who have to make a real effort to learn sign language and integrate themselves into the Deaf world. But they are too often categorized as oral deaf by other Deaf and hence marginalized. A last example concerns a number of hearing people involved with Deafness. Among these, we find the hearing children of Deaf parents, sign-speech interpreters, signing parents of Deaf children, signing friends of the Deaf, etc. Even though they are objectively members of both the hearing and of the Deaf world (see the three biculturalism criteria given above), many hesitate to identify themselves overtly with Deaf culture. And yet, they too should be able to claim their membership in both the hearing and the Deaf world.

This said, things are slowly changing. The final word is given to Emerton (1996), a Deaf sociologist, who writes that Deaf people are far more heterogeneous than they were before. He claims that no longer can one categorize people as hearing or deaf, oral or manual. He continues by stating (1996: 143, 144), "People who grew up in the 'oral tradition' now sign openly without embarrassment. Hard-of-hearing people no longer have to pretend that they are either hearing or deaf.... Many deaf people today are, as a result of their upbringing, a blend of two cultures and they choose to participate in both worlds. They are bicultural. The new social identity of Deaf people is now or will soon be a bicultural identity.... The bicultural deaf (or hearing) needs to be able to move back and forth between these groups with a minimum of interference and without the concomitant discomforts of marginality".

13.3 The Deaf child[1]

At the time of writing this book, few Deaf children in the world receive a bilingual upbringing from their earliest years on. Most are brought up "oral" although some few do come into contact with sign language in their youth or adolescence, usually by unofficial means (e.g. contact with other Deaf children). Many attain adulthood without having been given the chance of mastering both sign language and the majority language. In the following section, we will explain why it is so important for Deaf children to be able to grow up bilingual in sign language and the oral language.

13.3.1 Why Deaf children need to be bilingual

There is widespread agreement among parents, caretakers, language pathologists, and educators that language is central to Deaf children's lives, and more precisely that:

- Deaf children should have complete access to language as early as possible. This said, not all agree unfortunately on how to give language to children: some advocate a strictly oral approach aided with hearing aids and implants whereas others defend a bilingual

---

[1] This section is based in part on the short paper I wrote, "The right of the deaf child to grow up bilingual" which appeared in four publications in English: *Deaf Worlds*, 1999, 15 (2): 29–31; *WFD NEWS*, 2000, 13 (1): 14–15; *The Endeavor*, 2000, 1: 28–31; *Sign Language Studies*, 2001, 1 (2): 110–14. It has also been translated into some thirty different languages and has been published in numerous countries around the world.

approach (sign and speech) in which sign language plays an important role in the early years of the Deaf child (see below).

- Deaf children should develop ties and communicate fully with their parents and family members as soon as possible. Language is central when establishing and solidifying social and personal ties between children and their parents. Deaf children must be able to communicate with them by means of a natural language as soon, and as fully, as possible. It is with language that much of the parent–child affective bonding takes place.

- Deaf children need to develop a number of cognitive abilities in infancy. Again language is central here. It is through language that children develop cognitive abilities that are critical to their personal development. Among these we find various types of reasoning, abstracting, memorizing, etc. The absence of language can have major negative consequences on children's cognitive development.

- Deaf children must acquire world knowledge, and this is done in large part through language. As they communicate with parents, caretakers, and family members, information about the world will be processed and exchanged. It is this knowledge, in turn, which serves as a basis for the activities that take place in school. It is also world knowledge which facilitates language comprehension; there is no real language understanding without the support of this knowledge.

- Deaf children should be able to communicate fully with the surrounding world. Like hearing children, they must be able to communicate with those who are part of their lives (parents, brothers and sisters, peers, teachers, various adults, etc.). Communication must take place at an optimal rate of information in a language that is appropriate to the interlocutor and the situation.

- Finally, for some (including this author), Deaf children should be allowed to acculturate into two worlds, the world of the hearing and the world of the Deaf. Through language, they must progressively become members of both the hearing and of the Deaf world. They should be able to identify, at least in part, with the hearing world which is almost always the world of their parents and family members (90 percent of deaf children have hearing parents). But they should also come into contact as early as possible with the world of the Deaf, their other world. It is important that Deaf children feel comfortable in these two worlds and that they be able to identify with each as much as possible.

Despite these agreed upon goals (with the exception of the last one which some do not agree with), bilingualism and biculturalism have not usually been the route followed by those involved in nurturing and educating Deaf children. The reasons for this are of two kinds: misunderstandings concerning bilingualism and sign language, and the lack of acceptance of certain realities by many professionals working with the Deaf, most notably members of the medical world.

Misunderstandings concerning bilingualism are many. First, we still find the outdated view that bilingualism is the near-perfect mastery of two or more languages (see Chapter 2). And yet, we now know that bilingualism is simply the regular use of two or more languages and that fluency is rarely equivalent in the bilingual's languages. Second, it is still thought that bilingualism is a rare phenomenon even though we now know that half the world's population (or even more) is bilingual. Third, there is still the idea that bilingualism has negative consequences on the linguistic and cognitive development of children. And yet, there is very real evidence that the brain is made to be multilingual; instead of being a problem, bilingualism in children is a linguistic and social enrichment.

The misunderstandings concerning sign language are also numerous. For example, despite all the research done on the subject in the last forty years (in the United States, England, Scandinavia, etc.), some still think that sign language is not a real language. And yet, it has been shown, over and over again, that sign language has all the linguistic characteristics of a human language. Another myth is that sign language will hinder the development of the oral language in Deaf children. As we will see below, the reverse is true; it helps the acquisition of the oral language, directly and indirectly, in addition to being a natural means of communication for the Deaf child. Finally, it has been maintained by some that if one defends sign language, one must be opposed to the oral language. In fact, most of those who defend sign language want the Deaf child to also acquire an oral language to the highest level of fluency.

As concerns realities that are difficult to accept, three come to mind. The first is that most Deaf people belong to two worlds: the hearing world and the Deaf world. Deaf children are destined therefore to be bilingual and bicultural. The second is that a strictly oral education often fails to meet its aims: many Deaf children do not develop their oral language sufficiently for unhindered communication with the outside world; they often drop behind in school and do not acquire the kind of knowledge they need in adult life. The third reality is that counting solely on technological progress and oral monolingualism is gambling on the development of the Deaf child, and it is ignoring the child's need to belong to the two worlds that are his or hers, to varying degrees at least.

We will argue below that a sign language–oral language bilingualism is the only way that Deaf children will meet their many needs, that is, communicate early on with their parents, develop their cognitive abilities, acquire knowledge of the world, communicate fully with the surrounding world, and acculturate into the world of the hearing and of the Deaf. This bilingualism involves the sign language used by the Deaf community and the oral language used by the hearing majority. The latter language will be acquired in its written, and if possible, in its spoken modality. Depending on the child, the two languages will play different roles: some children will be dominant in sign language, others will be dominant in the oral language, and some will be balanced in their two languages. In addition, various types of bilingualism are possible since there are several levels of deafness and the language contact situation is itself complex (four language modalities, two production and two perception systems, etc.). This said, most deaf children will become bilingual and bicultural to varying degrees. In this sense, they will be no different from about half the world's population that lives with two or more languages. Just like other bilingual children, they will use their languages in their everyday lives and they will belong, to varying degrees, to two worlds—in this case, the hearing world and the Deaf world.

13.3.2 The role of sign language

Sign language must be the first language (or one of the first two languages) acquired by children who have severe hearing loss. It is a natural, fully developed language that ensures complete and full communication. The role it can play is of several kinds:

- As can be seen in Figure 13.4, sign language triggers the Human language capacity which then influences oral language development. (The arrows that emanate from the sign language box are much thicker than the arrows that come from the oral language box, indicating a better flow in the former case.) A well triggered Human

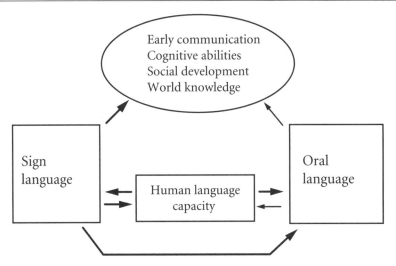

FIGURE 13.4 The strong role of sign language (shown by thicker arrows) in triggering the Deaf child's Human language capacity and hence in helping in the development of the oral language

language capacity (Chomsky's Language acquisition device or LAD) will prevent later language pathologies, if it takes place early enough. As Fischer (1998) writes, our capacity for language is innate but it must be triggered by exposure to actual language early enough. Children with severe delays in their first language acquisition (feral children, retarded children, etc.) have problems acquiring various aspects of language after the critical period, which Fischer defines as that age after which not everybody can learn particular aspects of a language, especially without explicit instruction. Since the notion of a critical period applies to any natural language, oral or sign, Fischer stresses that children or adults who acquire sign language late have more difficulties than those who acquire it early. We also know that children exposed to sign language from birth show better acquisition of the oral language: their Human language capacity has been triggered early enough and it can, in turn, help with the acquisition of the oral language.

• Sign language will allow early and full communication between Deaf children and their caretakers—and this at an optimal rate of communication. We know that, despite many years of spoken language therapy, the speech of Deaf children and adolescents is often labored, slow, and not fully intelligible. In addition, listening or lip reading is rarely optimal; it is very tiring and involves a lot of guessing. Signing, on the other hand, allows communication to take place fully and at an optimal rate.

- Another benefit of sign language is the important role it plays in the deaf child's cognitive and social development as well as the acquisition of world (encyclopedic) knowledge. This is depicted in the top part of Figure 13.4 by a thicker arrow coming from the sign language box. Knowledge of the oral language is usually so poor that it cannot play the same role as sign language.

- Sign language will also facilitate the acquisition of the oral language, be it in its spoken or written modality. It is well known that a first language that has been acquired normally, be it oral or signed, will greatly enhance the acquisition and use of a second language. This is depicted by the arrow in the bottom part of Figure 13.4 linking sign language and the oral language directly. Sign language can be used overtly in class to clarify difficulties, explain exercises, summarize texts and stories, etc. It is also a means of communication to talk about language (metalanguage). With sign language, and through the use of "chaining" (sign–meaning–finger spelling–orthography), a link between a concept and the written language word can be made. In addition, various sign language characteristics and processes can be shown to have equivalents in the oral language (e.g. the notion of a lexical item, simple sentence structures, anaphora); discourse skills developed when signing (organizing a narrative or a story, participating in a debate, etc.) can be transferred to the written modality; and, finally, various forms of sign writing can be used to introduce children to the written representation of the oral language. We should note that Strong and Prinz (1997), among others, have found a significant positive correlation between ASL (American Sign Language) competency and English literacy levels, that is, as ASL skills increased, so did English literacy.

- A final contribution of sign language is that it allows Deaf children to acculturate into the Deaf world (one of the two worlds to which he/she belongs) as soon as contact is made with that world.

Knowing sign language is a guarantee that Deaf children will have mastered at least one language fully in their youth. As stated above, despite considerable effort on the part of Deaf children and of the professionals that surround them, and despite the use of various technological aids, it is a fact that many Deaf children have great difficulties producing and perceiving an oral language in its spoken modality. Having to wait several years to reach a satisfactory level that might never be attained, and in the meantime denying the Deaf child access to a language that meets his/her immediate needs (sign language), is basically taking the risk that the child will fall behind in his/her development, be it linguistic, cognitive, social, or personal.

13.3.3 The role of the oral language

Being bilingual means knowing and using two or more languages. The deaf child's other language will be the oral language used by the hearing world to which he/she also belongs. This language, in its spoken and/or written modality, is the language of the child's parents, brothers and sisters, extended family, future friends, employers, etc. When those who interact with the child in everyday life do not know sign language, it is important that communication nevertheless takes place and this can only happen in the oral language. It is also this language, in its written modality mainly, that will be an important medium for the acquisition of knowledge. Much of what we learn is transmitted via writing, be it at home or more generally at school. In addition, the Deaf child's academic success and his/her future professional achievements will depend in large part on a good mastery of the oral language, in its written and, if possible, spoken modality.

In sum, it is crucial that those who take care of Deaf children (parents, educators, language pathologists, doctors) allow them to acquire two languages, the sign language of the Deaf community (as a first language when the hearing loss is severe) and the oral language of the hearing majority. It is equally important that Deaf children and adolescents be given every opportunity to learn about the cultures they belong to, that they be able to interact with these cultures, and that they be able to go through the process of choosing the culture, or preferably, the cultures, they wish to identify with. Searls and Johnston (1996), themselves Deaf and the parents of Deaf children, are of the same opinion when they write: "today we as parents want our children to experience and take advantage of both Deaf and hearing worlds" (1996: 222). To achieve this, the child must be in contact with the two communities (hearing and Deaf) and must feel the need to learn and use both languages and discover both cultures. Counting solely on the hearing culture and on an oral approach to language, because of recent technological advances, is betting on the Deaf children's future. It is putting at risk their cognitive, linguistic, and personal development and it is negating their need to acculturate into the two worlds to which they belong. Early contact with the two languages and cultures will give them more guarantees than contact with just one language and one culture, whatever their future will be, and whichever world they choose to live in (in case it is only one of them).

PART VI

Methodological Issues in Bilingualism Research

Introduction

This last part contains two chapters, both of which are reprints of papers that appeared in *Bilingualism: Language and Cognition*. In Chapter 14, "Methodological and Conceptual Issues", it is argued that, because the field of bilingualism is still relatively new, studies in the linguistics, psycholinguistics, language development, and neurolinguistics of bilingualism have often produced conflicting results. It is suggested that some of the difficulties encountered by researchers could have been lessened, if not avoided, had close attention been paid to methodological and conceptual issues. Among the issues covered are bilingual participants, language mode, stimuli, and tasks as well as models of bilingual representation and processing. Each issue is dealt with in the following way: first it is explained; then the problems it causes are discussed, and, finally, tentative solutions are proposed. Examples are taken from descriptive and experimental studies of normal bilingual adults and children as well as bilinguals suffering from aphasia and dementia.

Chapter 15, "Imaging Bilinguals", is a dialogue between two neuroscientists (Thomas Münte and Antoni Rodriguez-Fornells) and two language scientists (Ping Li and myself). The object of the discussion is a paper which appeared in *Nature* in 2002, "Brain potential and functional MRI evidence for how to handle two languages with one brain" by A. Rodriguez-Fornells, M. Rotte, H.-J. Heinze, T. Nösselt, and T. Münte. The intention of the authors is to start bridging the gap between the two sciences they represent on a number of methodological and theoretical issues. First, a short summary of the paper is given by the two neuroscientists. This is followed by a critical commentary offered by the language scientists. The neuroscientists respond, and a final comment is offered by the language scientists. The four authors conclude that a two-way collaboration between neurosciences and language sciences should be encouraged in order to make headway in our understanding of language processing and representation in bilinguals.

14

Methodological and Conceptual Issues*

Most researchers who have studied both monolinguals and bilinguals would undoubtedly agree that working with bilinguals is a more difficult and challenging enterprise. Many reasons come to mind as to why this might be so: bilingualism has been studied less extensively than monolingualism; theoretical models in areas such as bilingual competence, language development, and processing are less well developed; conceptual notions and definitions show a great deal of variability; specific methodological considerations have to be taken into account; and so on. One outcome of this situation is that research dealing with bilinguals has often produced conflicting results. In the field of experimental psycholinguistics, for example, some researchers have proposed that language processing is selective (e.g. Scarborough *et al.* 1984; Gerard and Scarborough 1989) while others have suggested that it is non-selective (e.g. Altenberg and Cairns 1983; Beauvillain and Grainger 1987); some studies have shown evidence for a language-independent lexicon (e.g. Kolers 1966; Schwanenflugel and Rey 1986) while others have supported language-dependent lexicons (Tulving and Colotla 1970; Taylor 1971); some papers propose that lexical representation is best explained by a word association model or a concept mediation model (both proposed by Potter *et al.* 1984) while others put forward a revised hierarchical model (Kroll and Stewart 1994) or a conceptual feature model (de Groot 1992); some researchers have shown that code-switches in continuous text take time to produce and

* This chapter is a reprint of Grosjean, F. (1998a). "Studying bilinguals: Methodological and conceptual issues", *Bilingualism: Language and Cognition* 1 (2): 131–49. The author wishes to thank Cambridge University Press for permission to reprint it here. The appendix is reprinted from: Grosjean, F. (1989). "Neurolinguists, beware! The bilingual is not two monolinguals in one person", *Brain and Language* 36: 3–15. Copyright: Academic Press. The author wishes to thank Elsevier for permission to reprint it here.

perceive (e.g. Macnamara 1967; Macnamara and Kushnir 1971) while others have shown the opposite (Wakefield *et al.* 1975; Chan *et al.* 1983). In the field of bilingual language development, some studies have found evidence that children who acquire two languages simultaneously go through a fusion stage (e.g. Volterra and Taeschner 1978; Redlinger and Park 1980) while others have questioned this stage (Meisel 1989; Paradis and Genesee 1996), and, in the field of neurolinguistics, such questions as hemispheric lateralization and localization of language in bilinguals have been disputed (for a critical review, see Zatorre 1989), as has the inability of some bilingual aphasics to control the production of mixed language in a monolingual environment (e.g. compare Perecman 1984 with Grosjean 1985b). This list is not exhaustive and other controversial findings bear on such topics as variability in code-switching patterns in various communities, perceptual boundaries in bilingual listeners, the existence or not of an input or output switch in bilinguals, the lexical routes taken when bilinguals are translating from their weaker language into their stronger language, and so on.

In what follows, it will be suggested that some of the difficulties encountered by researchers, and some of the conflicting results they have obtained, could perhaps have been lessened, if not avoided, had close attention been paid to methodological and conceptual issues. Among the issues covered are participants, language mode, stimuli, tasks, and models. Concerning participants, I will review the main defining characteristics of the bilingual individual (language history, language proficiency, language use, etc.), list the problems that are encountered in choosing participants, and show that some factors that are not always taken into account in studies clearly affect the results obtained. With regard to language mode, I will describe the language modes bilinguals find themselves in, and show how this affects such issues as code-switching patterns in bilingual speech, the independence or interdependence of language representation, language fusion in very young bilingual children, mixing in aphasics, and so on. As concerns stimuli, I will question the comparability of stimuli within and across studies, and will show how some of their characteristics need to be controlled for. As for tasks, I will examine the side-effects that some of them induce, what it is they are tapping into, and what aspects of the results are task-specific. I will end with a discussion of the advantages but also the problems of models of bilingual representation and processing, such as the monolingual outlook of some, their use of discrete classifications, the absence of certain components or levels, and the scarcity of global models. (For lack of space, issues such as data collection procedures in naturalistic environments and the transcription and categorization of bilingual speech as well as the problems associated with the statistical analysis of these kinds of data, will not be addressed here.)

Each issue will be dealt with in the following way: first it is explained, then the problems it causes are discussed, and, finally, tentative solutions for future research are proposed. Several points need to be made. First, a lot of what follows has been stated in one way or another over the years by researchers in the field. I will try to do justice to their comments and suggestions but I will probably not be able to refer to everyone concerned for lack of space. If this chapter can act as an echo chamber for the field and create further discussion and action around these issues, it will have served its purpose. Second, even though the discussion of each issue will end with suggestions for solutions, it is clear that these are quite tentative and that it is the field as a whole that will solve the problems that have been raised (all researchers have to struggle with these issues and finding solutions is a common challenge). Finally, even though I will mainly consider experimental studies done with adult bilinguals, I will also cover work done with speakers recorded in more natural environments and children, as well as with aphasic and demented patients. Thus, of the five issues that will be discussed, three (participants, language mode, and models) concern all researchers working on the bilingual individual and two (stimuli and tasks) are primarily of interest to experimentalists.

14.1 Participants

14.1.1 Issue

Most researchers would probably agree that bilinguals, that is those people who use two (or more) languages (or dialects) in their everyday lives, can be characterized by a number of general features. First, they are usually influenced by what has been called the complementarity principle (Grosjean 1997b), that is, the fact that they usually acquire and use their languages for different purposes, in different domains of life, with different people. Second, and as a direct consequence of this first characteristic, bilinguals are rarely equally fluent in all language skills in all their languages. Level of fluency depends in large part on the need for and use of a language (and a particular skill). Third, some bilinguals may still be in the process of acquiring a language (or language skill), whereas others have attained a certain level of stability. Fourth, the language repertoire of bilinguals may change over time: as the environment changes and the needs for particular language skills also change, so will their competence in these skills. Finally, bilinguals interact both with monolinguals and with other bilinguals and they have to adapt their language behavior accordingly (see the section on language mode).

Even though some research questions may be able to abstract away individual differences that exist among bilinguals (e.g. theoretical questions dealing with aspects of the bilingual's grammars), many others will not be able to do so. Among these differences we find:

- *Language history and language relationship*: Which languages (and language skills) were acquired, when, and how? Was the cultural context the same or different? What was the pattern of language use? What is the linguistic relationship between the bilingual's languages?
- *Language stability*: Are one or several languages still being acquired? Is the bilingual in the process of restructuring (maybe even losing) a language or language skill because of a change of linguistic environment? Has a certain language stability been reached?
- *Function of languages*: Which languages (and language skills) are used currently, in what context, for what purpose, and to what extent?
- *Language proficiency*: What is the bilingual's proficiency in each of the four skills in each language?
- *Language mode*: How often and for how long is the bilingual in a monolingual mode (i.e. when only one language is active) and in a bilingual mode (i.e. when both languages are active)? When in a bilingual mode, how much code-switching and borrowing is taking place?
- *Biographical data*: What is the bilingual's age, sex, socioeconomic, and educational status, etc.?

Of course, many other factors can be added to this list but these are the ones that are most often mentioned in the bilingualism literature.

14.1.2 Problems

Two main problems relate to the participants issue. The first is that some researchers, admittedly only a few, do not yet fully share the field's understanding of who bilinguals really are, and the second is that the factors that have been taken into account when choosing participants are often diverse, insufficient, or controversial. As concerns the first problem, some people still feel that bilinguals have or should have equal and perfect fluency in each of their languages (what has been called the two monolinguals in one person viewpoint; Grosjean 1985a, 1989); others still see language mixing as an anomaly, be it in children acquiring their languages simultaneously or successively, or in adult bilinguals; and others still fail to remember that many bilinguals are also bicultural and that their languages will reflect this dimension. The consequences are that erroneous claims may be made about a particular bilingual behavior, inappropriate comparisons may be made with monolinguals, and exceptional cases may be taken to apply to bilinguals in general. Three examples taken from the literature will illustrate this. First, in a study pertaining to spontaneous translation and language mixing in a polyglot aphasic, Perecman (1984) finds various types of language mixing at all levels of linguistic description in the patient under study. Basing herself on earlier work by Weinreich (1966), who unfortunately did not differentiate between interferences and code-switching, she states that language mixing is inappropriate switching from one language to another and that these "errors" can also be found in normal polyglots. However, language mixing in the form of code-switches and borrowings in bilingual interactions has long been known to be perfectly normal behavior among bilinguals interacting with one another (Poplack 1980; Grosjean 1982).

A second example concerns the so-called "semilingualism" of certain bilingual children. Supposedly these children possess less than native-like skills in both languages. They show quantitative deficiencies such as smaller vocabularies when compared to monolingual children, they deviate from monolingual norms, they mix their languages a lot, and so on (see Romaine 1989 for a survey and a critical review of the question). What proponents of "semilingualism" need to ask themselves before classifying a child in this category are the following three questions: Is the child still in the process of becoming bilingual (either learning two languages simultaneously or learning a second language and most probably restructuring the first one)? Is the child mostly in a bilingual mixed-language mode at home and is he or she just discovering the monolingual version of one or the other language (in the school environment, for example)? Finally, has the child been meeting his or her communicative needs up to then (before entering school, for example)? Answers to these questions will probably show that the "semilingual" child is in the process of adjusting to such things as a new social context, a new language, new language skills and language varieties, new domains of use, etc. One should also remember that the complementarity principle will explain, as it does for the bilingual adult, why the child will never become two monolinguals in one person (Grosjean 1997b).

A third example comes from the field of psycholinguistics. In a study on speech segmentation, Cutler *et al.* (1992) used participants who they reported were as bilingual in English and French as they could find: they were accepted as native speakers of French by other speakers of French and accepted as native speakers of English by other speakers of English, they used both languages on an everyday basis, and they had been exposed to both languages simultaneously from one year of age. The authors concluded that their participants had, to all intents and purposes, equally perfect command of the two languages. The participants were tested on English and French stimuli but, in the authors' words, the results produced "a puzzling picture" as they were not really comparable to those of either monolingual group. The authors decided, therefore, to subdivide the participants into subgroups (we will return to how they did this below) since, they report, the overall analysis left them with no obvious point of departure for interpretation of the bilingual results. The point to make here is that bilinguals are speaker-hearers in their own right who will often not give exactly the same kinds of results as monolinguals. One should be ready to accept this and maybe not always seek alternative solutions.

The second problem that relates to participants is that the factors that have been taken into account when choosing participants are often diverse, insufficient, or controversial. On the first problem, diversity, one only needs to examine the "Participants" section of most papers to realize that they are chosen very differently from one study to the next. Some researchers put the stress on fluency and use various scales or tests to evaluate their bilinguals; others stress language use (which languages are used with whom and for what); still others put the emphasis on language stability (whether their participants are still learning a language or not) and in what context they learned their two (or more) languages; and a few give their participants actual screening tests (reading aloud, counting, understanding a passage, etc.) in addition to presenting biographical data. What is clear is that, because the information is so diverse and the tools of assessment so different, we probably have very different bilinguals in the studies published. Some participants are still acquiring their second language (using language learners is a phenomenon that is on the increase), some are strongly dominant in one language, some others appear to be equally fluent in the spoken but not in the written modality, and a few appear to be quite balanced and active bilinguals. This variability is found between groups and is present within groups also.

At times the information given about participants is simply insufficient to get an idea of who they are. For example, in an often-cited study by Caramazza and Brones (1980) that deals with the bilingual lexicon, we are only told that the Spanish-English bilinguals were native speakers of Spanish who ranged in their self-ratings of bilingual fluency from good to excellent (mean rating of 5.5 on a 7-point scale). No explanation is given as to what "bilingual fluency" means and none of the factors listed above (language history, language stability, function of languages, etc.) are mentioned. This problem of insufficient information is especially present in studies that deal with aphasic and demented patients. Very little information is given about the patient after the onset of the pathology and even less about him or her prior to it. For example, Perecman (1984) simply gives us the age of the patient (HB), where he was born, the order of acquisition of his languages, and the fact that English was the language he used primarily from age eighteen on. We know nothing about the patient's proficiency in the four language skills in each language prior to his aphasia, the function of his languages, the amount of language mixing he did with other bilinguals, etc. (In the Appendix to this chapter we list a series of questions that need to be asked when assessing the bilingual aphasic's language knowledge and use prior to and after injury.) The same problem is also present in child language studies (see e.g. Redlinger and Park 1980; Vihman 1985), where little is said about the children's proficiency in each language (admittedly harder to assess), the function of their languages, the amount of time they spent using the languages with monolinguals and bilinguals, and so on (see de Houwer 1990 for a critical review).

Finally, a few studies take into account controversial factors when choosing or dividing up their participants. One approach that comes to mind is the one used by Cutler et al. (1992) to break their participants down into two groups, a French-dominant and an English-dominant group. It should be recalled that these fluent and balanced bilinguals had been chosen because they had equally perfect command of their two languages. The authors tried out several approaches to divide them up and finally found one that produced interpretable data according to them: they asked participants to indicate which language they would choose to keep if they developed a serious disease and their life could only be saved by a brain operation which would have the unfortunate side-effect of removing one of their languages. One could discuss at length whether such a question is appropriate (after all, isn't a person bilingual because he or she needs two or more languages in his or her everyday life?), but what should be stressed here is that we have no evidence concerning the validity of such a question for assessing language dominance. As a consequence, we do not really know what kinds of participants fell into each of the two groups. One unfortunate outcome is that replicating the results with similar groups of participants will be very difficult. This is exactly what Kearns (1994) found when she used the same type of highly fluent participants whom she also broke down into subgroups using the same question. Whereas her "French dominant" participants did not show the classic crossover interaction with French stimuli (what has since been called the French syllable effect), Cutler et al.'s "French dominant" participants did show it.[1] In addition, and surprisingly, Kearns' "English dominant" participants showed a syllable effect with French stimuli whereas Cutler et al.'s participants did not. In sum, what is at stake here is not dividing up participants into subgroups in order to better understand the results obtained but rather the approach that is used to do so.

The problem of participant selection and description would be less crucial if we did not have evidence that the defining factors listed above (i.e. language history, language stability, function of languages, etc.) are important. In fact, this evidence does exist: concerning the language history and language relationship factor, Segalowitz (1997) shows that there is considerable variability between participants in L2 learning and that this has an impact on language knowledge and language processing; Mayo, Florentine, and Buus (1997) present data showing that perception in noise is affected by age of acquisition of the second

---

[1] According to Frauenfelder and Kearns (1997), a syllable effect is generally characterized as a significant interaction of target type and word type. Participants are faster or more accurate in detecting targets which correspond exactly to the first syllable of a word than targets which correspond to more or less than the first syllable. The authors add that, according to a more stringent criterion, to be able to infer a syllable effect there must be a significant crossover interaction between target type and word type.

language; de Groot (1995) suggests that recent use, but also disuse, of a language affects one's lexical representations, etc. As concerns language stability, Kroll and Curley (1988) and Chen and Leung (1989) both show that the processing paths followed during simple word translation are different in language learners and bilinguals who have attained a certain stability and fluency in their languages. As for language function, it is a well-known fact that certain domains of the lives of bilinguals are usually covered exclusively by one language (e.g. work, religion, sports, etc.) and that many bilinguals simply do not have translation equivalents in their other language for these domains, especially if they did not acquire either language in school. Regarding language proficiency, Poplack (1980) shows that one obtains different code-switching patterns depending on how fluent speakers are in their two languages (see also the four switching styles described by Bentahila and Davies (1991) that depend in part on proficiency); Dornic (1978) shows that various linguistic tasks given to bilinguals take more time and are harder to accomplish in their non-dominant language; de Groot (1995) reports that the effect found with a bilingual Stroop test depends on the participants' language proficiency; Lanza (1992) demonstrates that the type of mixing young bilingual children do depends on their language dominance; Zatorre (1989) argues that less lateral cerebral asymmetry found in some studies for a bilingual's non-dominant language could be due to comprehension problems (and not laterality reasons); Hyltenstam (1991) finds a relationship in demented patients between proficiency in a language and the ability to keep to it separate from the other language; and so on. As for the language mode factor (to which we will return in the next section), Genesee (1989) makes the point that more mixing takes place in children who hear both languages used interchangeably by the same interlocutors. Finally, it is a well-known fact that certain biographical variables such as sex and handedness play an important role in language laterality studies (Zatorre 1989; Vaid and Hall 1991).

14.1.3 Tentative solutions

Concerning the first problem, the lack of understanding of who bilinguals really are, all that can be said is that there are a sufficient number of general introductions to the field to help researchers not to fall into this trap (see e.g. Grosjean 1982; Beatens-Beardsmore 1986; Appel and Muysken 1987; Edwards 1995; Romaine 1989). As for the second problem, factors that have to be taken into account in choosing participants, one can always make bilingual assessment measures covariate variables during the analysis of results or allow participants to be their own control when the study permits it (which is not often the case). But the main solution will no doubt be for the field to agree on the kind of information that should be reported to describe the main types of bilinguals used (adult bilinguals, second language learners, bilingual children, polyglot aphasics, or demented patients, etc.). For example, papers in experimental psycholinguistics could be expected (if not required) to have an appendix containing the following information on the group(s) used: biographical data (mean age, number of males and females, educational level of participants); language history (age participants started acquiring each skill in each language; manner of acquiring the languages, etc.); language stability (skills in the languages still being actively acquired); function of languages (which languages are used and in what contexts); proficiency (proficiency ratings in the four skills in the participants' languages); and language mode (amount of time spent in the monolingual and in the bilingual mode). Each of these factors may have an impact on processing and representation and should therefore be assessed. Of course, much of the information can be collected via questionnaires by means of scales and can be reported numerically (central tendencies and dispersions). For other domains, one may choose to add or take out factors and one could even think of adding actual performance measures. Two points need to be made. First, it is important that, if self-rating scales are used, differences in the way people rate themselves be controlled for. It appears to be the case that, due to various factors, some individuals, and even some groups, have no problem using endpoints of scales, and sometimes overrate themselves, while others are more conservative in their self-evaluation. Anchoring scales properly will therefore be very important for comparison across groups. For example, one could use as a yardstick native speakers of a language. Second, it appears crucial to distinguish between language learners in an academic setting who do not usually interact socially with their two languages and who therefore are not really bilingual (at least yet), and people who are acquiring a language in a natural environment and who are using both languages on a regular basis. The former should be characterized as "language learners" and maybe not as "novice" or "non-fluent" bilinguals, at least until they start using both languages on a regular basis.

14.2 Language mode[2]

14.2.1 Issue

As we saw in Chapter 4, language mode is the state of activation of the bilingual's languages and language processing mechanisms at a given point in time. In their everyday lives, bilinguals find themselves in various language modes that correspond to points on a monolingual–bilingual mode continuum (see Figure 4.1). This state is controlled by such variables as who the bilingual is speaking or listening to, the situation, the topic, the purpose of the interaction, and so on. At one end of the continuum, bilinguals are in a totally monolingual language mode in that they are interacting only with (or listening only to) monolinguals of one—or the other—of the languages they know. One language is active and the other is deactivated. At the other end of the continuum, bilinguals find themselves in a bilingual language mode in that they are communicating with (or listening to) bilinguals who share their two (or more) languages and language mixing may take place (i.e. code-switching and borrowing). In this case, both languages are active but the one that is used as the main language of processing (the base or matrix language) is more active than the other. These are endpoints but bilinguals also find themselves at intermediary points depending on the factors mentioned above. It should be noted that bilinguals differ among themselves as to the extent they travel along the continuum; some rarely find themselves at the bilingual end whereas others rarely leave this end (for example, bilinguals who live in communities where mixed language is the norm).

Everything that pertains to speakers also pertains to listeners or readers. For example, and whatever the base language, if listeners determine (consciously or not), or find out as they go along, that what they are listening to can contain elements from the other language, they will put themselves partly in a bilingual mode, that is, activate both their languages (with the base language being more strongly activated). This is also true of readers, whether they are reading a continuous text or looking at individual lexical items interspersed with items from the other language. Simply knowing that there is a possibility that elements from the other language will be presented (in an experiment, for example) will move the bilingual away from the monolingual endpoint

---

[2] The original section on Language Mode has been reduced here and slightly rewritten so as to avoid too much overlap with what is said in Chapter 4. We also refer back to the latter chapter when necessary.

of the continuum. Just one guest word in a stream of base-language words can increase this displacement towards the bilingual endpoint (see Chapter 5 for a more extensive discussion of this).

Evidence for the language mode continuum concept is starting to be quite extensive. For example, in a production study described in Chapter 5, Grosjean (1997a) manipulated the language mode participants were in when retelling stories that contained code-switches. He found that the three dependent measures (number of base-language syllables, number of guest-language syllables, and number of disfluencies produced) were all affected by the language mode the speakers were in. In a developmental study, Lanza (1992) found that the same child mixed languages much more when in a bilingual context (represented by her father) than in a monolingual context (represented by her mother). As for evidence from an adult naturalistic setting, this can be found in a study by Treffers-Daller (1998) that is described below and mentioned in Chapter 4.

14.2.2 Problems

Because the mode a bilingual is in corresponds to a state of activation of the bilingual's languages and language processing mechanisms, it has an impact both on language production (maintenance or change of the base language, amount and type of language mixing that takes place, etc.) and on language perception (speed of processing of a language, access to one or to both lexicons, role of the less activated language, etc.). It appears critical therefore that one control for the mode participants are in when they are being recorded or tested experimentally. This has not been the case very often as can be seen by examining examples from a number of different domains (see Chapter 4 for additional examples).

In a first domain, research on interferences (also known by some as transfers; for a review see Odlin 1989), the mode that bilingual participants are in when interferences are observed, has rarely been reported. Thus, what might appear on the surface as an interference could also be a code-switch or a borrowing produced by the speaker who is aware that his or her interlocutor knows the other language (to some extent at least). For example, although "baving" (from the French verb "baver" (to dribble)), produced in an English monolingual mode, is probably the result of the deactivated language "intruding" upon the language being spoken (an interference, therefore), in a bilingual mode it is either an interference or, more probably, the normal access of a word in the less activated lexicon and its integration into the base language (a borrowing). It is now widely recognized that in Weinreich's (1966) classical work on bilingualism, the concept of interference covered the whole range of possible bilingual productions (true interferences in both the monolingual and the bilingual mode as well as code-switches and borrowings in the bilingual mode). This is also clearly the case with the interferences discussed by Taeschner (1983) in her study of two bilingual children. In sum, to have any chance of identifying interferences correctly one needs to be sure that the data collected come from a truly monolingual mode. (See Grosjean 1998b for further discussion of this.)

A second domain of study in which it is important to know where bilinguals are positioned on the language mode continuum concerns natural interview situations. This information is not often given in the description of the interview setting and yet, as we saw in Chapter 4, Treffers-Daller (1998), among others, has shown that, depending on the speaker's position on the continuum (based on the interlocutor, the topic, the situation, etc.), different types of language behavior will be obtained. In her study, as we saw, she placed the same speaker, a Turkish-German bilingual, in three different positions by changing the context and the interlocutors, and she found quite different code-switching patterns. For example, when the participant was speaking to another bilingual he did not know well, his code-switches were less numerous, more peripheral, and contained various types of pauses (the latter have been called flagged switches). However, when the participant interacted with a very close bilingual friend, the code-switches were more numerous, they were both intra- and intersentential, and they were produced without hesitations or special highlighting (these have been termed fluent switches). Based on these results (also observed by Poplack 1981 in a different context), Treffers-Daller concludes that the language mode continuum concept may offer a new approach to studying variable code-switching patterns within and between communities (e.g. Poplack 1985; Bentahila and Davies 1991) because it can help predict the frequency and type of switching that takes place.

A third domain where the language mode needs to be controlled for is experimental psycholinguistics. Several domains of research are concerned, but I will concentrate here on the language representation issue. This pertains to whether bilinguals have an integrated semantic memory for their two languages (also called a shared or a common store) or whether they have two separate, independent semantic systems. Several studies have addressed this question. For example, Schwanenflugel and Rey (1986) used a cross-language priming task in which Spanish-English bilinguals saw the prime word "body" and immediately afterwards had to say whether the following item, either "brazo" (arm) or "arm", was a word or not. The authors found that whether the prime and the following word (the target) belonged to the same or different languages had no effect on the amount of priming, and they concluded that concepts in the bilingual individual are represented by a language neutral conceptual system. In a more recent study, Fox (1996) used flanker words to prime targets and found an equal level of negative priming for monolingual and bilingual word pairs. She also concluded that mental representations of words in a bilingual's two languages are integrated within a shared representational system. Although both studies were carefully conducted and produced reliable data, it is difficult to tease apart in the results obtained what is due to the representational issue and what is caused by the language mode variable. The bilinguals were probably not in a monolingual mode when they were tested. Participants knew they were being tested as bilinguals and they saw words in the two languages. Because of this, they had probably activated both their languages (consciously or unconsciously) and were thus in a bilingual mode. (The same argument can be made about masked priming studies if considerable care is not taken to put participants in a monolingual mode.) If both languages are active, bilinguals are then in a position to react as quickly to targets in the language of the prime (or flanker word) as to targets in the other language (all other things being equal). No claim is being made here concerning the substantive issue of shared as opposed to separate semantic stores or, more concretely, which language(s) is/are primed in within- and between-language experimental studies. The only point being put forward is that the language mode variable can certainly influence, and maybe sometimes even account for, the results obtained. (The same is probably true of studies examining selective versus non-selective processing in bilinguals as will be seen later.)

Another domain of research which has not always controlled for language mode sufficiently concerns simultaneous language acquisition in bilingual children. As we saw in Chapter 4 (Section 4.3.1), it has been proposed by some researchers that children who acquire two languages simultaneously go through an early fusion stage in which the languages are in fact one system (one lexicon, one grammar, etc.).

This position has been criticized by other researchers who claim that the children were often in a bilingual mode, i.e. the caretakers were usually bilingual themselves and were probably overheard using both languages, separately or in a mixed form, by the children, if not actually mixing their languages with them (see Goodz 1989). In addition, the context in which the recordings were made for the studies probably induced language mixing. If one examines the procedure followed by Redlinger and Park (1980) and Vihman (1985), for example, it is clear that the recording context was rarely (if ever) monolingual. In the first study, the investigator spoke the same languages as two of the bilingual children and, in addition, the children's parents appear to have been present; and in the second study, the person doing the taping was the mother of the child (Raivo) and she was herself bilingual. In both cases, therefore, the children were in a bilingual context which induced a bilingual mode and hence language mixing. It is interesting to note that Lanza (1992) shows clear differences in mixing behavior for the same child when interacting with two different adults, one of whom prefers a monolingual interaction and one who accepts language mixing. (See Genesee *et al.* 1996, already mentioned in Chapter 4, for a similar type of study where the adult interlocutors were two monolinguals (one in each language) and one bilingual.)

A final domain in which language mode is a crucial variable is language pathology. For example, in the domain of bilingual aphasia, several case studies have been published of patients who appear to mix languages inappropriately. Perecman (1984), for instance, states that the language of her patient (HB) was strongly marked by language mixing. The author writes that HB shifted from one language to another during the course of a single conversation and within the same utterance. However, we learn in the same paper that language mixing was particularly pronounced when the investigator (or investigators, it is unclear if there were one or two) shifted from one language to another within the same conversation or task, and we are actually given an extract from a dialogue in which the investigator switches languages! As was stated in a response to Perecman's paper (Grosjean 1985b), it is interesting to speculate how much language switching HB would have produced had the investigator been totally monolingual. (See the Appendix to this chapter for indications of what to assess prior to and after injury.) It seems only appropriate that a bilingual aphasic who is in a bilingual context, and who is faced with production problems, should use language mixing as a strategy to enhance communication (as would normal bilinguals). Another example comes from language production in bilinguals who suffer from dementia. Hyltenstam (1991), for instance, presents formally elicited data gathered from Finnish-Swedish patients recorded in what he states is a monolingual interaction (with a native speaker of each language) as well as in a bilingual interaction. The Swedish interactant was indeed monolingual but the Finnish one was also a speaker of Swedish, as we learn later in the paper. It is not surprising therefore to find in the Finnish productions language patterns ranging from monolingual Finnish utterances to mixed Finnish-Swedish utterances. It should be noted that mixing also took place in the Swedish monolingual interactions but these can clearly be attributed to the patients' dementia. One cannot say the same thing concerning mixing in the Finnish interactions.

To conclude, failure to control for the bilingual mode factor produces at best highly variable data due to the fact that participants are probably situated at various points along the monolingual–bilingual continuum, and at worst ambiguous data given the confound between this factor and the variable under study.

14.2.3 Tentative solutions

Language mode is a variable to be studied independently (one will need to investigate ways of determining the bilingual's position on the continuum, among other things) but it is also a variable to control for. Failure to do so has important implications for the way in which findings are interpreted. In what follows, I will summarize what is stated in Chapter 4 (Section 4.3.2) on language mode as a control variable. As concerns the monolingual mode, two inappropriate approaches should be avoided. The first is to put the participants simply in a "language set" (also called erroneously a "language mode") by giving them instructions in one language, getting them to do preliminary tasks in that language, occasionally presenting reminders in that language, giving them monolingual stimuli, etc. What this does is to activate a particular base language but it in no way guarantees a particular position on the monolingual–bilingual mode continuum.[3] The second

[3] Interestingly, and with hindsight, the participants who were tested in Soares and Grosjean's (1984) study, "Bilinguals in a monolingual and a bilingual speech mode: The effect on lexical access", were never in a totally monolingual mode. This is because they knew the study dealt with bilingualism and they were accustomed to code-switching with one of the experimenters. Instructions in each of the two languages and practice sentences in these languages did help to establish the base language (or language set) in the

approach, which has been used a lot with bilingual children, second language learners, and aphasic or demented patients, has been to hide the experimenter's or interviewer's bilingualism. This is a dangerous strategy as subtle cues such as facial expression and body language can give away the interlocutor's comprehension of the other language. In addition, it will not prevent occasional slip-ups such as responding in the "wrong" language or showing in one's response that what has been said in that language has been understood.

As we stated in Chapter 4, the solution to the monolingual mode problem is unfortunately not quite as easy as one would like it to be. For interview situations, if the researcher is interested in observing how a bilingual can produce just one language (something a bilingual often has to do), then the interviewer must be completely monolingual in that language (and not feign to be so). In addition, the situation must be monolingual and there must not be any other person present who knows the other language. For more experimental situations, the difficulty is how to prevent the bilingual from activating, to some extent at least, the other language. As we saw in Chapter 5, Section 5.2, it is unfortunately far too easy to put a participant, involuntarily, in a bilingual mode in an experiment. If interest is shown in the participant's bilingualism, if he or she is tested in a laboratory that works on bilingualism, if the experimenter is bilingual, or if the participant sees or hears stimuli from both languages, then any one of these factors is sufficient to put the participant in a bilingual mode and hence activate the two languages, albeit to differing degrees. Such questions as the independence or interdependence of the bilingual's language systems or the "automatic" influence of one language on the other (selective versus non-selective processing) cannot be studied adequately if this is so, even if precautions such as masking primes are taken (e.g. Bijeljac-Babic *et al.* 1997). One possibility that we proposed in Chapter 4 would be to intermix bilingual participants with monolingual participants in a monolingual experiment (for example, a study that is part of a course requirement) and, once the experiment is done, and after the fact only, to go back to the list of participants and extract the bilinguals. In addition, care will have to be taken that the stimuli presented do not give the aim away. Of course, one can also make the bilingual mode an independent variable and use two or more intermediary levels of

"monolingual" parts of the study. This, added to the fact that the stimuli were in only one language, probably pushed the participants towards the monolingual endpoint of the continuum. Whether they actually reached that monolingual endpoint is doubtful, however.

the continuum (e.g. Grosjean 1997a), but there is no guarantee that the most monolingual level will be monolingual enough to make claims about non-selective processing or interdependent representations.

As concerns the bilingual endpoint of the language mode continuum, we recommended in Chapter 4 that care be taken that the participants are totally comfortable producing, or listening to, mixed language. This can be done by having bilingual experimenters or interviewers who belong to the same bilingual community as the participants and, if possible, who know them well. They should interact with the participants in mixed language and the situation should be conducive to mixed language (no monolinguals present, a relaxed non-normative atmosphere, etc.).

14.3 Stimuli

14.3.1 Issue

Stimuli used in bilingual studies, such as syllables, words, phrases, and sentences, differ in a number of ways within and between languages. For example, words can differ on graphic form, frequency of graphic form, frequency and density of graphic form neighbors, phonetic form, frequency of phonetic form, frequency and density of phonetic form neighbors, syntactic categories and frequency of these categories, meanings of the various syntactic forms, concreteness–abstractness, animacy, etc. For instance, if one takes French "pays" (country) and English "pays", two homographs taken from a study conducted by Beauvillain and Grainger (1987), one notices that although both graphic forms are quite frequent, English "pays" probably has more graphic form neighbors than French "pays". As for the phonetic form, the two are quite different as English /peɪz/ contains a diphthong and a terminal consonant whereas French /pei/ has two vowels and no final consonant. The phonetic form frequency is probably quite similar in the two languages but the English form has more neighbors than the French form. As concerns syntactic categories, English "pays" is an inflected verb and a very rarely found noun in its plural form. As for French "pays", it is only a noun and it is far more frequent than the English noun. Moving on to meaning, the English verb form of "pays" has four meanings and the noun form has two meanings. The French noun "pays" has three meanings and they are all different from the English noun meanings. Finally, there is a certain diversity as to concreteness and animacy of the various French and English meanings. Thus, as can be seen from this apparently simple case, stimuli will differ considerably from one another.

14.3.2 Problems

Three problems surround stimuli in bilingual studies: differences in the stimuli used across studies, differences in stimuli used within studies, and factors that need to be controlled for in stimulus selection. As concerns differences in stimuli used across studies, what are often thought to be similar stimuli are unfortunately not always that similar. For example, much work has been done with cognates, defined by Crystal (1991) as linguistic forms that are historically derived from the same source as other language forms. When one compares how different researchers define the concept, one finds very large differences. For example, concerning the graphemic form of cognate pairs, de Groot (1995) says it is similar, Caramazza and Brones (1979) say it is identical, Sánchez-Casas *et al.* (1992) talk of a large degree of overlap, and Beauvillain and Grainger (1987) say it is the same. As concerns meaning, the labels used respectively are: similar, same, large degree of overlap, and similar. Finally, with respect to phonology, de Groot says it is similar, Caramazza and Brones state that it is different (!), and the two other studies do not give any information on this factor. Because of the problem of understanding what is meant by "similar", "same", and "large degree of overlap", and based on the fact that words often have several meanings with different frequencies, among other things, it is no surprise that differences are found across studies (especially if the tasks used call on all the linguistic aspects of cognates, including phonology). In fact, Votaw (1992) shows the complexity of the issue in a six-cell table in which she presents three levels of shared form and three levels of shared meaning. Even though she does not refer to phonological form and to multi-meaning cognates, the table is useful for observing which cells are covered by the different studies that have used cognates. What has just been said about cognates also pertains to other "similar" stimuli across studies.

Concerning differences in stimuli within studies, the issue is one of variability. An example comes from the homographs used by Beauvillain and Grainger (1987). We have already seen that English "pays" and French "pays" share the noun category (although the English word is very much more frequent as a verb), and that as nouns the meanings are different in the two languages. When we compare this pair with another pair that was used in the same study, English "lame" and French "lame" (blade), we find another pattern of differences. English "lame" is an adjective and a verb (and also a very rare noun) whereas French "lame" is only a noun. The cause of this variability is quite understandable (there is only a small set of homographs to choose from in the two languages), but if variability within a study is too large, it can reduce the effect that is sought or actually make it disappear.

As for factors that need to be controlled for during stimulus preparation, several have been mentioned in recent years, making studies which do not control for them somewhat problematic. For example, concreteness is an important variable both in neurolinguistics and psycholinguistics. In the former domain, Zatorre (1989) reports that concrete nouns are processed more bilaterally than abstract nouns. In psycholinguistics, de Groot (1992) has shown that concrete words are translated faster than abstract words. She also states that cognates and infrequent words are more likely to be translated by means of the word–word association route. Sholl (1995) has shown that animacy has clear effects on word translation: animate concepts are translated more rapidly then inanimate concepts. As for Grainger and Beauvillain (1987), they put forward the orthographical uniqueness of a word as a factor. In a lexical decision task, they showed a cost for language mixing in word lists; mixed lists produced longer reaction times than pure lists. The cost disappeared, however, when the words in each language were orthographically unique to that language. Finally, in research on spoken word recognition of code-switches and borrowings, a number of factors have been found to play a role, as we saw in Chapter 10: phonotactics and language phonetics (Grosjean 1988; Li 1996), interlanguage neighbor proximity (Grosjean 1988), and sentential context (Li 1996). Not controlling for such factors (at least the more important ones) can lead to weak effects or no effects, to different or contradictory results across studies, and to the difficulty of replicating published studies.

14.3.3 Tentative solutions

At least four well established solutions known to most researchers in psycholinguistics can be used to solve or lessen the stimuli problem. The first but also the hardest is to control for as many linguistic factors as possible when choosing stimuli; the second is to replicate the results using a new set of stimuli; and the third is to use stimuli as their own control when possible (although one must avoid repetition effects across conditions). Finally, the fourth, and probably the most appropriate for cross-study comparisons, is simply to reuse the stimuli that have appeared in an already published study so as to replicate the results or to show that some specific independent variable can modify the outcome of the experiment.

A long-term solution to the problem would be for the field to start putting together normalized stimuli for pairs of languages, such as lists of cognates and homographs controlled on a number of variables, word frequency counts, and word association lists obtained from bilingual groups, etc. This kind of information already exists in monolingual research and it provides many advantages, not least that the experimenter can spend more time on other aspects of the study.

14.4 Tasks

14.4.1 Issue

Experimental tasks used to study bilinguals range from those used in production studies (reading continuous text or lists aloud, retelling stories, naming pictures under various conditions, giving word associations, etc.), to those used in perception and comprehension studies (free recall, syllable identification and discrimination, Stroop tests, eye tracking, word priming, lexical decision, translation, etc.), all the way to those in hemispheric lateralization studies (dichotic listening, hemifield presentation, concurrent activity tasks, etc.).

14.4.2 Problems

Some problems are common to monolingual and bilingual research such as those that relate to strategic versus automatic processes involved in the task, the metalinguistic nature of the task, its processing locus, the allocation of attention during the task, etc. There is also much debate around such questions as the size of the SOA (stimulus onset asynchrony), the blocking or not of stimuli, the proportion of filler items, etc. I will concentrate, however, on three specific problems. The first concerns how certain tasks activate both the bilingual's languages and hence create a confound between the bilingual mode the participant is in and the variable under study; the second deals with the question of what certain tasks are tapping into; and the third concerns which aspects of the results depend on the task itself and which on the variable being studied.

As concerns the first problem, it is clear that such tasks as the bilingual Stroop test, bilingual word priming, bilingual association production, bilingual category matching, word translation, and so on, all activate both languages in the bilingual. In the bilingual Stroop test, one cannot perceive the word "red" written in green and respond "vert" ("green" in French) without having both languages activated. In the bilingual category matching task, one cannot see the name of a category in one language (e.g. "furniture") and then an instance of that category in another language (e.g. "silla", or "chair" in Spanish), without activating both languages. This becomes a very real problem when the question being studied pertains to such issues as selective versus non-selective processing, the independence or the interdependence of the bilingual's language systems, or one versus two lexicons. If one is interested in these issues, one should be careful not to activate the other language by using a task that does just that. When this occurs, it becomes difficult to disentangle what is due to normal bilingual representation and processing, and what is due to the bilingual language mode induced by the task.

For example, as mentioned briefly in Chapter 4, Beauvillain and Grainger (1987) wanted to find evidence for the presence or absence of language-selective access of interlexical homographs during visual word perception. To do this, in the first experiment, they presented pairs of words in two conditions. In the related condition, the first word (the context word) was a homograph in English and French (e.g. "coin", which means "corner" in French) and it was followed by a test word (e.g. "money") that could be primed by its English meaning but not its French meaning. In the unrelated condition, the context word was only an English word (not a homograph) and the test word had no relationship to it. The participants were told that the first word would always be a French word and they were never informed of the presence of homographs (the pairs were mixed in with filler pairs). They were asked to do a lexical decision on the second item and were informed that it would be an English word or non-word. The authors hypothesized that selective access would be confirmed if the context word in the related condition ("coin") was found not to facilitate the test word ("money"); if there was facilitation, however, then non-selective access would be confirmed. The results showed that facilitation was in fact obtained, that is, that reaction times were faster in the related than in the unrelated condition. This was replicated in a second experiment and the authors concluded that lexical access in bilinguals is not initially language-selective.

The problem, of course, is that, despite the instructions which were meant to force participants to ignore the meaning of the homograph in the other language, the bilinguals needed their two languages to do the task, that is, to read the context word in French and then decide whether the second word was an English word or not. To do this, they had to put themselves in a bilingual language mode and activate both their lexicons. (It should be noted that, as they were tested as bilinguals, they were probably already in a bilingual mode before the experiment even started.) It is no surprise, therefore, that a result indicating non-selective processing was obtained (the same comment can be made about another well-known study which examined the same question, that of Altenberg and Cairns 1983). Recently, Dijkstra *et al.* (1998) have shown that interlingual homographs may be recognized faster than, slower than, or as fast as monolingual control words depending on task requirements and language intermixing. Even though they did not account for their findings in terms of language mode, it is clear that both these variables affect the mode and hence the results obtained. What one can conclude from this is that, whenever possible, tasks or conditions that activate both languages should not be used to study issues such as selective versus non-selective processing, or the independence versus the interdependence of the bilingual's language systems.

The second problem that concerns tasks is that it is difficult to know what tasks are tapping into: language processing, language representation, or both? It is interesting to note that most monolingual studies that use priming tasks, lexical decision, or the Stroop test are basically aimed at understanding processing, that is how words are accessed in the lexicon. The findings that have come out of this research have mainly been used to build processing models and not representational models. However, probably because of an early interest in bilingual language representation, these same tasks are often used to study representation in bilinguals. Unless one espouses a view that equates processing with representation (something that becomes very difficult to defend at higher language levels), one should try to come to grips with this second, highly delicate, problem. Unfortunately, the field is hesitant about the issue and we find researchers using identical tasks to tap into representation and processing. For example, Beauvillain and Grainger (1987) used priming with lexical decision to get at the selective access issue, whereas Schwanenflugel and Rey (1986) used this same task (with minor procedural differences) to get at the representational issue. If a task is indeed reflecting representation, then we need to know which level of representation it is reflecting. For example, in lexical representation research, we have to know which of the following four levels is being tapped into: the lexeme level, the lemma level, the conceptual level, or the encyclopedic level (which is outside the lexicon).

The third problem concerns which aspects of the results depend on the specific processing demands of the task itself and which on the variable being studied. Many conflicting results in the literature, in particular those concerning the one versus two lexicons issue, can be accounted for in terms of this problem. It will be recalled that in the 1960s and 1970s an extensive debate took place around whether bilinguals have one language-independent store or whether they have two language-dependent stores. Much evidence was collected for each hypothesis, but little by little researchers started realizing that there was a confound between the tasks used to study the question and the question itself. Kolers and Gonzalez (1980) were among the first to state that two different issues had become confused in the study of bilingual memory: the issue of representation, its commonness across languages or its means dependency, and the way the issue is tested. They suggested that the bilingual's linguistic representations are independent or dependent to the degree that particular skills are utilized in a given context or task. Scarborough *et al.* (1984) stated practically the same thing when they wrote that a bilingual might appear to have a separate or an integrated memory system depending upon how task demands control encoding or retrieval strategies (see also Durgunoglu and Roediger 1987). Since then the focus has shifted away from the one versus two lexicons question to how the bilingual's lexical representation might be organized (see e.g. Potter *et al.* 1984; Kroll and Stewart 1994; de Groot 1992), but the problem of what the task is doing has not disappeared completely, as can be seen in discussions by Fox (1996) and Kroll and de Groot (1997), among others. The task effect is also present in neurolinguistics where it has been shown that orthographic comparisons yield consistent left visual field advantages while phonological and syntactic judgments give right visual field advantages (Vaid 1983, 1987; Zatorre 1989).

14.4.3 Tentative solutions

The first problem mentioned, the fact that certain tasks activate both of the bilingual's languages, is very difficult to solve if one is interested in issues such as selective processing or the independent nature of language representation in bilinguals. If that is the case, one must make sure that the task is not artefactually activating the bilingual's two languages and/or processing systems. The task must be monolingual in nature and must not involve processes such as cross-language priming, perception in one language and production in the other, etc. If the question of interest is different, such as whether distinct groups of bilinguals behave differently when perceiving or producing language, then the dual language activation nature of the task should simply be controlled for.

The other two problems (what it is that tasks are reflecting and which aspects of the results are task specific) can be addressed by having a very good understanding of the tasks used in bilingualism research: what issues can be studied with them, which variables can be tested, what the dependent measures are, the advantages and problems of the tasks, and so on. It would be important one day to develop a guide to bilingual research paradigms along the lines of the one proposed by Grosjean and Frauenfelder (1997) for spoken word recognition paradigms. Finally, several paradigms can be used to obtain converging evidence, but one must keep in mind that similar effects, revealed by similar values of a dependent measure, may not always reflect similar processing routes and similar underlying representations.

14.5 Models

14.5.1 Issue

One of the main aims of research on bilingualism, whether descriptive, theoretical or experimental, is to develop models of how the bilingual's languages are acquired, represented, and processed. Since research started in the field, researchers have met this aim with proposals such as the coordinate, compound, subordinate distinction; the one versus two lexicons hypotheses; the switch or monitor proposals; various models of lexical representation; ventures to describe written and spoken word recognition in the bilingual; and the fused versus separate language development models of simultaneous language acquisition. By their very existence, these theoretical contributions have been a real asset to the field in that they attempt to step back from data to give a general description of a phenomenon. In addition, they allow other researchers to confirm or invalidate certain predictions and hence propose variants or new models. Their advantages therefore far outweigh their problems, as will be seen below.

14.5.2 Problems

A first problem that is slowly disappearing is that some models still have a monolingual view of the bilingual individual. Instead of accepting that bilinguals are specific speaker-hearers who, through the contact and interaction of two or more languages, are distinct from monolinguals (Grosjean 1985a; Cook 1992), some researchers still use a monolingual yardstick to describe aspects of bilingual behavior and representation. Earlier work on the input and output switches (reviewed in Grosjean 1982) was based in part on the notion that bilinguals had one language switched on, and the other switched off, but never the two switched on at the same time. And yet, it is now recognized that, in a bilingual language mode, both languages are active and the bilingual can produce mixed language utterances at the same rate as monolingual utterances (and, of course, decode them at that rate). This monolingual viewpoint can still be found in certain areas where it is expected that "dominant" bilinguals will behave in large part like monolinguals in their dominant language. Of course, this might be the case in some instances but one should be ready to accept bilingual specificities when they appear.

A second problem concerns the discrete classifications that are found in the field. For example, Weinreich's (1966) coordinate, compound, subordinate trichotomy and Ervin and Osgood's (1954) coordinate, compound dichotomy triggered much research. But contradictory findings and theoretical considerations have led various researchers to move away from these distinctions and hypothesize that, within the very same bilingual, some words in the two lexicons will have a coordinate relationship, others a compound relationship, and still others a subordinate relationship, especially if the languages were acquired in different cultural settings and at different times. Recent work on lexical representation in bilinguals appears to defend such a position (see various chapters in de Groot and Kroll 1997). The same kind of discrete classification problem can be found in the long debate that has surrounded the number of lexicons the bilingual possesses (reviewed by Grosjean 1982). Paradis' (1981, 1986) subset hypothesis was instrumental in helping researchers view this question in a different light, and recent proposals of lexical organization such as the word association model and the concept mediation model (Potter *et al.* 1984), the revised hierarchical model (Kroll and Stewart 1994), and the conceptual feature model (de Groot 1992) have also contributed to an improved understanding of the organization of the bilingual's lexical representations. It should be noted though that some researchers still propose that distinct groups of bilinguals are best characterized by just one of these models (or variants of it). It was later that de Groot (1995), based on an extensive review of the literature, came to the conclusion that *the* bilingual memory does not exist. The memory of every individual is likely to contain structures of various types and these structures will occur in different proportions across bilinguals. This will depend on factors such as level of proficiency of the languages known, the characteristics of the words, the strategy used to learn them, the context in which the languages are used, the age at which a language was acquired, and so on. In sum, one should be extremely wary of discrete classifications that do not do full justice to the representational and processing complexity found within the individual bilingual.

A third problem is that some models may not contain all the necessary components or levels needed. An example comes from work on lexical representation where most of the models proposed (see above) contain only two levels: a lexeme (or form) level and a conceptual (or meaning) level. And yet there is quite a bit of evidence in the literature that the lexicon contains a third level, the lemma level, that is situated between the lexeme and the conceptual level. Lemmas contain morphological and syntactic information about the word (Jescheniak and Levelt 1994; Myers-Scotton and Jake 1995). Kroll and de Groot (1997) have proposed to take this level into account and have presented the general outline of a distributed lexical/conceptual feature model of lexical representation in the bilingual that contains this level. At some point their model will probably have to take into account a fourth level (world knowledge), at least to explain the underlying operations that take place when participants are involved in paradigms that include non-linguistic operations (such as picture naming). Paradis (1995) states, as he has done repeatedly, that one of the major problems in the field has been the failure to distinguish between the meaning of words and non-linguistic representations. Based on research in neurolinguistics, he states that we must distinguish between the lexical meaning of words, which is a part of the speaker's linguistic competence, and conceptual representations, which are outside of implicit linguistic competence. (Note here that he uses the expression "lexical meaning" for what corresponds to the conceptual level in most models and "conceptual representation" for non-linguistic, world knowledge.) He adds that the conceptual system, where messages are elaborated before they are verbalized in the course of the encoding process, and where a mental representation is attained at the end of the decoding process, remains independent and isolable from the bilingual's language systems. It would be interesting to know whether tasks such as word repetition, word translation, and picture naming, for example, require access to this non-linguistic level. Some must (e.g. picture naming), whereas others may not have to do so.

A fourth problem is that the field has too few global models that give a general picture of bilingual competence, and bilingual production and perception as well as bilingual language acquisition. For example, until de Bot's (1992) attempt at adapting Levelt's (1989) 'Speaking' model to the bilingual, there was no general overall view of how the bilingual speaker goes from a prelinguistic message to actual overt speech. Even though de Bot's model still needs to give a clear account of how language choice is conducted, how the language mode is chosen and the impact it has on processing, how code-switches and borrowings are actually produced, how interferences occur, and so on, it has the very real quality of dealing with the complete production process and hence of encouraging debate in the field (e.g. de Bot and Schreuder 1993; Poulisse and Bongaerts 1994; Poulisse 1997). This is true also of Green's (1986) resources model of production for normal and brain-damaged bilinguals. In the domain of perception and comprehension, no model as broad as Marslen-Wilson and Tyler's (1987) interactive model or Forster's (1979) modular model of language processing has been proposed. However, headway is being made by two computational models that are relatively broad: a bilingual model of visual word recognition (BIA: Grainger and Dijkstra 1992; Dijkstra and van Heuven 1998), and a model of spoken word recognition in bilinguals (BIMOLA: Grosjean 1988; Léwy and Grosjean unpublished).

A final problem, which is admittedly in partial contradiction with the previous one, is that models are not always detailed or explicit enough. For example, Myers-Scotton (1993) has proposed a model, the Matrix Language Frame (MLF) Model, which states that a number of hierarchies, hypotheses, and principles govern the structuring of sentences containing code-switches. The model has attracted the attention and the interest of linguists and psycholinguists but, like other important models, it has also raised many questions. For example, Bentahila (1995) states that it is not specific enough on such things as what constitutes a matrix language, the difference the model makes between an extensive embedded language (EL) island and a change of matrix language, what a system morpheme is, and so on. For Bentahila, models must be explicit and their validity depends on clear definitions which are externally verifiable without circularity.[4]

14.5.3 Tentative solutions

If there is one issue for which solutions can only be tentative, it is the one which deals with models. This is by far the most delicate and complex issue raised so far, and what follows is only one researcher's viewpoint. First, and from what has been said, it is clear that any model will have to take into account the full complexity of the bilingual speaker-hearer as illustrated in the first two sections of this chapter (participants and language mode). For example, bilinguals should not be viewed as two monolinguals in one person or be classified once and for all into discrete linguistic or psycholinguistic categories. Second, it is crucial that general models be proposed. The field is in dire need of general theories of the bilingual speaker-hearer as well as of models of bilingual language acquisition and processing. Third, models must contain all the necessary components or levels needed and they must be as explicit as possible so that they can be put to the test. Fourth, it is important that cross-fertilization takes place between the various domains of bilingualism. A theoretical linguistics of bilingualism that attempts to account for the bilingual's competence, a developmental psycholinguistics that models how children acquire their two languages simultaneously or successively, a neurolinguistics of bilingualism that accounts for normal and pathological brain behavior, and a psycholinguistics that models processing in bilinguals can each bring a lot to the other domains and receive a lot from them. Finally, bilingual models will have to use, after being adapted, the new approaches and the new theories that are constantly being developed in the various fields of cognitive science primarily to study monolinguals. In return, these fields will be enriched by what is learned about bilinguals.

Concluding remark

Dealing with the methodological and conceptual issues that have been presented in this chapter will take time, work, and some inventiveness.

---

[4] It should be noted that Myers-Scotton (p.c.) reports that many issues raised by Bentahila are discussed and clarified in the "Afterword" of the 1997 paperback version of her book *Duelling Languages* (Myers-Scotton 1993).

The outcome, however, will be clearer and less ambiguous results as well as models that take into account the full complexity of the bilingual individual.

Appendix: Assessing the bilingual aphasic's language knowledge and use

The following is an extract (pp. 12–13) from Grosjean, F. (1989). "Neurolinguists, beware! The bilingual is not two monolinguals in one person", *Brain and Language* 36: 3–15. The author thanks Elsevier for permission to reprint it here.

A. Describing the bilingual prior to injury

Although everyone concurs that there are major difficulties involved in adequately describing a patient's bilingualism prior to injury, it is nevertheless important not to overlook certain critical questions. Some of these are:

- Which languages did the patient know before injury?
- How well did he or she know them (as a function of linguistic level, language skills, styles, etc.)?
- What were the languages used for, with whom, and for what?
- What kind of interferences occurred in the patient's speech when in a monolingual speech/language mode? When speaking language A? Language B?
- Which of these interferences were of a static nature? Which of a dynamic kind?
- How much time did the patient spend in a monolingual as opposed to a bilingual speech mode?
- How much mixing took place in the bilingual speech mode (if and when the patient was in that mode)?
- What kind of mixing occurred: speech borrowing, code-switching, or both?
- Who did the patient code-switch and borrow with?
- How good were the translation abilities of the patient, etc.?

B. Describing the bilingual after injury

Having assessed the patient's language knowledge and use before injury, it will be important to examine the patient in the speech modes he or she was involved in prior to injury.

1. The monolingual speech/language mode

In the sessions examining the monolingual mode, it will be important to deactivate the language not being tested. To do this, the patient will have to be tested in *each* of the two languages (if both were used monolingually) at *different times* and with different examiners *who do not know the other language at all*. Thus, in each case, the patient will understand that he or she is facing a monolingual interlocutor and can therefore only use one language. We should note that, in order to simulate the monolingual mode, many examiners "pretend" not to know the other language. This is quite inappropriate as the pretense is rarely foolproof and never lasts very long; the consequence is that the data obtained are usually ambiguous as they emanate from a conversation where the speech/language mode has changed from being monolingual to bilingual.

Keeping in mind the knowledge, use, and function of the languages prior to injury, it will now be possible to assess the impact of the injury on each of the two languages when they are used monolingually. Of particular interest will be the amount and type of language loss as well as the kind of interferences that now occur: are these different from those prior to injury? It will also be necessary to determine if the patient can keep his or her two languages separate in these monolingual testing situations: change of base language or actual code-switching with a monolingual examiner will be a sure sign that the mechanism that allows bilinguals to deactivate one language, when speaking the other, has been affected.

2. The bilingual speech/language mode

If the patient also operated in the bilingual speech mode before injury, he or she will need to be examined in that particular mode. To do this, a testing situation will need to be set up such that the patient feels comfortable code-switching and borrowing during the examination. One way of doing this is to adjoin to a *third* bilingual examiner (the first two being monolingual in either language A or B), some members of the patient's family, or close friends with whom he or she code-switched and borrowed before injury. In this bilingual mode, one should study the appropriateness of language choice and the ability to code-switch and borrow. Questions that need to be answered are:

- Does the patient speak the "wrong" language to a bilingual family member or close friend?

- Does he or she mix languages to the same extent as before?
- Are these mixes of the same type (code-switches, borrowings)?
- Are the code-switches still grammatically constrained?
- Do they belong to the same class: intersentential, intrasentential, single items, tags, etc.?
- Can the patient translate from one language to the other in the same way as he or she did before injury, etc.?

Examining bilinguals in their various speech/language modes and determining the exact nature of the deficit in these modes should help us better understand bilingual aphasia and, more generally, the neurolinguistics of bilingualism.

15

Imaging Bilinguals*

The Rodriguez-Fornells, Rotte, Heinze, Nösselt, and Münte (2002) paper published in *Nature*, "Brain potential and functional MRI evidence for how to handle two languages with one brain", is discussed in this chapter by two of its authors (T. F. Münte and A. Rodriguez-Fornells), both neuroscientists, and by two language scientists (F. Grosjean and P. Li). First, a short summary of the paper is given. This is followed by a critical commentary offered by the language scientists. The neuroscientists respond, and a final comment is offered by the language scientists. The four authors conclude that a two-way collaboration between neurosciences and language sciences should be encouraged in order to make headway in our understanding of language processing and representation in bilinguals.

15.1 Summary of the article

(by T. F. Münte and A. Rodriguez-Fornells)

Rodriguez-Fornells, A., Rotte, M., Heinze, H-J., Nösselt, T., and Münte, T. F. (2002). "Brain potential and functional MRI evidence for how to handle two languages with one brain", *Nature*, 415, 1026–9.

The starting point of our investigation was the long-standing notion that bilingual individuals need effective mechanisms to prevent interference from one language while processing material in the other (e.g. Penfield and Roberts 1959). To demonstrate how the prevention of interference is implemented in the brain we employed event-related

* This chapter is a reprint of Grosjean, F., Li, P., Münte, T., and Rodriguez-Fornells, A. (2003). "Imaging bilinguals: When the neurosciences meet the language sciences", *Bilingualism: Language and Cognition* 6: 159–65. The author wishes to thank Cambridge University Press as well as P. Li, T. Münte, and A. Rodriguez-Fornells for permission to reprint it here.

brain potentials (ERPs; see Münte *et al.* 2000 for an introductory review) and functional magnetic resonance imaging (fMRI) techniques, thus pursuing a combined temporal and spatial imaging approach. In contrast to previous investigations using neuroimaging techniques in bilinguals, which had been mainly concerned with the localization of the primary and secondary languages (e.g. Perani *et al.* 1998; Chee *et al.* 1999), our study addressed the dynamic aspects of bilingual language processing.

Bilingual speakers of Spanish and Catalan, with high proficiency in both languages, and monolingual Spanish participants, served as volunteers. In the main ERP and fMRI experiments, participants were shown a series of stimuli appearing one at a time in the middle of a video-screen. Stimulus lists comprised high and low frequency Spanish and Catalan words as well as pseudo-words, which were derived from either Spanish or Catalan words by changing one or several letters. Care was taken to exclude cognate words, that are very similar or identical in the two languages, from the stimulus material. Participants were instructed to press a button for Spanish words only and to withhold response for either Catalan or pseudo-words. Brain potentials were recorded from thirty-two scalp channels. The N400 component in the ERP was examined. Words from the target language (Spanish) showed a modulation of the N400 response (Kutas *et al.* 2000) as a function of word frequency in both bilingual and monolingual subject groups, while the brain potentials to the Catalan words did not show a frequency dependent modulation of the N400. In a control experiment, performed on a smaller number of bilingual subjects, the task was changed such that now the Catalan words had to be responded to, while Spanish and pseudo-words had to be ignored. This control experiment indicated that a modulation of the N400 to the Catalan words was now present, while no such effect was seen for the Spanish words. In a further control experiment we showed that these effects were independent of the requirement to respond. The lack of an N400 modulation for words from the non-target language in the bilingual subjects was taken to indicate that the meaning of these words had not been accessed by the bilinguals.

Event-related fMRI was performed using the same task as in the main ERP experiment, that is with Spanish words serving as a target, but introducing consonant strings (for example, "dfmvr") as an additional stimulus category. A first important finding was that neither the monolingual nor the bilingual group showed reliable differences between the activation pattern of pseudo-words and Catalan words. These stimuli were apparently treated very similarly by the two subject groups, thus corroborating the interpretation of ERP results, that is that Catalan words were in general not processed for meaning. Critically, only bilingual subjects showed activation of the left posterior inferior frontal area and the planum temporale, that is regions that have previously been found in experiments employing pseudo-word reading, phonological processing, and subvocal rehearsal (e.g. Petersen *et al.* 1989; Zatorre *et al.* 1992; Paulesu *et al.* 1993).

This brain activation pattern, together with the N400 data, suggested to us that bilinguals prevent interference by using the brain and cognitive machinery normally reserved for the reading of unknown or pseudo-words, that is the sublexical pathway (Coltheart *et al.* 1993), while at the same time inhibiting the direct access route from orthography to the lexicon. This interpretation was also supported by greater activation of an anterior prefrontal region in bilinguals, which is generally viewed as supporting inhibition (e.g. Bunge *et al.* 2001).

15.2 Commentary

(by F. Grosjean and P. Li)

"Two languages with one brain" is a fascinating topic that has naturally attracted the attention of neuroscientists who have access to the latest neuroimaging technologies. More than three-dozen "imaging bilinguals" articles have been published including the one by Rodriguez-Fornells *et al.* (2002; henceforth RF) which we discuss here. In what follows, we argue that the authors do not take into account crucial factors in bilingualism research and that they fail to interpret their data in terms of current theories of bilingual processing.

RF state that their monolingual speakers of Spanish and their Spanish/Catalan bilinguals were foreign students at two German universities. If that is the case, didn't both groups also know and use German and weren't they therefore bilingual and trilingual? What impact did this have on the results obtained? Such questions lead to the issue of what is meant by bilingual. In the language sciences, bilingualism is increasingly defined in terms of regular use of two or more languages (Grosjean 1994) and it does not necessarily imply equal proficiency in the languages known (as RF's study seems to imply). In addition, it is well established that language history, language stability, and the functions of each language, along with language mixing habits, all have an impact on processing results. The probable diversity of the subjects used by RF is further confounded by the unequal number of bilinguals in each experiment (e.g. fifteen in the main ERP study but only four in the first control!) and by the fact that some participated in several experiments and saw some of the same stimuli. In short, the RF results may be specific to the subjects used and may not be replicable with other bilinguals.

RF's starting point is that "bilinguals need effective mechanisms to prevent interference from one language while processing material in the other." This rather monolingual view of the bilingual fending off the other languages has been replaced by a much more dynamic view of bilingual language processing based on the language mode concept (Grosjean 1998a, 2001; Marian and Spivey 2003). In some situations the bilingual must indeed only process one language (the mode is close to being monolingual), but in others several languages are processed online with one taking the lead role (as in the case of mixed language where the base language is more active than the guest language; Li 1996). The bilinguals in RF's main ERP experiment were not in a monolingual mode: they had activated their Spanish lexicon to a greater extent but they were still processing Catalan words despite being asked to respond to Spanish words only. Bilinguals made more errors (i.e. false-positive responses) to high frequency Catalan words and were generally delayed in preparing a motor response compared to monolinguals as is evidenced by the lateralized readiness potentials (LRPs).

Why then were words from the non-target language "rejected" by the bilinguals? Probably not because they used a sublexical access route to the lexicon, as the authors speculate (there is no evidence in the literature that the lexical access mechanisms are any different in bilinguals and monolinguals), but for other reasons. First, in the main ERP and MRI experiments, since the task was to respond to Spanish words, it is possible that the Spanish lexicon was more active and the Catalan lexicon less so. This would help ensure response to Spanish words. Second, there were probably some graphemic cues specific to Catalan words that would exclude the latter from the process (e.g. the grave accent, letters such as "ç" and "x"; sequences such as "l.l", "ny", "ix", "ss", "tx", "tge", "lts"; etc.). Third, the high-frequency Spanish words may have got an extra boost by being more frequent than their counterparts in Catalan (95 versus 68.4 occurrences per million). These, and other reasons (e.g. the varying proportion of words from the two languages in the experiments), would speak less in favor of "rejection" than of reduced activation of the words in the non-target language. These words did not reach the required activation threshold and hence were usually not responded to (Dijkstra and van Heuven 1998).

RF end their paper with a statement that the generality of their findings should be tested with other experimental tasks. We can only concur with this, for the reasons given above, but also because the findings in bilingualism research and in brain imaging studies are often task specific (Joseph 2001).

The gap between the neurosciences and the language sciences of bilingualism will be narrowed if both sides define and choose their bilinguals with care, use carefully selected stimuli, control for language mode, employ tasks that tap into normal language processing, and build together coherent theories of bilingual language representation and processing.

15.3 Response

(by T. F. Münte and A. Rodriguez-Fornells)

The comments by Grosjean and Li (henceforth GL) can be divided into those pertaining specifically to our experiment and those that have a more general character. In the following, we will briefly address the specific issues and then turn to the more important general issues.

15.3.1 Comments on specific issues

We concur with GL that our Spanish/Catalan subjects with high proficiency in two languages represent a rather extreme case of bilingualism. While we can see that other studies with different aims might call for different subject groups, we still view Spanish/Catalan bilinguals to be ideal for our purpose, as we were interested in the mechanisms allowing bilinguals to preferentially process one language while suppressing the other. A high level of proficiency in both languages is needed in such a study, and in Spanish/Catalan subjects this proficiency is guaranteed by the educational policies in Catalunya. This has led to the use of these subjects in a great number of studies on bilingualism (e.g. Pallier *et al.* 1998; Perani *et al.* 1998; Sebastian-Galles and Soto-Faraco 1999; Costa *et al.* 2000; Pallier *et al.* 2001). Moreover, our subjects were assessed for current language habits by a questionnaire adapted from Weber-Fox and Neville (1997), which indicated regular use, as well as high proficiency, of both languages. We thus do not see how a "probable diversity" of the subjects could be responsible for our results.

GL also point out that the different number of subjects in the main and in the control ERP experiments might be problematic. Statistical power is not an issue here, however, as the control experiment has demonstrated the ability of subjects to switch between languages, and the ERP pattern can be reversed as a function of the instructions.

Furthermore, GL—with regard to the lateralized readiness potential (LRP)—remark that our Spanish/Catalan subjects were not in a monolingual mode. In fact, however, the LRP results of our study show NO LRP ACTIVITY for the words from the non-target language. This suggests that these words were effectively rejected. This view is supported by the findings for the N400 component (Kutas *et al.* 2000) not mentioned by GL in their comments. In the bilingual as well as in the monolingual subjects there was no N400 modulation for Catalan words in the main experiment, which suggests that Catalan words were NOT processed for meaning by the bilinguals. In addition, the first control experiment showed that bilinguals can effectively switch their strategy according to instructions and that at that point Spanish words were not processed for meaning.

This selective processing of Spanish or Catalan words in the bilinguals was interpreted by us in light of the brain activation patterns in bilinguals, which, as pointed out in our summary, were reminiscent of activations seen in experiments using pseudo-word reading. As these, by necessity, engage the phonological route, they suggested to us that bilinguals might use this route in order to block out the information from the non-target language. In their comments, GL disregard these results, however. By contrast, we believe that brain activation patterns can be highly informative because activations can be compared across multiple studies and tasks, as was done in our paper.

In any biological or psychological experiment a particular limited phenomenon is studied under particular limited conditions. Our experiment suggests how certain bilingual subjects behave in a certain situation (reading of mixed word lists with one language relevant). Other mechanisms might help bilinguals to keep their languages separate in other situations. Thus, our experiment is limited like virtually every other brain imaging and psycholinguistic experiment. In several further studies, we have therefore extended our work to test the monolingual versus bilingual mode during comprehension

(Rodriguez-Fornells *et al.* in preparation) as well as bilingual, Spanish/German, production in a picture naming task (Rodriguez-Fornells *et al.* 2005).

15.3.2 Comments on general issues

In their comments GL endorse a collaboration between the language sciences and the neurosciences for the study of bilingualism. We could not agree more but we would like to point out that such a collaboration should not be a one-way street with neuroscientists proving theories devised by language scientists. That such an approach falls significantly short of the possibilities of such a collaboration can be illustrated by the following recent example. A heated debate in psycholinguistics concerns the representation and processing of regular and irregular verb forms (Marcus *et al.* 1995; Marchman *et al.* 1997; Pinker 1997; Clahsen 1999). Some theorists have advocated single mechanism models that represent and process both classes of verbs within a single system, while other researchers have proposed dual mechanism models with separate paths for regular and irregular verbs. Pinker (1997) has gone so far as to call the regular and irregular formation of verb forms the "fruit fly of linguistics". Several research laboratories including our own (e.g. Penke *et al.* 1997; Münte *et al.* 1999b; Rodriguez-Fornells *et al.* 2001) have collected ERP and brain imaging data on regular and irregular word processing, which have been used by psycholinguists in support of single (Seidenberg and Hoeffner 1997) and dual mechanism models (Clahsen 1999) of morphological processing. However, as we have pointed out elsewhere (Münte *et al.* 1999a), the neuroscientific data on the matter suggest that *neither* a single *nor* a dual mechanism model appears to be entirely appropriate. For example, PET (positron emission tomograpic) studies by Jaeger *et al.* (1996) and Indefrey *et al.* (1997) have revealed that multiple (i.e. more than ten) brain areas distinguish between the processing of regular and irregular verbs. This, in turn, suggests that both classes of psycholinguistic models might give an incomplete picture of what computations are necessary to handle these different types of verbs. We have therefore proposed that the brain activation patterns seen in fMRI or PET as well as the modulations of the ERPs might be used to guide the development of more realistic psycholinguistic models. In the same way, of course, neuroscientific data, like the ones in our own study, might be used to stimulate and constrain psycholinguistic models addressing language processing in bilinguals, while these models in turn should be used to devise appropriate experiments. This will, we believe, eventually lead to a more fruitful collaboration between psycholinguists and neuroscientists.

On a more practical note, first time (psycholinguistic) users and consumers of neuroimaging or electrophysiological techniques may find that their experimental possibilities are limited by methodological constraints, for example, the necessity to have many trials per category or the problem of artifacts produced by vocalizations. These drawbacks are offset in our opinion by the fact that these techniques can deliver multidimensional spatio-temporal data on the timing, localization, and parceling of cognitive processes underlying bilingual language processing. Moreover, they can even deliver data on stimuli that do not require overt responses. They can thus be viewed as a useful extension rather than a replacement of more traditional experimentation in psycholinguistics.

To conclude, while naturally we do not agree with most of the criticisms raised by GL, we welcome very warmly their proposal for a more fruitful collaboration between psycholinguists and neuroscientists.

15.4 Reply to the response

(by P. Li and F. Grosjean)

Münte and Rodriguez-Fornells (henceforth MRF) provide us with a rather detailed response to our commentary. Although it contains many important points, we are not sure that MRF address the main issues we made in our commentary. Below, we first list the concerns we raised for which we do not see a response, and next we discuss MRF's comments on the other points we made.

There are a number of concerns for which we do not see a response. First, there is the fact that the monolingual speakers of Spanish were *not* in fact monolingual (they were probably bilingual) and that the Spanish/Catalan bilinguals were probably trilingual. It should be remembered that they were all foreign students in Germany at the time of the study and hence German—as a second language for the first group and as a third language for the second—could have played some role in the results obtained. Second, there is the fact that some of the subjects participated both in the main study and in the control study. Hence, we have no guarantee that the subjects' first experimental run did not influence the second (e.g. they may have remembered some items). Third, the bilinguals in the main ERP experiment were not in a monolingual mode and hence it is no surprise that the non-target language was showing some activity. This is apparent in the LRP onset latencies and in the errors made. MRF do not respond specifically to the language mode issue or to the latency and error data comment; they do, however, address the LRP activity issue to which we will return below. Fourth, we proposed that there were at least three bases for "rejecting" non-target language words: a more active target language lexicon, graphemic cues to the non-target language that helped to exclude it, and the higher frequency of some items in the target language. MRF do not address these factors. We believe that all of these concerns are important and that they might have influenced the results obtained.[1]

As for MRF's comments on the other points we made, we should first state that we did not question that their bilingual subjects were highly proficient in Catalan and Spanish or that these bilinguals were ideal for their study. Hence we will not discuss these two aspects but rather we will focus on MRF's other points (presented in italics below).

1. *The high proficiency of the bilinguals does away with the diversity criticism.* MRF appear to use the argument that their bilinguals were highly proficient in Catalan and Spanish to disagree with the fact that bilingual diversity could have had an impact on their results. However, language proficiency is just one factor in defining the diversity of bilinguals: others include language history, language stability, the functions of each language, and language mixing habits. These are well-accepted factors among researchers of bilingualism and have been shown to affect processing (see e.g. Grosjean 1998); they may well have had an impact on the Rodriguez-Fornells *et al.* (2002) results.

2. *The small number of subjects in the first control study is not a problem.* MRF believe that four subjects are sufficient for such a study. We have doubts, as would most cognitive scientists working with subject populations and using inferential statistics.

3. *The LRP results show no activity of the non-target language.* In our commentary we argue that the non-target language (Catalan) was still active, though to a lesser extent. This was clear from the LRP onset latencies and the higher error rate to high frequency Catalan

---

[1] A further possibility is that rejection occurs at a rather late stage and reflects a decision process. Von Studnitz and Green (2002) showed that reduction in interference can arise without reducing the lexical activation of the non-target language.

words. In fact, in their *Nature* paper, the authors acknowledge this when they write (p. 1027): "[the bilinguals] had some difficulty suppressing button presses to high-frequency irrelevant words." In their response, MRF do not address our concern but point out that (a) there was no LRP activity for Catalan words in the bilinguals, and (b) there was no ERP N400 modulation to Catalan words in both monolinguals and bilinguals. With regard to (a), we believe that there is a difference between no LRP activity and the inactivity of a language. LRP indicates the preparation of motor responses only, as is pointed out in Rodriguez-Fornells *et al.* (2002). In addition, there was a marked difference between monolinguals and bilinguals in terms of the amplitude and the speed to the target language. This clearly indicates that the bilinguals did not prepare their responses to the target language as effectively, due probably to the partial activation of the non-target language. With regard to (b), we note two important things. First, the authors use the difference between high and low frequency words in N400 as a measure of meaning access. (It should be recalled that, according to Kutas and Hillyard (1980), N400 is an ERP component that detects semantic violations or incongruity in sentence processing.) It is a big step to go from the presence or absence of a frequency effect to the presence or absence of meaning access; the interplay of the two is not as direct as the authors seem to suggest. Second, there is a major difference between monolinguals and bilinguals. Monolinguals have no N400 to either type of word (high or low frequency), while bilinguals have N400 to both. Moreover, in the control experiment with four subjects, the ERP patterns were of two sorts: for Spanish words, they were similar to those of the bilinguals in the main experiment; for Catalan words, they were similar to those of the monolinguals in the main experiment. Thus, there were general differences in ERP and N400 patterns between the monolinguals and the bilinguals that the authors did not discuss, and these differences could undermine the authors' interpretation of the general difference between the two groups in terms of dual-route access.

4. *The bilinguals might be using the phonological route to block out the information from the non-target language.* MRF's assignment of a "lexical" route to monolinguals and a "sublexical" route to bilinguals seems to be at odds with most known theories and results in monolingual and bilingual language processing studies.

For example, research by Perfetti and colleagues suggests that all monolinguals, even in phonologically non-transparent languages, use "sublexical" routes to access the mental lexicon (Perfetti *et al.* 1988; Tan and Perfetti 1998). We believe that a better explanation of Rodriguez-Fornells *et al.*'s (2002) results should be based on factors pointed out earlier, such as which lexicon was more active and the existence of graphemic cues specific to words of one language.

In conclusion, MRF point out that, "collaboration between the language sciences and the neurosciences . . . should not be a one-way street with neuroscientists proving theories devised by language scientists". Our intention in starting this dialogue with our colleagues is precisely to bridge the gap between the neurosciences and language sciences. Thus, we too are advocating a two-way collaboration (cf. the "if both sides define" paragraph in our commentary on p. 277). We know that this is a view shared by an increasing number of neuroscientists and language scientists (see Vaid and Hull 2002 for a review of the field as well as the 2001 special issue of *Bilingualism: Language and Cognition*, edited by David Green).

Appendix: List of publications on bilingualism and biculturalism by François Grosjean

1. General

(Describing bilingualism and the bilingual person, language mode, and the complementarity principle)

Grosjean, F. (1982). *Life with Two Languages: An Introduction to Bilingualism*. Cambridge, MA: Harvard University Press.

Grosjean, F. (1984). "Communication exolingue et communication bilingue", in B. Py (ed.) *Acquisition d'une Langue Etrangère III*. Paris: Presses de l'Université de Paris VIII and Encrages; Neuchâtel: Centre de Linguistique Appliquée, 49–61.

Grosjean, F. (1984). "Le bilinguisme: Vivre avec deux langues", *Bulletin de Linguistique Appliquée et Générale de l'Université de Besançon (Bulag)* 11: 4–25. Also in *Travaux Neuchâtelois de Linguistique (Tranel)* 7: 15–42.

Grosjean, F. (1985). "The bilingual as a competent but specific speaker-hearer", *Journal of Multilingual and Multicultural Development* 6: 467–77.

Grosjean, F. (1989). "The bilingual as a person", in R. Titone (ed.) *On the Bilingual Person*. Ottawa: Canadian Society for Italian Studies, 35–54.

Grosjean, F. (1992). "Another view of bilingualism", in R. Harris (ed.) *Cognitive Processing in Bilinguals*. Amsterdam: North-Holland, 51–62.

Grosjean, F. (1993, 1996, 2004). "Le bilinguisme et le biculturalisme: essai de définition", *Travaux Neuchâtelois de Linguistique (Tranel)*, 1993, 19: 13–42. Also in A. Gorouden and B. Virole (eds.) *Le bilinguisme aujourd'hui et demain*. Paris: Editions du CTNERHI, 2004, 17–50. German version in H. Schneider and J. Hollenweger (eds.) *Mehrsprachigkeit und Fremdsprachigkeit: Arbeit für die Sonderpädagogik?* Lucerne: Edition SZH, 1996, 161–84.

Grosjean, F. (1994, 1997, 1999, 2001, 2003). "Individual bilingualism", in R. Asher (ed.) *The Encyclopedia of Language and Linguistics*. Oxford: Pergamon Press, 1994, 1656–60. Also in *Applied Linguistic Studies in Central Europe* (University of Veszprem, Hungary), 1997, 103–13; in B. Spolsky (ed.) *Concise Encyclopedia of Educational Linguistics*. Oxford: Pergamon Press, 1999, 284–90; in R. Mesthrie (ed.) *Concise Encyclopedia of Sociolinguistics*. Oxford: Pergamon Press, 2001, 10–16. Slovak version in J. Stefanik (ed.) *Individualny bilingvizmus*. Bratislava: Academic Electronic Press, 2003, 39–48.

Grosjean, F. (1997). "The bilingual individual", *Interpreting: International Journal of Research and Practice in Interpreting* 2: 163–87.

Grosjean, F. (1999). "Le bilinguisme: une compétence communicative à part entière", *Educateur Magazine* 12: 18–21.

Grosjean, F. (2001, 2007). "The bilingual's language modes", in J. Nicol (ed.) *One Mind, Two Languages: Bilingual Language Processing*. Oxford: Blackwell, 2001, 1–22. Also in Li Wei (ed.) *The Bilingual Reader*, 2nd edn. London: Routledge, 2007, 428–49.

Grosjean, F. (2002, 2003). "Interview". *The Bilingual Family Newsletter* 2002, 19: 4–7, and 2002, 20: 1–7. Hungarian version in *Hungarian Journal of Applied Linguistics* 2002, 1: 103–14. Italian version in *Education et sociétés plurilingues*, 2003, 15: 85–97.

Grosjean, F. (2004). "Le bilinguisme et le biculturalisme: quelques notions de base", in C. Billard, M. Touzin, and P. Gillet (eds.) *Troubles spécifiques des apprentissages: l'état des connaissances*. Paris: Signes Editions, 2–9.

2. Language restructuring

Grosjean, F. and Py, B. (1991). "La restructuration d'une première langue: l'intégration de variantes de contact dans la compétence de migrants bilingues", *La Linguistique* 27: 35–60.

Py, B. and Grosjean, F. (2002). "Variantes de contact, restructuration et compétence bilingue: approche expérimentale", in V. Castellotti and B. Py (eds.) *La notion de compétence en langue*. Lyon: ENS Editions, 19–27.

3. Language processing

(Psycholinguistics, speech perception, and production)

Soares, C. and Grosjean, F. (1984). "Bilinguals in a monolingual and a bilingual speech mode: The effect on lexical access", *Memory and Cognition* 12: 380–6.

Grosjean, F. and Soares, C. (1986). "Processing mixed language: Some preliminary findings", in J. Vaid (ed.) *Language Processing in Bilinguals: Psycholinguistic and Neuropsychological Perspectives*. Hillsdale, NJ: Lawrence Erlbaum, 145–79.

Grosjean, F. (1987). "Vers une psycholinguistique du parler bilingue", in G. Lüdi (ed.) *Devenir Bilingue—Parler Bilingue*. Tübingen: Niemeyer, 115–32.

Grosjean, F. (1988). "Exploring the recognition of guest words in bilingual speech", *Language and Cognitive Processes* 3: 233–74.

Bürki-Cohen, J., Grosjean, F., and Miller, J. (1989). "Base language effects on word identification in bilingual speech: Evidence from categorical perception experiments", *Language and Speech* 32: 355–71.

Grosjean, F. and Miller, J. (1994). "Going in and out of languages: An example of bilingual flexibility", *Psychological Science* 5: 201–6.

Grosjean, F. (1995). "A psycholinguistic approach to code-switching: The recognition of guest words by bilinguals", in L. Milroy and P. Muysken (eds.) *One Speaker, Two Languages: Cross-Disciplinary Perspectives on Code-Switching*. Cambridge: Cambridge University Press, 259–75.

Grosjean, F. (1997, 2000, 2003). "Processing mixed language: Issues, findings, and models", in A. M. B. de Groot and J. F. Kroll (eds.) *Tutorials in Bilingualism: Psycholinguistic Perspectives*. Mahwah, NJ: Lawrence Erlbaum Associates, 1997, 225–54. Also in Li Wei (ed.) *The Bilingual Reader*. London: Routledge, 2000, 443–69. Slovak version in J. Stefanik (ed.) *Individualny bilingvizmus*. Bratislava: Academic Electronic Press, 2003, 193–214.

Grosjean, F. (1998). "The on-line processing of speech: Lexical access in bilinguals", in P. Bhatt and R. Davis (eds.) *The Linguistic Brain*. Toronto: Canadian Scholars' Press, 3–12.

Guillelmon, D. and Grosjean, F. (2001). "The gender marking effect in spoken word recognition: The case of bilinguals", *Memory and Cognition* 29: 503–11.

4. Biculturalism

Grosjean, F. (1983, 1984, 1989). "Quelques réflexions sur le biculturalisme", *Pluriel*, 1983, 36: 81–91. Also in *Bulletin de Linguistique Appliquée et Générale de l'Université de Besançon (Bulag)*, 1984, 11: 86–97; and *Paroles d'Or: Revue de l'Association Romande des Logopédistes Diplômés*, 1989, 4: 3–6.

Grosjean, F. (1990). "Etre biculturel: une identité qui exclut la naturalisation?", in P. Centlivres (ed.) *Devenir Suisse: adhésion et diversité culturelle des étrangers en Suisse*. Geneva: Georg, 243–52.

Grosjean, F. (2007). "La personne biculturelle: un premier aperçu", *Contacts sourds entendants* 2: 17–44.

5. Bilingualism of the Deaf

(Bimodal bilingualism)

Grosjean, F. (1986). "Bilingualism", in *Gallaudet Encyclopedia of Deaf People and Deafness*, vol 3. New York: McGraw-Hill, 179–82.

Grosjean, F. (1992, 1993, 1998). "The bilingual and the bicultural person in the hearing and in the deaf world", *Sign Language Studies*, 1992, 77: 307–20. French version: *Nouvelles Pratiques Sociales*, 1993, 6: 69–82. German version: *Das Zeichen*, 1993, 24: 183–9. Danish version: Hansen, B. (ed.) *Samspil Mellem dove og Horende*. Copenhagen: Center for Tegnsprog og Tengtottet Kommunikation, 1998, 101–9.

Grosjean, F. (1994). "Sign bilingualism: Issues", in R. Asher (ed.) *The Encyclopedia of Language and Linguistics*. Oxford: Pergamon Press, 3889–90.

Grosjean, F. (1996). "Living with two languages and two cultures", in I. Parasnis (ed.) *Cultural and Language Diversity and the Deaf Experience*. Cambridge: Cambridge University Press, 20–37.

Grosjean, F. (1999, 2000, 2003). "The right of the deaf child to grow up bilingual", *Deaf Worlds*, 1999, 15(2): 29–31. Also in *WFD News*,

2000, 13(1): 14–15; *The Endeavor*, 2000, 1: 28–31; *Sign Language Studies*, 2001, 1(2): 110–14. French version: *Langage et pratiques*, 1999, 23: 1–15; *Bulletin ASPEDA* (Association Suisse des Parents d'Enfants Déficients-Auditifs), 1999, 1: 8–11; *Surdités*, 2000, 3: 90–3. German version: *Das Zeichen*, 1999, 47: 64–6; *Forum Logopädie*, 1999, 4: 18–19; *Bulletin ASPEDA* (Schweizerische Vereinigung der Eltern hörgeschädigter Kinder), 1999, 1: 8–11. Hungarian version: *Modern Nyelvoktatás*, 1999, 4: 5–8. Italian version: *Parole e Segni*, 2000, 10(1): 44–6; *Saggi Child Development and Disabilities*, 2003, 1: 65–8. Portuguese version: *Revista da FENEIS* (Federation of Education and Integration of the Deaf, Brazil), 2000, 2(6): 26–7. Serbian version: *Glas Tisine*, 2000, 24(6): 11. Slovak version: *Efeta*, 2000, 10(1): 17–18. *Slovensky Gong*, 2000, 2: 7–8. Spanish version: *El bilingüismo de los Sordos*, 2000, 1(4): 15–18.

Grosjean, F. (2003). "Le bilinguisme, clé de l'égalité des chances pour les sourds", *Sourd d'aujourd'hui* 6: 10–11.

Grosjean, F. (2004). "Bilinguisme, biculturalisme et surdité", in A. Gorouden and B. Virolle (eds.) *Le bilinguisme aujourd'hui et demain* Paris: Editions du CTNERHI, 51–70.

Grosjean, F. (2007). "La personne biculturelle: un premier aperçu". See Biculturalism.

6. Neurolinguistics and aphasia

Soares, C. and Grosjean, F. (1981). "Left hemisphere language lateralization in bilinguals and monolinguals", *Perception and Psychophysics* 29: 599–604.

Grosjean, F. (1985). "Polyglot aphasics and language mixing: A comment on Perecman (1984)", *Brain and Language* 26: 349–55.

Grosjean, F. (1989). "Neurolinguists, beware! The bilingual is not two monolinguals in one person", *Brain and Language* 36: 3–15.

Marty, S. and Grosjean, F. (1998). "Aphasie, bilinguisme et modes de communication", *APHASIE und verwandte Gebiete* 12: 8–28.

Grosjean, F., Li, P., Münte, T., and Rodriguez-Fornells, A. (2003). See Methodological and conceptual issues.

7. Methodological and conceptual issues

Grosjean, F. (1990). "The psycholinguistics of language contact and code-switching: Concepts, methodology and data", in *Papers for the Workshop on Concepts, Methodology and Data. Network on Code-Switching and Language Contact*. Strasbourg: European Science Foundation, 105–16.

Grosjean, F. (1998, 2004). "Studying bilinguals: Methodological and conceptual issues", *Bilingualism: Language and Cognition*, 1998, 1: 131–49. Also in T. K. Bhatia and W. C. Ritchie (eds.) *The Handbook of Bilingualism*. Oxford: Blackwell Publishing, 2004, 32–63.

Grosjean, F. (1998). "Transfer and language mode. Commentary of Natascha Müller, 'Transfer in bilingual first language acquisition'", *Bilingualism: Language and Cognition* 1: 175–6.

Grosjean, F., Li, P., Münte, T., and Rodriguez-Fornells, A. (2003). "Imaging bilinguals: When the neurosciences meet the language sciences", *Bilingualism: Language and Cognition* 6: 159–65.

8. Bilingualism: Language and Cognition

(The journal published by Cambridge University Press)

Grosjean, F., Kroll, J., Meisel, J., and Muysken, P. (1998). "Editorial", *Bilingualism: Language and Cognition* 1: iii–iv.

Grosjean, F. (2007). "Starting BLC: 1996–1998", *Bilingualism: Language and Cognition* 10: 3–6.

References

Altenberg, E. and Cairns, H. (1983). "The effects of phonotactic constraints on lexical processing in bilingual and monolingual subjects", *Journal of Verbal Learning and Verbal Behavior* 22: 174–88.

Altmann, G. (1990). *Cognitive Models of Speech Processing: Psycholinguistic and Computational Perspectives*. Cambridge, MA: MIT Press.

Ann, J. (2001). "Bilingualism and language contact", in C. Lucas (ed.) *The Sociolinguistics of Sign Languages*. Cambridge: Cambridge University Press, 33–60.

Appel, R. and Muysken, P. (1987). *Language Contact and Bilingualism*. London: Edward Arnold.

Baetens Beardsmore, H. (1986). *Bilingualism: Basic Principles*. Clevedon: Multilingual Matters.

Bates, E., Devescovi, A., Hernandez, A., and Pizzamiglio, L. (1996). "Gender priming in Italian", *Perception and Psychophysics* 58: 992–1004.

Bates, E., Devescovi, A., Pizzamiglio, L., d'Amico, S., and Hernandez, A. (1995). "Gender and lexical access in Italian", *Perception and Psychophysics* 57: 847–62.

Bates, E. and Liu, H. (1997). "Cued shadowing", in F. Grosjean and U. Frauenfelder (eds.) *A Guide to Spoken Word Recognition Paradigms*. Hove, England: Psychology Press, 577–83.

Battison, R. (1978). *Lexical Borrowing in American Sign Language*. Silver Spring, MD: Linstok Press.

Beauvillain, C. and Grainger, J. (1987). "Accessing interlexical homographs: Some limitations of a language-selective access", *Journal of Memory and Language* 26: 658–72.

Bentahila, A. (1995). "Review of C. Myers-Scotton: *Duelling Languages: Grammatical Structure in Codeswitching*", *Language* 71: 135–40.

Bentahila, A. and Davies, E. (1991). "Constraints on code-switching: A look beyond grammar", *Papers for the Symposium on Code-switching in Bilingual Studies: Theory, Significance and Perspectives*. Strasbourg: European Science Foundation, 369–404.

Bernstein, M. Maxwell, M., and Matthews, K. (1985). "Bimodal or bilingual communication?", *Sign Language Studies* 47: 127–40.

Bijeljac-Babic, R., Biardeau, A., and Grainger, J. (1997). "Masked orthographic priming in bilingual word recognition", *Memory and Cognition* 25: 447–57.

Bishop, M. and Hicks, S. (2005). "Orange eyes: Bimodal bilingualism in hearing adults from Deaf families", *Sign Language Studies* 5: 188–230.

Blair, D. and Harris, R. (1981). "A test of interlingual interaction in comprehension by bilinguals", *Journal of Psycholinguistic Research* 10: 457–67.

Blank, M. A. (1980). "Measuring lexical access during sentence processing", *Perception and Psychophysics* 28: 1–8.

Bradley, D. and Forster, K. (1987). "A reader's view of listening", *Cognition* 25: 103–34.

Bunge, S. A., Ochsner, K. N., Desmond, J. E., Glover, G. H., and Gabrieli, J. D. (2001). "Prefrontal regions involved in keeping information in and out of mind", *Brain* 124: 2074–86.

Bürki-Cohen, J., Grosjean, F., and Miller, J. (1989). "Base language effects on word identification in bilingual speech: Evidence from categorical perception experiments", *Language and Speech* 32: 355–71.

Cacciari, C., Carreiras, M., and Barbolini Cionini, C. (1997). "When words have two genders: Anaphor resolution for Italian functionally ambiguous words", *Journal of Memory and Language* 37: 517–32.

Caixeta, P. (2003). L'impact de la compétence linguistique du bilingue en L2 sur le mode langagier: une étude de production. Master's Thesis, Institute of Linguistics, Neuchâtel University, Switzerland.

Caramazza, A. and Brones, I. (1979). "Lexical access in bilinguals", *Bulletin of the Psychonomic Society* 13: 212–14.

Caramazza, A. and Brones, I. (1980). "Semantic classification by bilinguals", *Canadian Journal of Psychology* 34: 77–81.

Caramazza, A., Yeni-Komshian, G., Zurif, E., and Carbone, E. (1973). "The acquisition of a new phonological contrast: The case of stop consonants in French-English bilinguals", *Journal of the Acoustical Society of America* 54: 421–8.

Carroll, S. (1989). "Second-language acquisition and the Computational Paradigm", *Language Learning* 39: 535–94.

Chan, M., Chau, H., and Hoosain, R. (1983). "Input/output switch in bilingual code-switching", *Journal of Psycholinguistic Research* 12: 407–16.

Chee, M. W. L., Caplan, D., Soon, C., Sriram, N., Tan, E., Thiel, T., and Weekes, B. (1999). "Processing of visually presented sentences in Mandarin and English studied with fMRI", *Neuron* 23: 127–37.

Chen, H.-C. and Leung, Y.-S. (1989). "Patterns of lexical processing in a non-native language", *Journal of Experimental Psychology: Learning, Memory, and Cognition* 15: 316–25.

Chomsky, N. and Halle, M. (1968). *The Sound Pattern of English*. New York: Harper and Row. (Reprinted: Cambridge, MA: MIT Press, 1991).

Clahsen, H. (1999). "Lexical entries and rules of language: A multidisciplinary study of German inflection", *Behavioral Brain Sciences* 22: 991–1013.

Clyne, M. (1967). *Transference and Triggering*. The Hague: Marinus Nijhoff.

Clyne, M. (1972). *Perspectives on Language Contact*. Melbourne: Hawthorne Press.

Cohen, J., MacWhinney, B., Flatt, M., and Provost, J. (1993). "PsyScope: An interactive graphic system for designing and controlling experiments in the psychology laboratory using Macintosh computers", *Behavior Research Methods, Instruments, and Computers* 25: 257–71.

Colé, P. and Segui, J. (1994). "Grammatical incongruency and vocabulary types", *Memory and Cognition* 22: 387–94.

Cole, R. and Jakimik, J. (1978). "Understanding speech: How words are heard", in G. Underwood (ed.) *Strategies of Information Processing.* London and San Diego: Academic Press, 67–116.

Coltheart, M., Curtis, B., Atkins, P., and Haller, M. (1993). "Models of reading aloud: Dual-route and parallel-distributed processing approaches", *Psychological Review* 100: 589–608.

Content, A., Mousty, P., and Radeau, M. (1990). "BRULEX: Une base de données lexicales informatisées pour le français écrit et parlé", *L'Année Psychologique* 90: 551–66.

Cook, V. (1992). "Evidence for multicompetence", *Language Learning* 42: 557–91.

Corbett, G. (1991). *Gender.* Cambridge: Cambridge University Press.

Costa, A., Caramazza, A., and Sebastian-Galles, N. (2000). "The cognate facilitation effect: Implications for models of lexical access", *Journal of Experimental Psychology: Learning, Memory and Cognition* 26: 1283–96.

Crystal, D. (1991). *A Dictionary of Linguistics and Phonetics.* Oxford: Blackwell.

Cutler, A., Mehler, J., Norris, D., and Segui, J. (1992). "The monolingual nature of speech segmentation by bilinguals", *Cognitive Psychology* 24: 381–410.

Dagenbach, D. and Carr, T. (1994). *Inhibitory Processes in Attention, Memory, and Language.* San Diego, CA: Academic Press.

Davis, J. (1989). "Distinguishing language contact phenomena in ASL interpretation", in C. Lucas (ed.) *The Sociolinguistics of the Deaf Community.* New York: Academic Press, 85–102.

De Bot, K. (1992). "A bilingual production model: Levelt's 'speaking' model adapted", *Applied Linguistics* 13: 1–24.

De Bot, K. and Schreuder, R. (1993). "Word production and the bilingual lexicon", in R. Schreuder and B. Weltens (eds.) *The Bilingual Lexicon.* Amsterdam: John Benjamins, 191–214.

De Groot, A. M. B. (1992). "Bilingual lexical representation: A closer look at conceptual representations", in R. Frost and L. Katz (eds.) *Orthography, Phonology, Morphology and Meaning.* Amsterdam: Elsevier, 389–412.

De Groot, A. M. B. (1995). "Determinants of bilingual lexicosemantic organisation", *Computer Assisted Language Learning* 8: 151–80.

De Groot, A. M. B. and Kroll, J. F. (eds.) (1997). *Tutorials in Bilingualism: Psycholinguistic Perspectives.* Mahwah, NJ: Lawrence Erlbaum Associates.

De Houwer, A. (1990). *The Acquisition of Two Languages from Birth: A Case Study*. Cambridge: Cambridge University Press.

Delaporte, Y. (2002). *Les sourds, c'est comme ça*. Paris: Maison des sciences de l'homme.

Delattre, P. (1965). *Comparing the Phonetic Features of English, French, German and Spanish: An Interim Report*. Heidelberg, Germany: Julius Groos Verlag.

Delattre, P. (1966). *Studies in French and Comparative Phonetics*. The Hague: Mouton.

Dell, F. (1985). *Les règles et les sons*. Paris: Hermann.

Dijkstra, T. and van Hell, J. G. (2003). "Testing the language mode hypothesis using trilinguals", *International Journal of Bilingual Education and Bilingualism* 6: 2–16.

Dijkstra, T. and van Heuven, W. (1998). "The BIA model and bilingual word recognition", in J. Grainger and A. Jacobs (eds.) *Localist Connectionist Approaches to Human Cognition*. Mahwah, NJ: Lawrence Erlbaum, 189–225.

Dijkstra, T., van Jaarsveld, H., and ten Brinke, S. (1998). "Interlingual homograph recognition: Effects of task demands and language intermixing", *Bilingualism: Language and Cognition* 1: 51–66.

Domenighetti, C. and Caldognetto, D. (1999). Le rôle de la langue de base dans la reconnaissance des alternances codiques chez les bilingues. Unpublished Master's Thesis, Language Pathology Program, Neuchâtel University, Switzerland.

Dornic, S. (1978). "The bilingual's performance: Language dominance, stress and individual differences", in D. Gerver and H. Sinaiko (eds.) *Language Interpretation and Communication*. New York: Plenum. 259–71.

Durgunoglu, A. and Roediger, H. (1987). "Test differences in accessing bilingual memory", *Journal of Memory and Language* 26: 377–91.

Edwards, J. (1995). *Multilingualism*. London: Routledge.

Elman, J., Diehl, R., and Buchwald, S. (1977). "Perceptual switching in bilinguals", *Journal of the Acoustical Society of America* 62: 971–4.

Emerton, E. G. (1996). "Marginality, biculturalism and social identity of deaf people", in I. Parasnis (ed.) *Cultural and Language Diversity and the Deaf Experience*. Cambridge: Cambridge University Press, 136–45.

Emmorey, K., Borinstein, H., and Thompson, R. (2003). Bimodal bilingualism: Code-blending between spoken English and American Sign Language. Paper presented at the 4th International Symposium on Bilingualism, Tempe, Arizona, USA.

Ervin, S. and Osgood, C. (1954). "Second language learning and bilingualism", *Journal of Abnormal and Social Psychology* 49(suppl.): 139–46.

Fischer, S. (1998). "Critical periods for language acquisition: Consequences for deaf education", in A. Weisel (ed.) *Issues Unresolved: New Perspectives on*

Language and Deaf Education. Washington, DC: Gallaudet University Press, 9–26.

Forster, K. (1976). "Accessing the mental lexicon", in R. Wales and E. Walker (eds.) *New Approaches to Language Mechanism.* Amsterdam: North-Holland, 139–74.

Forster, K. (1979). "Levels of processing and the structure of the language processor", in W. Cooper and E. Walker (eds.) *Sentence Processing.* Hillsdale, NJ: Lawrence Erlbaum Associates, 27–85.

Foss, D. (1969). "Decision processes during sentence comprehension: Effects of lexical item difficulty and position upon decision times", *Journal of Verbal Learning and Verbal Behavior* 8: 457–62.

Foss, D. and Blank, M. (1980). "Identifying the speech codes", *Cognitive Psychology* 12: 1–31.

Fox, E. (1996). "Cross-language priming from ignored words: Evidence for a common representational system in bilinguals", *Journal of Memory and Language* 35: 353–70.

Frauenfelder, U. and Kearns, R. (1997). "Sequence Monitoring", in F. Grosjean and U. Frauenfelder (eds.) *A Guide to Spoken Word Recognition Paradigms.* Hove, UK: Psychology Press, 665–74.

Frauenfelder, U. and Tyler, L. (1987). *Spoken Word Recognition.* Cambridge, MA: MIT Press.

Gal, S. (1979). *Language Shift: Social Determinants of Linguistic Change in Bilingual Austria.* London and San Diego: Academic Press.

Gasser, C. (2000). Exploring the Complementarity Principle: The case of first generation English-German bilinguals in the Basle area. Master's Thesis, English Linguistics, University of Basle, Switzerland.

Genesee, F. (1989). "Early bilingual development: One language or two?", *Journal of Child Language* 16: 161–79.

Genesee, F., Boivin, I., and Nicoladis, E. (1996). "Talking with strangers: A study of bilingual children's communicative competence", *Applied Psycholinguistics* 17: 427–42.

Genesee, F., Nicoladis, E., and Paradis, J. (1995). "Language differentiation in early bilingual development", *Journal of Child Language* 22: 611–31.

Gerard, L. and Scarborough, D. (1989). "Language-specific lexical access of homographs by bilinguals", *Journal of Experimental Psychology: Learning, Memory, and Cognition* 15: 305–15.

Girard, E. (1995). Intégration de variantes de contact dans la compétence de bilingues de deuxième génération. Master's Thesis, Language Pathology Program, University of Neuchâtel, Switzerland.

Gollan, T. and Frost, R. (2001). "Two routes to grammatical gender: Evidence from Hebrew", *Journal of Psycholinguistic Research* 30: 627–51.

Goodz, N. (1989). "Parental language mixing in bilingual families", *Journal of Infant Mental Health* 10: 25–44.

Grainger, J. and Beauvillain, C. (1987). "Language blocking and lexical access in bilinguals", *Quarterly Journal of Experimental Psychology* 39A: 295–319.

Grainger, J. and Dijkstra, T. (1992). "On the representation and use of language information in bilinguals", in R. Harris (ed.) *Cognitive Processing in Bilinguals*. Amsterdam: Elsevier, 207–20.

Green, D. (1986). "Control, activation, and resource: A framework and a model for the control of speech in bilinguals", *Brain and Language* 27: 210–23.

Green, D. (1998). "Mental control of the bilingual lexico-semantic system", *Bilingualism: Language and Cognition* 1: 67–81.

Green, D. (ed.) (2001). "The cognitive neuroscience of bilingualism", *Bilingualism: Language and Cognition* 4: 101–201.

Grosjean, F. (1980). "Spoken word recognition processes and the gating paradigm", *Perception and Psychophysics* 28: 267–83.

Grosjean, F. (1982). *Life with Two Languages: An Introduction to Bilingualism*. Cambridge, MA: Harvard University Press.

Grosjean, F. (1985a). "The recognition of words after their acoustic offset: Evidence and implications", *Perception and Psychophysics* 38: 299–310.

Grosjean, F. (1985b). "Polyglot aphasics and language mixing: A comment on Perecman (1984)", *Brain and Language* 26: 349–55.

Grosjean, F. (1985c). "The bilingual as a competent but specific speaker-hearer", *Journal of Multilingual and Multicultural Development* 6: 467–77.

Grosjean, F. (1986). "Bilingualism", in *Gallaudet Encyclopedia of Deaf People and Deafness*. Vol. 3. New York: McGraw-Hill, 179–82.

Grosjean, F. (1988). "Exploring the recognition of guest words in bilingual speech", *Language and Cognitive Processes* 3: 233–74.

Grosjean, F. (1989). "Neurolinguists, beware! The bilingual is not two monolinguals in one person", *Brain and Language* 36: 3–15.

Grosjean, F. (1992). "The bilingual and the bicultural person in the hearing and in the deaf world", *Sign Language Studies* 77: 307–20.

Grosjean, F. (1994). "Individual bilingualism", in R. Asher (ed.) *The Encyclopedia of Language and Linguistics*. Oxford: Pergamon Press, 1656–60.

Grosjean, F. (1996). "Living with two languages and two cultures", in I. Parasnis (ed.) *Cultural and Language Diversity and the Deaf Experience*. Cambridge: Cambridge University Press, 20–37.

Grosjean, F. (1997a). "Processing mixed language: Issues, findings, and models", in A. M. B. de Groot and J. F. Kroll (eds.) *Tutorials in Bilingualism: Psycholinguistic Perspectives*. Mahwah, NJ: Lawrence Erlbaum Associates, 225–54.

Grosjean, F. (1997b). "The bilingual individual", *Interpreting: International Journal of Research and Practice in Interpreting* 2: 163–87.

Grosjean, F. (1998a). "Studying bilinguals: Methodological and conceptual issues", *Bilingualism: Language and Cognition* 1: 131–49.

Grosjean, F. (1998b). "Transfer and language mode. Commentary of Natascha Müller, 'Transfer in bilingual first language acquisition' ", *Bilingualism: Language and Cognition* 1: 175–6.

Grosjean, F. (2001). "The bilingual's language modes", in J. Nicol (ed.) *One Mind, Two Languages: Bilingual Language Processing*. Oxford: Blackwell, 1–22.

Grosjean, F. and Frauenfelder, U. (eds.) (1997). *A Guide to Spoken Word Recognition Paradigms*. Hove: Psychology Press.

Grosjean, F. and Miller, J. (1994). "Going in and out of languages: An example of bilingual flexibility", *Psychological Science* 5: 201–6.

Grosjean, F. and Py, B. (1991). "La restructuration d'une première langue: l'intégration de variantes de contact dans la compétence de migrants bilingues", *La Linguistique* 27: 35–60.

Grosjean, F. and Soares, C. (1986). "Processing mixed language: Some preliminary findings", in J. Vaid (ed.) *Language Processing in Bilinguals: Psycholinguistic and Neuropsychological Perspectives*. Hillsdale, NJ: Lawrence Erlbaum, 145–79.

Grosjean, F., Dommergues, J.-Y., Cornu, E., Guillelmon, D., and Besson, C. (1994). "The gender marking effect in spoken word recognition", *Perception and Psychophysics* 56: 590–8.

Gumperz, J. (1970). "Verbal strategies in multilingual communication", in J. Alatis (ed.) *Bilingualism and Language Contact*. Washington, DC: Georgetown University Press, 129–47.

Gurjanov, M., Lukatela, G., Lukatela, K., Savic, M., and Turvey, M. (1985). "Grammatical priming of inflected nouns by the gender of possessive adjectives", *Journal of Experimental Psychology: Learning, Memory, and Cognition* 11: 692–701.

Hakuta, K. (1986). *Mirror of Language: The Debate on Bilingualism*. New York: Basic Books.

Handschin, K. (1994). "L'influence de la langue de base dans la perception des alternances codiques: le cas de la consonne initiale du mot", *Travaux neuchâtelois de linguistique (TRANEL)* 21: 51–60.

Harris, R. (1992). *Cognitive Processing in Bilinguals*. New York: North-Holland.

Hasselmo, N. (1970). "Code-switching and modes of speaking", in G. Gilbert (ed.) *Texas Studies in Bilingualism*. Berlin: Walter de Gruyter, 179–210.

Haugen, E. (1956). *Bilingualism in the Americas: A Bibliography and Research Guide*. Alabama: University of Alabama Press.

Haugen, E. (1969). *The Norwegian Language in America: A Study in Bilingual Behavior*. Bloomington, IN: University of Indiana Press.

Hernandez, A., Bates, E., and Avila, L. (1994). "On-line sentence interpretation in Spanish-English bilinguals: What does it mean to be 'in between'?", *Applied Psycholinguistics* 15: 417–46.

Howes, D. (1957). "On the relation between the intelligibility and frequency of occurrence of English words", *Journal of the Acoustical Society of America* 29: 296–305.

Hyltenstam, K. (1991). "Language mixing in Alzeimer's dementia", *Papers for the Workshop on Constraints, Conditions and Models*. Strasbourg: European Science Foundation, 221–58.

Indefrey, P., Brown, C., Hagoort, P., Herzog, H., Sach, M., and Seitz, R. J. (1997). "A PET study of cerebral activation patterns induced by verb inflection", *NeuroImage* 5(suppl.): 548.

Jaccard, R. and Cividin, V. (2001). Le principe de complémentarité chez la personne bilingue: le cas du bilinguisme français-italien en Suisse Romande. Master's Thesis, Language Pathology Program, University of Neuchâtel, Switzerland.

Jaeger, J., Lockwood, A., Kemmerer, D., Van Valin, R., Murphy, B., and Khalak, H. (1996). "A positron emission tomographic study of regular and irregular verb morphology in English", *Language* 72: 451–97.

Jakubowicz, C. and Faussart, C. (1998). "Gender agreement in the processing of spoken French", *Journal of Psycholinguistic Research* 27: 597–617.

Jescheniak, J. and Levelt, W. (1994). "Word frequency effects in speech production: Retrieval of syntactic information and of phonological form", *Journal of Experimental Psychology: Learning, Memory, and Cognition* 20: 824–43.

Joseph, J. (2001). "Functional neuroimaging studies of category specificity in object recognition: A critical review and meta-analysis", *Cognitive, Affective, and Behavioral Neuroscience* 1: 119–36.

Joshi, A. (1985). "Processing of sentences with intra-sentential code-switching", in D. Dowty, L. Kartunen, and A. Zwicky (eds.) *Natural Language Processing: Psychological, Computational and Theoretical Perspectives*. Cambridge: Cambridge University Press.

Kannapel, B. (1974). "Bilingualism: A new direction in the education of the deaf", *Deaf American* June: 9–15.

Kearns, R. (1994). Prelexical Speech Processing by Mono- and Bilinguals. Unpublished doctoral dissertation. Cambridge University, Cambridge.

Kettrick, C. and Hatfield, N. (1986). "Bilingualism in a visuo-gestural mode", in J. Vaid (ed.) *Language Processing in Bilinguals*. Hillsdale, NJ: Lawrence Erlbaum Associates, 253–73.

Kirk, R. (1967). *Experimental Design: Procedures for the Behavioral Sciences*. Belmont, CA: Brooks/Cole.

Kolers, P. (1966). "Reading and talking bilingually", *American Journal of Psychology* 3: 357–76.

Kolers, P. and Gonzalez, E. (1980). "Memory for words, synonyms, and translations", *Journal of Experimental Psychology: Human Learning and Memory* 6: 53–65.

Kroll, J. F. and Curley, J. (1988). "Lexical memory in novice bilinguals: The role of concepts in retrieving second language words", in M. Gruneberg, P. Morris, and R. Sykes (eds.) *Practical Aspects of Memory*, Vol. 2. London: Wiley, 389–95.

Kroll, J. F. and de Groot, A. M. B. (1997). "Lexical and conceptual memory in the bilingual: Mapping form to meaning in two languages", in A. M. B. de Groot and J. F. Kroll (eds.) *Tutorials in Bilingualism: Psycholinguistic Perspectives*. Mahwah, NJ: Lawrence Erlbaum Associates, 169–99.

Kroll, J. F. and Stewart, E. (1994). "Category interference in translation and picture naming: Evidence for asymmetric connections between bilingual memory representations", *Journal of Memory and Language* 33: 149–74.

Kučera, F. and Francis, W. (1967). *Computational Analysis of Present Day American English*. Providence, RI: Brown University Press.

Kutas, M. and Hillyard, S. (1980). "Reading senseless sentences: Brain potentials reflect semantic incongruity", *Science* 207: 203–5.

Kutas, M., Federmeier, K. D., Coulson, S., King, J. W., and Münte, T. F. (2000). "Language", in J. T. Cacioppo, L. G. Tassinary, and G. G. Berntson (eds.) *Handbook of Psychophysiology*, 2nd edn. Cambridge: Cambridge University Press, 576–601.

Ladd, P. (2003). *Understanding Deaf Culture: In Search of Deafhood*. Clevedon: Multilingual Matters.

Ladefoged, P. (1975). *A Course in Phonetics*. New York: Harcourt Brace Jovanovich.

Lanza, E. (1992). "Can bilingual two-year-olds code-switch?' *Journal of Child Language* 19: 633–58.

Le Robert Oral-Ecrit. (1989). Paris: Les dictionnaires Le Robert.

Lee, D. (1983). Sources and Aspects of Code-Switching in the Signing of a Deaf Adult and her Interlocutors. Unpublished doctoral dissertation, University of Texas at Austin.

Levelt, W. (1989). *Speaking: From Intention to Articulation*. Cambridge, MA: MIT Press.

Léwy, N. and Grosjean, F. (unpublished). The computerized version of BIMOLA: A bilingual model of lexical access. Laboratoire de traitement du langage et de la parole, Université de Neuchâtel, Switzerland.

Li, P. (1996). "Spoken word recognition of code-switched words by Chinese-English bilinguals", *Journal of Memory and Language* 35: 757–74.

Liberman, A. M., Harris, K. S., Hoffman, H. S., and Griffith, B. C. (1957). "The discrimination of speech sounds within and across phoneme boundaries", *Journal of Experimental Psychology* 54: 358–68.

Lipski, J. (1978). "Code-switching and the problem of bilingual competence", in M. Paradis (ed.) *Aspects of Bilingualism*. Columbia, SC: Hornbeam Press, 263–77.

Lipski, J. (1982). "Spanish–English language switching in speech and literature: Theories and models", *Bilingual Review/Revista Bilingue* 9: 191–212.

Lisker, L. and Abramson, A. (1964). "A cross-language study of voicing in initial stops: Acoustical measurements", *Word* 20: 384–422.

Lucas, C. (ed.) (1989). *The Sociolinguistics of the Deaf Community*. New York: Academic Press.

Lucas, C. and Valli, C. (1992). *Language Contact in the American Deaf Community*. New York: Academic Press.

Ludérus, S. (1995). Language choice and language separation in bilingual Alzeimer patients. Ph.D. Dissertation. Amsterdam: University of Amsterdam.

McClelland, J. and Elman, J. (1986). "The TRACE model of speech perception", *Cognitive Psychology* 18: 1–86.

McClelland, J. and Rumelhart, D. (1981). "An interactive activation model of context effects in letter perception: Part 1. An account of basic findings", *Psychological Review* 88: 375–407.

McClure, E. (1977). "Aspects of code-switching in the discourse of bilingual Mexican–American children". Technical Report No. 44, Center for the Study of Reading. Urbana-Champaign, IL: University of Illinois.

Mackey, W. (1968). "The description of bilingualism", in J. Fishman (ed.) *Readings in the Sociology of Language*. The Hague: Mouton, 554–84.

Macnamara, J. (1967). "The bilingual's linguistic performance: A psychological overview", *Journal of Social Issues* 23: 59–77.

Macnamara, J. and Kushnir, S. (1971). "Linguistic independence of bilinguals: The input switch", *Journal of Verbal Learning and Verbal Behavior* 10: 480–7.

McQueen, J., Cutler, A., Briscoe, T., and Norris, D. (1995). "Models of continuous speech recognition and the contents of the vocabulary", *Language and Cognitive Processes* 10: 309–32.

Marchman, V. A., Plunkett, K., and Goodman, J. (1997). "Overregularization in English plural and past tense inflectional morphology: A response to Marcus (1995)". *Journal of Child Language* 24: 767–79.

Marcus, G. F., Brinkmann, U., Clahsen, H., Wiese, R., and Pinker, S. (1995). "German inflection: The exception that proves the rule", *Cognitive Psychology* 29: 189–256.

Marian, V. and Spivey, M. (2003). "Competing activation in bilingual language processing: Within- and between-language competition", *Bilingualism: Language and Cognition* 6: 97–115.

Marslen-Wilson, W. (1984). "Function and process in spoken word recognition: A tutorial review", in H. Bouma and D. G. Bouwhuis (eds.) *Attention and Performance X: Control of Language Processes*. Hillsdale, NJ: Lawrence Erlbaum Associates, 125–50.

Marslen-Wilson, W. (1987). "Functional parallelism in spoken word-recognition", *Cognition* 25: 71–102.

Marslen-Wilson, W. and Tyler, L. (1987). "Against modularity", in J. Garfield (ed.) *Modularity in Knowledge Representation and Natural Language Understanding*. Cambridge, MA: MIT Press, 37–62.

Marslen-Wilson, W. and Welsh, A. (1978). "Processing interactions and lexical access during word recognition in continuous speech", *Cognitive Psychology* 10: 29–63.

Marty, S. and Grosjean, F. (1998). "Aphasie, bilinguisme et modes de communication", *APHASIE und verwandte Gebiete* 12: 8–28.

Mayo, L., Florentine, M., and Buus, S. (1997). "Age of second-language acquisition and perception of speech in noise", *Journal of Speech, Language, and Hearing Research* 40: 686–93.

Meisel, J. (1989). "Early differentiation of languages in bilingual children", in K. Hyltenstam and L. Obler (eds.) *Bilingualism Across the Lifespan: Aspects of Acquisition, Maturity and Loss*. Cambridge: Cambridge University Press, 13–40.

Miller, G. and Isard, S. (1963). "Some perceptual consequences of linguistic rules", *Journal of Verbal Learning and Verbal Behavior* 2: 217–88.

Miller, J. L., Green, K., and Schermer, T. M. (1984). "A distinction between the effect of sentential speaking rate and semantic congruity on word identification", *Perception and Psychophysics* 36: 329–37.

Morton, J. (1969). "Interaction of information in word recognition", *Psychological Review* 76: 165–78.

Morton, J. and Long, J. (1976). "Effect of word transitional probability on phoneme identification", *Journal of Verbal Learning and Verbal Behavior* 15: 43–51.

Münte, T. F., Rodriguez-Fornells, A., and Kutas, M. (1999a). "One, two, or many mechanisms: The brain's processing of complex words", *Behavioral Brain Science* 22: 415–17.

Münte, T. F., Say, T., Clahsen, H., Schiltz, K., and Kutas, M. (1999b). "Decomposition of morphologically complex words in English: Evidence from event-related brain potentials", *Cognitive Brain Research* 7: 241–53.

Münte, T. F., Urbach, T. P., Düzel, E., and Kutas, M. (2000). "Event-related brain potentials in the study of human cognition and neuropsychology", in F. Boller, J. Grafman and G. Rizzolatti (eds.) *Handbook of Neuropsychology*, 2nd edn. vol. 1. Amsterdam: Elsevier, 139–235.

Myers-Scotton, C. (1993). *Duelling Languages: Grammatical Structure in Codeswitching*. Oxford: Oxford University Press.

Myers-Scotton, C. and Jake, J. (1995). "Matching lemmas in a bilingual language competence and production model: Evidence from intrasentential codeswitching", *Linguistics* 33: 981–1024.

Nicoladis, E. and Genesee, F. (1998). "Parental discourse and codemixing in bilingual children", *The International Journal of Bilingualism* 2: 85–9.

Nooteboom, S. (1981). "Lexical retrieval from fragments of spoken words: Beginnings versus endings", *Journal of Phonetics* 9: 407–24.

Norris, D. (1994). "Shortlist: A connectionist model of continuous speech recognition", *Cognition* 52: 189–234.

Obler, L. and Albert, M. (1978). "A monitor system for bilingual language processing", in M. Paradis (ed.) *Aspects of Bilingualism*. Columbia, SC: Hornbeam Press, 105–13.

Odlin, T. (1989). *Language Transfer: Cross-Linguistic Influence in Language Learning*. Cambridge: Cambridge University Press.

Ohman, S. (1966). "Perception of segments of VCCV utterances", *Journal of the Acoustical Society of America* 40: 979–88.

Padden, C. and Humphries, T. (1988). *Deaf in America: Voices from a Culture*. Cambridge, MA: Harvard University Press.

Pallier, C., Colome, A., and Sebastian-Galles, N. (2001). "The influence of native-language phonology on lexical access: Exemplar-based versus abstract lexical entries", *Psychological Science* 12: 445–9.

Pallier, C., Sebastian-Galles, N., Dupoux, E., Christophe, A., and Mehler, J. (1998). "Perceptual adjustment to time-compressed speech: A cross-linguistic study", *Memory and Cognition* 26: 844–51.

Paradis, J. and Genesee, F. (1996). "Syntactic acquisition in bilingual children: Autonomous or interdependent?", *Studies in Second Language Acquisition* 18: 1–25.

Paradis, M. (1977). "Bilingualism and aphasia", in H. Whitaker and H. Whitaker (eds.) *Studies in Neurolinguistics*, vol. 3. New York: Academic Press, 65–121.

Paradis, M. (1980). "The language switch in bilinguals: Psycholinguistic and neurolinguistic perspectives", in P. Nelde (ed.) *Languages in Contact and Conflict*. Weisbaden: Franz Steiner Verlag, 501–6.

Paradis, M. (1981). "Contributions of neurolinguistics to the theory of bilingualism", in R. Herbert (ed.) *Applications of Linguistic Theory in the Human Sciences*. Department of Linguistics, Michigan State University, 180–211.

Paradis, M. (1986). "Bilingualism", in T. Husén and T. N. Poselthwaite (eds.) *International Encyclopedia of Education*. Oxford: Pergamon Press, 489–93.

Paradis, M. (1989). "Bilingual and polyglot aphasia", in F. Boller and J. Grafman (eds.) *Handbook of Neuropsychology*, vol. 2. Amsterdam: Elsevier, 117–40.

Paradis, M. (1995). "Introduction: The need for distinctions", in M. Paradis (ed.) *Aspects of Bilingual Aphasia*. Oxford: Pergamon Press, 1–9.

Paulesu, E., Frith, C., and Frackowiak, R. (1993). "The neural correlates of the verbal component of working memory", *Nature* 362: 342–5.

Pearlmutter, N., Garnsey, S., and Bock, K. (1999). "Agreement processes in sentence comprehension", *Journal of Memory and Language* 41: 427–56.

Penfield, W. (1959). "The learning of languages", in W. Penfield and L. Roberts (eds.) *Speech and Brain-Mechanisms*. Princeton, NJ: Princeton University Press.

Penfield, W. and Roberts, L. (1959). *Speech and Brain Mechanisms*. Princeton, NJ: Princeton University Press.

Penke, M., Weyerts, H., Gross, M., Zander, E., Münte, T. F., and Clahsen, H. (1997). "How the brain processes complex words: An event-related potential study of German verb inflections", *Cognitive Brain Research* 6: 37–52.

Perani, D., Paulesu, E., Galles, N. S., Dupoux, E., Dehaene, S., Bettinardi, V., Cappa, S. F., Fazio, F., and Mehler, J. (1998). "The bilingual brain: Proficiency and age of acquisition of the second language", *Brain* 121: 1841–52.

Perecman, E. (1984). "Spontaneous translation and language mixing in a polyglot aphasic", *Brain and Language* 23: 43–63.

Perfetti, C. A., Bell, L. C., and Delaney, S. M. (1988). "Automatic (prelexical) phonetic activation in silent word reading: Evidence from backward masking", *Journal of Memory and Language* 27: 59–70.

Petersen, S., Fox, P., Posner, M., Mintun, M., and Raichle, M. (1989). "Positron emission tomographic studies of the processing of single words", *Journal of Cognitive Neuroscience* 1: 153–70.

Pfaff, C. (1979). "Constraints on language mixing: Intrasentential code-switching and borrowing in Spanish/English", *Language* 55: 291–318.

Pinker, S. (1997). "Words and rules in the human brain", *Nature* 387: 547–8.

Pollack, I. and Pickett, J. (1963). "The intelligibility of excerpts from conversation", *Language and Speech* 6: 165–71.

Poplack, S. (1980). "Sometimes I'll start a sentence in Spanish Y TERMINO EN ESPAÑOL: Towards a typology of code-switching", *Linguistics* 18: 581–618.

Poplack, S. (1981). "Syntactic structure and social function of code-switching", in R. Duran (ed.) *Latino Discourse and Communicative Behavior*. Norwood, NJ: Ablex, 169–84.

Poplack, S. (1985). "Contrasting patterns of code-switching in two communities", in H. Warkentyne (ed.) *Methods V: Papers from the V International Conference on Methods in Dialectology*. Victoria, BC: University of Victoria Press, 363–86.

Poplack, S., Sankoff, D., and Miller, C. (1988). "The social correlates and linguistic processes of lexical borrowing and assimilation", *Linguistics* 26: 47–104.

Potter, M., So, K-F., von Eckhardt, B., and Feldman, L. (1984). "Lexical and conceptual representation in beginning and proficient bilinguals", *Journal of Verbal Learning and Verbal Behavior* 23: 23–8.

Poulisse, N. (1997). "Language production in bilinguals", in A. M. B. de Groot and J. F. Kroll (eds.) *Tutorials in Bilingualism: Psycholinguistic Perspectives*. Mahwah, NJ: Lawrence Erlbaum Associates, 201–24.

Poulisse, N. and Bongaerts, T. (1994). "First language use in second language production", *Applied Linguistics* 15: 36–57.

Preston, M. and Lambert, W. (1969). "Interlingual interference in a bilingual version of the Stroop Color–Word task", *Journal of Verbal Learning and Verbal Behavior* 8: 295–301.

Redlinger, W. and Park, T. (1980). "Language mixing in young bilinguals", *Journal of Child Language* 7: 337–52.

Reiser, M. and Wirth, N. (1992). *Programming in Oberon: Steps Beyond Pascal and Modula*. Wokingham, UK: Addison-Wesley.

Repp, B. H. (1981). "On levels of description in speech research", *Journal of the Acoustical Society of America* 69: 1462–4.

Repp, B. H. (1984). "Categorical perception: Issues, methods, findings", in N. J. Lass (ed.), *Speech and Language: Advances in Basic Research and Practice*, Vol. 10. New York: Academic Press, 243–335.

Repp, B. H., and Liberman, A. M. (1987). "Phonetic category boundaries are flexible", in S. N. Harnad (ed.) *Categorical Perception*. New York: Cambridge University Press, 89–112.

Rodriguez-Fornells, A., Clahsen, H., Lleo, C., Zaake, W., and Münte, T. F. (2001). "Event-related brain responses to morphological violations in Catalan", *Cognitive Brain Research* 11: 47–58.

Rodriguez-Fornells, A., Corral, M. J., Escera, C., and Münte, T. F. (in preparation). "Monolingual vs. bilingual reading modes in bilinguals: Are we able to switch-off completely?"

Rodriguez-Fornells, A., Rotte, M., Heinze, H.-J., Noesselt, T., and Münte T. F. (2002). "Brain potential and functional MRI evidence for how to handle two languages with one brain", *Nature* 415: 1026–9.

Rodriguez-Fornells, A., van der Lugt, A., Rotte, M., Britti, B., Heinze, H. J., and Münte, T. F. (2005). "Second language interferes with word production in fluent bilinguals: Brain potential and functional imaging evidence", *Journal of Cognitive Neuroscience* 17: 422–33.

Rogers, M. (1987). "Learners' difficulties with grammatical gender in German as a foreign language", *Applied Linguistics* 8: 48–74.

Romaine, S. (1989). *Bilingualism*. London: Blackwell.

Rubenstein, H. and Pollack, I. (1963). "Word predictability and intelligibility", *Journal of Verbal Learning and Verbal Behavior* 2: 147–58.

Salamin, C. (2003). Le bilinguisme et le biculturalisme des personnes sourdes: description, représentations et comparaison avec des personnes entendantes. Master's Thesis, Language Pathology Program, Université de Neuchâtel, Switzerland.

Salasoo, A. and Pisoni, D. (1985). "Interaction of knowledge sources in spoken word identification", *Journal of Memory and Language* 24: 210–31.

Sánchez-Casas, R., Davis, C., and García-Albea, J. (1992). "Bilingual lexical processing: Exploring the cognate/non-cognate distinction", *European Journal of Cognitive Psychology* 4: 293–310.

Scarborough, D., Gerard, L., and Cortese, C. (1984). "Independence of lexical access in bilingual word recognition", *Journal of Verbal Learning and Verbal Behavior* 23: 84–99.

Schmidt, R. (1986). "Was weiss der Artikel vom Hauptwort? Ein Beitrag zur Verarbeitung syntaktischer Beziehungen beim Lesen", *Zeitschrift für Experimentelle und Angewandte Psychologie* 23: 150–63.

Schreuder, R. and Weltens, B. (1993). *The Bilingual Lexicon*. Philadelphia: John Benjamins.

Schwanenflugel, P. and Rey, M. (1986). "Interlingual semantic facilitation: Evidence for a common representational system in the bilingual lexicon", *Journal of Memory and Language* 25: 605–18.

Scotton, C. and Ury, W. (1977). "Bilingual strategies: The social functions of code-switching", *Linguistics* 193: 5–20.

Searls, C. and Johnston, D. (1996). "Growing up deaf in deaf families: Two different experiences", in I. Parasnis (ed.) *Cultural and Language Diversity and the Deaf Experience*. Cambridge: Cambridge University Press, 201–24.

Sebastian-Galles, N. and Soto-Faraco, S. (1999). "On-line processing of native and non-native phonemic contrasts in early bilinguals", *Cognition* 72: 111–23.

Segalowitz, N. (1997). "Individual differences in second language acquisition", in A. M. B. de Groot and J. F. Kroll (eds.) *Tutorials in Bilingualism: Psycholinguistic Perspectives*. Mahwah, NJ: Lawrence Erlbaum Associates, 85–112.

Segui, J., Mehler, J., Frauenfelder, U., and Morton, J. (1982). "The word frequency effect and lexical access", *Neuropsychologia* 20: 615–27.

Seidenberg, M. S. and Hoeffner, J. H. (1997). "Evaluating behavioral and neuroimaging data on past tense processing", *Language* 74: 104–22.

Shillcock, R., Lindsey, G., Levy, J., and Chater, N. (1992). "A phonologically motivated input representation for the modeling of auditory word perception in continuous speech", *Proceedings of the 14th Annual Conference of the Cognitive Science Society*. Hillsdale, NJ: Lawrence Erlbaum, 408–13.

Sholl, A. (1995). Animacy Effects in Picture Naming and Bilingual Translation: Perceptual and Semantic Contributions to Concept Mediation. Unpublished doctoral dissertation, University of Massachusetts, Amherst.

Soares, C. and Grosjean, F. (1984). "Bilinguals in a monolingual and a bilingual speech mode: The effect on lexical access", *Memory and Cognition* 12: 380–6.

Spivey, M. and Marian, V. (1999). "Cross talk between native and second languages: Partial activation of an irrelevant lexicon", *Psychological Science* 10: 281–4.

Stokoe, W. (1969). "Sign language diglossia", *Studies in Linguistics* 21: 27–41.

Strong, M. and Prinz, P. (1997). "A study of the relationship between American Sign Language and English literacy", *Journal of Deaf Studies and Deaf Education* 2: 37–46.

Taeschner, T. (1983). *The Sun is Feminine: A Study on Language Acquisition in Bilingual Children*. Berlin: Springer-Verlag.

Tan, L. H. and Perfetti, C. (1998). "Phonological codes as early sources of constraints in reading Chinese: A review of current discoveries and theoretical accounts", *Reading and Writing* 10: 165–220.

Taylor, I. (1971). "How are words from two languages organized in bilinguals' memory?", *Canadian Journal of Psychology* 25: 228–40.

Timm, L. (1975). "Spanish–English code-switching: el porque y how-not-to", *Romance Philology* 28: 473–82.

Treffers-Daller, J. (1998). "Variability in code-switching styles: Turkish-German code-switching patterns", in R. Jacobson (ed.) *Code-switching Worldwide*. Berlin: Mouton de Gruyter, 177–97.

Tulving, E. and Colotla, V. (1970). "Free recall of trilingual lists", *Cognitive Psychology* 1: 86–98.

Tyler, L. and Wessels, J. (1983). "Quantifying contextual contributions to word-recognition processes", *Perception and Psychophysics* 34: 409–20.

Tyler, L. and Wessels, J. (1985). "Is gating an on-line task? Evidence from naming latency data", *Perception and Psychophysics* 38: 217–22.

Vaid, J. (1983). "Bilingualism and brain lateralization", in S. Segalowitz (ed.) *Language Functions and Brain Organization*. New York: Academic Press, 315–39.

Vaid, J. (1987). "Visual field asymmetries for rhyme and syntactic category judgments in monolinguals and fluent early and late bilinguals", *Brain and Language* 30: 263–77.

Vaid, J. and Hall, D. (1991). "Neuropsychological perspectives on bilingualism: Right, left and center", in A. Reynolds (ed.) *Bilingualism, Multiculturalism and Second Language Learning*. Hillsdale, NJ: Lawrence Erlbaum Associates, 81–112.

Vaid, J. and Hull, R. (2002). "Re-envisioning the bilingual brain using functional neuroimaging: Methodological and interpretive issues", in F. Fabbro (ed.) *Advances in the Neurolinguistic Study of Bilingualism*. Udine, Italy: Forum, 315–55.

Valdes Fallis, G. (1976). "Social interaction and code-switching patterns: A case study of Spanish/English alternation", in G. Keller, R. Teschner, and S. Viera (eds.) *Bilingualism in the Bicentennial and Beyond*. New York: Bilingual Press/Editorial Bilingue, 53–85.

Van Berkum, J. (1996). *The Psycholinguistics of Grammatical Gender*. Nijmegen, The Netherlands: Nijmegen University Press.

Van Hell, J. G. (1998). Cross-language processing and bilingual memory organization. Doctoral thesis, University of Amsterdam.

Van Hell, J. G. and Dijkstra, T. (2002). "Foreign language knowledge can influence native language performance in exclusively native contexts", *Psychonomic Bulletin and Review* 9: 780–9.

Van Heuven, W., Dijkstra, T., and Grainger, J. (1998). "Orthographic neighborhood effects in bilingual word recognition", *Journal of Memory and Language* 39: 458–83.

Vihman, M. (1985). "Language differentiation by the bilingual infant", *Journal of Child Language* 12: 297–324.

Volterra, V. and Taeschner, R. (1978). "The acquisition and development of language by bilingual children", *Journal of Child Language* 5: 311–26.

Von Studnitz, R. and Green, D. (2002). "Interlingual homograph interference in German-English bilinguals: Its modulation and locus of control", *Bilingualism: Language and Cognition* 5: 1–24.

Votaw, M. (1992). "A functional view of bilingual lexicosemantic organization", in R. Harris (ed.) *Cognitive Processing in Bilinguals*. Amsterdam: Elsevier, 299–321.

Wakefield, J., Bradley, P., Yom, B., and Doughtie, B. (1975). "Language switching and constituent structure", *Language and Speech* 18: 14–19.

Weber-Fox, C. and Neville H. J. (1997). "Maturational constraints on functional specializations for language processing: ERP and behavioral evidence in bilingual speakers", *Journal of Cognitive Neuroscience* 8: 231–56.

Webster's Ninth New Collegiate Dictionary. (1991). Springfield, MA: Merriam-Webster.

Weil, S. (1990). Choix de langue et alternance codique chez le bilingue en situations de communication diverses: une étude expérimentale. Master's Thesis, Institute of Romance Studies, Basle University, Switzerland.

Weinreich, U. (1966). *Languages in Contact: Findings and Problems.* The Hague: Mouton.

Woolford, E. (1983). "Bilingual code-switching and syntactic theory", *Linguistic Inquiry* 14: 520–36.

Woutersen, M. (1997). Bilingual Word Perception. Ph.D. Dissertation. Nijmegen: University of Nijmegen.

Zatorre, R. (1989). "On the representation of multiple languages in the brain: Old problems and new directions", *Brain and Language* 36: 127–47.

Zatorre, R. J., Evans, A. C., Meyer, E., and Gjedde, A. (1992). "Lateralisation of phonetic and pitch discrimination in speech processing", *Science* 256: 846–9.

Index